WOMEN AND LOW PAY

WOMEN AND LOW PAY

Edited by

Peter J. Sloane

First published 1980 by
THE MACMILLAN PRESS LTD
London and Basingstoke
Companies and representatives
throughout the World

Printed in Hong Kong

British Library Cataloguing in Publication Data

Women and low pay
  1. Wages – Women
  I. Sloane, Peter James
  331.4′2   HD6061

ISBN 0–333–26817–2

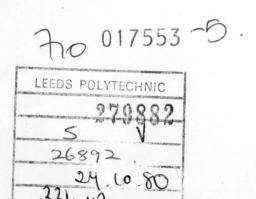

Contents

Preface   vii

Notes on the Contributors   viii

1 Introduction *P. J. Sloane*   1

2 Low Pay amongst Women—the Facts *P. J. Sloane and
  W. S. Siebert*   9

3 Relative Female Earnings in Great Britain and the Impact of
  Legislation *B. Chiplin, M. M. Curran and C. J. Parsley*   57

4 The Structure of Labour Markets and Low Pay for Women
  P. J. Sloane   127

5 Low Pay and Female Employment in Canada with Selected
  References to the USA *M. Gunderson and H. C. Jain*   165

6 Shortcomings and Problems in Analyses of Women and Low
  Pay *W. S. Siebert and P. J. Sloane*   223

Index   253

Preface

In its terms of reference of 22 June 1976 the Royal Commission on the Distribution of Income and Wealth was instructed by the Government to analyse the current situation with respect to low incomes in respect of individuals, households and families. It was also to consider past trends, particularly over the previous five years, in such incomes and the economic, social and other factors giving rise to them. The Commission duly presented its findings in Report no. 6, Lower Incomes, Cmnd. 7175, May 1975. In order to assist it in this task the editor (together with his associates) was invited to prepare a number of papers relating to the distribution of female employment incomes falling below the level of the lowest decile of the distribution for full-time manual men. The five papers contained in the book represent the results of this work, suitably revised for publication and taking into account the comments of the staff of the Commission. We are grateful to the Commission for giving permission for the publication of this material, but would stress that the contents are the responsibility of the authors and should not be taken to reflect either the views of the Royal Commission or those of individual members of its staff. I am also grateful to Jean Beggs for typing assistance and Lucy Docherty for help in preparing the index.

The author and publishers wish to thank the following who have kindly given permission for the use of copyright material: George Allen & Unwin (Publishers) Ltd. for the table from *Labour Markets Under Different Employment Conditions* by D. Mackay; The Controller of Her Majesty's Stationery Office for statistics from HMSO publications; Southern Economics Journal for data from *Southern Economics Journal*, 1973; The University of Chicago Press for data from the table by Leibowitz 'Home Investments in Children' in *Journal of Political Economy*, 1974; The University of Wisconsin Press for data from the table in *Journal of Human Resources* (© 1975 by the Regents of the University of Wisconsin); and John Wiley & Sons Inc for data from the table by Parsons 'Intergenerational Wealth Transfers and the Educational Decisions of Male Youth' in *Quarterly Journal of Economics*, 1975.

November 1978   P. J. SLOANE

Notes on the Contributors

P. J. SLOANE is Professor of Economics and Management, Paisley College, Scotland, having formerly held lecturing posts at the University of Aberdeen and the University of Nottingham. In 1973–4 he was seconded to the Department of Employment's Unit for Manpower Studies as economic adviser and in 1978 was Visiting Professor in the Faculty of Business, McMaster University, Canada, on a Commonwealth Fellowship. He has acted as consultant to the National Board for Prices and Incomes, Commission on Industrial Relations, Office of Manpower Economics, Social Science Research Council, Commission of the European Communities, International Labor Office and Organisation for Economic Co-operation and Development. He is co-author (with B. Chiplin) of *Sex Discrimination in the Labour Market* (Macmillan, 1976) and in addition to various papers on labour market discrimination his publications encompass the areas of wage drift, the economics of professional team sports, real and money wages, patterns of working hours and manpower policy.

B. CHIPLIN is Lecturer in the Department of Industrial Economics at the University of Nottingham. During 1978 he was a Visiting Professor in the Department of Economics, State University of New York at Buffalo. His publications include: (with P. J. Sloane) *Sex Discrimination in the Labour Market* (Macmillan, 1976); (with D. S. Lees) *Acquisitions and Mergers: Government Policy in Europe* (1975); and papers in the *American Economic Review, Economic Journal, British Journal of Industrial Relations*, amongst others. He has acted as consultant to a number of government institutions and private organisations.

M. CURRAN is now a Research Fellow in the Department of Sociology and Social Administration, University of Durham, engaged in a study of the inner city labour market. She was previously a research assistant in the Department of Industrial Economics, University of

Nottingham on an SSRC project concerning sex discrimination and female employment.

M. GUNDERSON is Associate Professor of Economics, University of Toronto, Center for Industrial Relations, Faculty of Management Studies and Scarborough College. He is a graduate of Queens University, Kingston, Ontario and the University of Wisconsin, Madison. He has published extensively on the labour market behaviour of women, manpower training and the impact of institutional constraints on the labour market.

H. C. JAIN is Associate Professor, Faculty of Business, McMaster University, Hamilton, Ontario. In 1975 he was a member of the Equal Value Committee of the Ontario Ministry of Labour. He was previously a Research Consultant with the Canada Department of Labour, Director of Research for the Nova Scotia Department of Labour and Research Assistant with the Federal Reserve Bank of Minneapolis. He has published many articles on the subjects of manpower resources, manpower policy and planning, pay and employment discrimination and industrial relations and is the author of *Contemporary Issues in Canadian Personnel Administration* (1974).

C. J. PARSLEY currently holds a visiting position in the Department of Economics at the University of Guelph, Ontario, Canada. He previously held a temporary post in the Department of Economics, Queen Mary College, London after working as a research assistant in the Department of Industrial Economics, University of Nottingham on an SSRC project on sex discrimination and female employment.

W. S. SIEBERT is Lecturer in Economics at the University of Stirling. He holds degrees from the University of Cape Town and London School of Economics and has held lecturing posts at the University of Birmingham and Paisley College. He has published articles on discrimination and occupational licensing and is co-author (with J. T. Addison) of *The Market for Labor: An Analytical Treatment* (1979).

1 Introduction

P. J. SLOANE

There are several reasons why it is informative to examine low pay in the context of female employment. First, there is the fact that, whatever definition of low pay one cares to adopt, women as a group predominate amongst this category of worker. This in turn means that any policy designed to improve the situation of the low paid worker is likely to have a disproportionate effect on the female workforce. Secondly, concern over problems of inequality of opportunity for the growing female labour force has led to the introduction in Britain, following the North American legislative pattern, of the Equal Pay Act in 1970 and the Sex Discrimination Act in 1975. Examination of the most disadvantaged section of the female labour force might, therefore, highlight problems relating to the adequacy of this legislation and equally enable some judgement to be made over the potential of such measures for reducing the numbers of low paid women. Thirdly, poverty is a problem which relates to family circumstances, and thus the role of married women, and more particularly single parent women, in relieving poverty through their participation in the labour force is clearly of some significance.

These factors suggest in turn that there are a number of ways in which we may define low pay relative to female employment. The first definition would relate to some estimate of the subsistence level of income. Thus, the Royal Commission on the Distribution of Income and Wealth took as its benchmark for low income weekly earnings at or below the lowest decile of the earnings of full-time manual men. This approximates to two-thirds of the average earnings of men in full-time manual work and to that level of net earnings (after tax and cash benefits) which would be sufficient to provide a married couple with two children with an income at least equal to that obtainable under the system of supplementary benefit. A second definition of low pay would compare female earnings with male earnings. The fact that average male earnings exceed those of females across the whole spectrum of occupations and industries is an established feature of both the British and North American labour markets considered in this book. The gap between the two may be attributed to a variety of causes, including the different occupational and industrial distributions of the sexes, differences between the sexes in education, skill and motivation, and the influence of sex discrimination. A third definition would consider cases where women were low paid relative to their level of productivity. This could occur where employers discriminated against women, thereby depressing the demand for female labour below that implied by its level of productivity or where women were subject to monopsonistic labour markets such that wages fell below the value of the marginal product of labour on account of inelasticity of supply (i.e. exploitation of labour). All three cases are considered in the five subsequent chapters.

Chapters 2 and 3 analyse data from the New Earnings Survey (NES) which, with the exception of 1969, has appeared annually since 1968 and is the most comprehensive source of information on the distribution of earnings. The former chapter concentrates on the current status of low paid women as revealed in the 1976 NES, low pay being defined here as payment below £40 per week.[1] The latter chapter concentrates on changes in the male/female earnings ratio over the last decade and attempts to assess the effects of government policy on this ratio. It is possible to characterise a low paid female job as involving unskilled, manual work, possibly undertaken on a part-time basis, in a small establishment in the service sector within a low paying region; typically there will be an absence of payment-by-results, overtime working, shift-work and collective agreement, or the job is located in the Wage Council sector. A low paid person is typically young or elderly and lacking in education and relevant experience. The main problem, however, appears to be not so much that some women are paid much less than others, but that women as a whole have much lower pay than men. Thus, analysis of the distributions of male and female earnings indicates that their shapes are broadly similar. Hence, in general it can be suggested that the poor pay position of women relative to men owes more to the position of the female earnings distribution to the left of the male than to differences in 'shape' between the two distributions. Consequently, redistributive policies which are directed towards the lower 'tails' of the male and female distributions, without attempting to shift the whole female distribution closer to the male, will have little effect on the male/female earnings ratio. Chapter 4 concentrates on the analysis of the structure of labour markets, particularly in the form of internal labour markets and dual labour markets, in the belief that an examination of the institutional framework of the unit of employment can cast considerable light on differences in treatment between men and women. Whilst every attempt is made to draw on relevant British material in this chapter, much of the analysis of necessity draws on American work and data. Chapter 5 deals explicitly with the North American experience, which is particularly relevant to the British case in so far as implementation of the legislation is more longstanding and parts of it are very similar in form to the British. The Canadian and US evidence does not, however, point to an unambiguous narrowing of the male/female earnings gap over time. Indeed, there is some evidence to suggest that the reverse has occurred. The gap does not appear to have narrowed during periods of prosperity and tight labour markets, nor in response to tighter enforcement of the equal pay legislation. The final chapter examines various theoretical shortcomings and data problems relating to analyses of women and low pay, focusing on schooling functions, dualism and crowding, monopsony, hiring standards and imperfect information.

Before considering some of these factors in more detail it is useful to highlight the extent to which women predominate amongst the low paid in Britain. The Royal Commission was able to obtain unpublished data from the New Earnings Survey which compares adult men (aged over 21) and women (aged over 18) whose pay was not affected by absence in the survey period in terms of the low pay definition of earnings equal to or less than the lowest decile of full-time manual men. This is reproduced below as Table 1.1 and reveals that, although there is a striking preponderance of women amongst the low paid, the relative position of both manual and non-manual women improved markedly between 1970 and 1977. Thus, whilst in April 1970 about 70 per cent of all women were low paid according to the above definition, by 1977 the figure had fallen to about 50 per cent. Of course, it might be objected that low pay amongst women is less serious from the point of view of family poverty since many women will be second wage earners. This fact was recognised by the Royal Commission which itself pointed out that over half the households and families in the lowest quarter of the income distribution contained no wage earner. Nonetheless, it went on to suggest that low earnings remain an important cause of low income among families with children, with nearly 70 per cent of earners in lower income households being 'low paid'. Further, one half of all one parent families as compared with one fifth of two parent families were in the lowest quarter of the distribution of equivalent net family incomes. According to the 1971 Census of Population there were 512,000 one

TABLE 1.1   Percentage of low-paid workers in various sex and skill groups
April 1970 and April 1977 (Great Britain)

Category of Worker		Percentage of group who are low paid		Percentage of low paid workers falling within each group	
		1970	*1977*	*1970*	*1977*
Male :	Manual	10	10	18	19
	Non-manual	5	7	5	9
Female:	Manual	85	68	33	26
	Non-manual	58	46	44	46
				100	100

SOURCE
Royal Commission on the Distribution of Income and Wealth, Report no. 6, *Lower Incomes*, Cmnd., 7175 (HMSO, May 1978).

parent families headed by women and Family Expenditure Survey data suggest that approximately one in three such mothers works full-time and one in seven part-time. Such facts led three members of the Royal Commission[2] to point out that one reason why low pay did not emerge as a more important cause of low family income was that married women's earnings lifted families out of lower income levels. They advocated, therefore, the monitoring of the availability of work for married women and access to provisions such as nurseries designed to facilitate such women's participation in the labour force. This accords with the findings of Chapter 5 where it is also suggested that labour force participation by married women in North America may be a prerequisite for raising families from poverty and that it is becoming increasingly archaic to regard women's earnings as secondary or supplementary.[3]

For some purposes it is useful to adopt the threefold classification of Chapter 6 and distinguish cases where average earnings differ because of varying personal characteristics acquired prior to entry into the labour force, factors affecting employment in differing jobs given education, and differences in pay given the job. Taking the first of these, General Household Survey data suggest that, whilst women are less well educated than men, the returns to educational advancement are actually higher for women than for men at the lower educational levels. In Canada, by contrast, the average duration of education is slightly higher for the female than for the male labour force. However, the type of education experienced is quite dissimilar. Also in line with British experience (at least at the lower educational levels) the percentage increase in annual earnings associated with a year of education is greater for women than for men. These features suggest that increasing education could ameliorate the position of low paid women. To the extent that pre-entry factors such as education are important determinants of earnings, it would appear that it is necessary to change the attitude of society towards the role of men and women not only in the labour market but also in household work.

Turning to factors influencing employment in the labour market given education, Chapters 2 and 5, in particular, suggest that there is a considerable amount of industrial and occupational segregation between the sexes with large numbers of women being found in industries and occupations closely related to household tasks. As far as occupations are concerned, low earnings seem to be explained in large part by the relative failure of women to advance up the career hierarchy of broad occupational groups. Whilst there are substantial differences in the percentage of low paid men and women, certain occupations are low paid for men as well as women. Indeed, as far as occupations are concerned there is no overwhelming evidence that women are unduly concentrated in low paying occupations (or industries), excluded from high paying male occupations (or industries) or concentrated in occupations (or industries) where the male earnings differential is particularly high. Only part-time women are clearly distributed unfavourably in relation to men occupationally and industrially.

The structuring of the labour market, as discussed in Chapter 4, may also militate against women's prospects of high earnings. Whilst fragmentary evidence suggests that the internal labour market is less significant in Britain than in North America, it is likely to be more significant for non-manual occupations, in which most women are found and for large firms from which women are more than proportionately excluded. Since internal labour markets occur in cases of high capital intensities and specific training, the quality of the labour force becomes crucial and hiring practices will play a more central role. However, in situations where it is not possible to judge individual performance prior to entry into the labour force, various screening devices will be utilised which may be based on sex or credentialism (the use of educational qualifications as a proxy for employability). Alternatively, self-selection devices (such as wage structures favouring slow quitters) may be utilised to dissuade certain groups (e.g. women) from applying for vacancies. The possibility that such stereotypes may become outdated is increased by the fact that the results of employment tests are rarely validated in Britain in the context of job performance. Under the related dual labour market concept it is held that women are concentrated into the secondary sector of the labour market and deprived of opportunities for entry into 'good' jobs. Even where women do gain entry into the primary sector it is likely to be into the 'subordinate primary' rather than the 'independent primary' (management) sector. Whilst in primary jobs seniority provisions mean that wages generally increase with age, in the secondary sector variations in hours will play a more important role in determining incomes. There is as yet, however, limited evidence for the existence of a dual labour market in Britain. It is likely that the occurrence of monopsonistic labour markets is more crucial to the relative pay of women given the fact that a married woman's job search is often constrained by her husband's employment. Locational factors are significant in so far as the percentage of low paid women does vary considerably by region and employment in conurbations has a positive effect on earnings levels.

Returning to the third aspect—differences in pay given the job—it must be borne in mind that men's earnings are increased relative to women's by the fact that relatively more men than women are in receipt of overtime, payment-by-results and shift premium payments and also by the fact that the size of such payments is generally higher for men. Further, age, as already noted above, is highly significant in determining the level of pay. NES data reveals that mean female manual earnings in the age ranges 18 to 24 and 60 to 64 fall below the definition of low pay and, whilst non-manual women actually fare better than men in the younger age group, the pattern of their earnings is the same as that of manual women. Human capital models applied at establishment level suggest that low earnings can at least partly be explained by low levels of human capital investment, including on-the-job training. More particularly one of the most important explanations for the low pay of women is their lack of cumulated work experience, most notable in the case of married women. Indeed, attempts to measure discrimination at the place of work find little difference in treatment between single men and single women. In general, it is, however, difficult to separate out efficiency criteria from discrimination, since marital status could itself be a proxy for commitment to work.

In addition to the above it is necessary to consider the fact that women are less likely to be unionised than men and consequently covered by some form or other of collective agreement. NES data for

1973 reveal that a significantly greater number of manual (though not non-manual) women than men are not covered by a collective agreement and analysis of these data suggests that the existence of a collective agreement may reduce the incidence of low pay. In Chapter 5 it is pointed out that the total effect of unionisation may well be to lower the ratio of female to male wages, because the union impact on wages (relative to non-union wages) may be dominated by the effect of the larger proportion of males organised in unions. Unionisation may itself foster labour market segmentation by causing overcrowding in non-unionised female jobs, in which case unionisation of women could be an effective means of improving the wages of low paid women.

It must also be noted that the female/male earnings ratio in Britain has in general increased over the period 1969–76, reversing its slight decline for earlier years (Chapter 3). The increase in the ratio has been most marked over the years 1974–6, with NES data showing a 16.7 per cent increase (9.21 percentage points) since 1973. A number of economic and social factors could have contributed towards this improvement in the relative position of women. However, changes in the industrial and occupational distribution of the labour force do not appear to have been significant and, whilst changes in the age distribution have played some part, well over 90 per cent of the change remains to be explained. The marked improvement in relative female earnings during the 1970s coincides with the introduction of the Equal Pay Act in 1970 and later with the Sex Discrimination Act in 1975. It is difficult to assess the direct contribution of this legislation but it does not seem to have been particularly marked and the results of American studies suggest that too much should not be expected in this direction. The years of improvement also coincide with periods of incomes policy involving flat rate elements. Calculation of the possible effects of such policies suggests that they could have made an important contribution to the improvement of relative female earnings. However, this does not imply that such policies are the most efficient way of improving the welfare of the female population, for they may create pressures in the labour market which could ultimately prove highly detrimental.

Explanations for the low pay of women are many and varied. Amongst other factors discrimination, lack of human capital, breaks in length of service, monopsonistic labour markets, limits on geographical mobility, job and enterprise segregation, exclusion from internal labour markets, dual labour markets, lack of productivity and concentration on household duties have been held to play a significant role. Therefore, one would incline to the view put forward by the Royal Commission that 'the present state of knowledge does not point with certainty to any single explanation as to why some families and individuals have lower incomes than others'. In turn, this suggests that no single policy will in itself be sufficient to improve the pay position of women relative to men to any marked extent. Further, the preponderance of women in the low-paid sector would seem to rule out one possible policy measure—a national minimum wage—since if such a measure were to be effective in relieving poverty it would have to be fixed at a level which would raise the earnings of a substantial number of male heads of household. But to achieve this would require adjustment to the pay of approaching half of the female workforce, with major effects on the level of employment and the rate of inflation. To some extent equal pay legislation can, of course, be seen as a form of minimum wage for women, but experience so far, as seen above, does not suggest that this is capable of closing the gap in male/female earnings to any major extent. Given the current division of labour in the household, attention should perhaps be focused more outside the labour market than within as far as future policies are concerned. Changing family roles and the aspirations of women may, however, be difficult to achieve and certainly should be regarded as a long-run rather than a short-run policy objective.

NOTES

1. At April 1976, 10 per cent of full-time male manual workers earned less than £43.60 per week (excluding those whose pay was affected by absence), but the published NES distribution of earnings data do not reveal how many women earned an amount at or below this figure. £40 is the closest figure for which the relevant information is provided.
2. See Addendum to Cmnd., 7175, op. cit., by Doughty, Lea and Wedderburn on working women and the role of low pay.
3. The authors point out that female-headed families have a much higher incidence of poverty than male-headed families and the relative position is worsening, since by 1974 female-headed families constituted 30 per cent of poor families compared with only 18 per cent in 1969.

2 Low Pay amongst Women—the Facts

P. J. SLOANE AND W. S. SIEBERT

INTRODUCTION

In this paper low pay amongst women is taken to refer to those whose pay falls below the level of the lowest decile of the distribution of employment incomes of full-time manual men. A major source of information on the distribution of employment income is the New Earnings Survey, and this paper concentrates in the main on the results of the April 1976 survey, supplemented where necessary by other sources including the General Household Survey. However a number of features of the NES survey must be borne in mind in interpreting these results:

(i) The information relates to a single pay period and is not necessarily representative of pay over a longer period. It generally excludes the value of payments in kind and income received from other concurrent employment.

(ii) The number of variables for which cross-classification is available is small,[1] and in particular it contains no information on the level of education of the employees in the sample.

(iii) According to the Office of Manpower Economics[2] it is deficient in terms of the response from small employers. Since such employers tend to be low paying, and women tend to be over-represented here (see below), this might cause us to over-estimate average female pay.

(iv) Occupational categories are broad, so that women are likely to be classified as being in the same occupational group as men, although differences in the work are such as to amount to a material difference under the terms of the Equal Pay Act 1970.

These factors are all important, but clearly one can only use the data

9

which are available. Attention is focused on weekly earnings inclusive of overtime for most of the analysis (though results for hourly earnings are also provided where appropriate). This follows the approach adopted by earlier studies which have suggested that results are not fundamentally different for men and women when the analysis is conducted in terms of hourly rather than weekly earnings.[3] Most analyses of the distribution of earnings in the NES exclude employees whose earnings for the pay period were affected by absence as these tend to distort the numbers in the lower ranges of weekly earnings. Moreover, the data relate to adult employees. In this respect it should be noted that males aged 21 and over at the beginning of the year of the survey are described as adult · men, whereas females aged 18 and over at the beginning of the year are defined as adult women.[4] We can, however, check the extent to which this biases the results. In the case of average gross weekly earnings adult manual women earned 61 per cent of adult male earnings in 1976. Comparing those in both groups aged 18 and over the figure was 62 per cent and aged 21 and over 61 per cent. The comparable figure for non-manual employees was 60 per cent as opposed to 61 and 63 per cent. In the case of average hourly earnings, excluding the effect of overtime, manual adult women earned 71 per cent of male adult earnings, whilst the figure for those in both groups aged 18 and over and aged 21 and over was 72 per cent in each case. For non-manual employees the comparable figure was 63 per cent as opposed to 64 and 66 per cent. It appears, therefore, that the failure to use a common starting age for men and women depresses the female/male earnings ratio between 0 and 3 percentage points.

A further problem in using NES data relates to the definition of low pay adopted in this paper. It is not possible from the published figures to analyse earnings distribution data for women earning less than the lowest male decile earnings figure. However, data are available for the percentage of employees earning less than certain figures which approximate to the lowest decile for male employees. Thus in terms of gross *weekly* earnings 10 per cent of manual men earned less than £43.60. It therefore seems reasonable to examine those groups of women, both manual and non-manual, who earned less than £40 in April 1976. This comprises 56 per cent of manual women, 38.2 per cent of non-manual women and 43.2 per cent of all women. In terms of gross *hourly* earnings (including overtime pay and overtime hours) 10 per cent of manual men earned less than 102.6p. In the light of this figure it seems reasonable to take a figure of 100p as the low pay threshold; in this case 52.3 per cent of manual, 30.3 per cent of non-manual and 36.6

per cent of all women earned less than this figure. There is the advantage of simplicity in adopting the same figure for both manual and non-manual employees, and yet—in the light of the very different employment experience of each group—to consider each group separately.

It is also apparent from the above figures that the problem of low pay, if such exists, is largely a problem of the low pay of women. But as the NBPI observed, one cannot ignore the social significance of the fact that men's earnings are normally the main source of family incomes, whilst this is true only for a minority of women. Notwithstanding this there are two aspects of low pay as far as women are concerned—the pay of women relative to men and the pay of low paid women relative to higher paid women. Before turning to the latter it is necessary to examine how far women's pay is depressed relative to that of men because of a relatively unfavourable employment distribution in relation to both occupation and industry. This relates to what has been termed the 'crowding hypothesis', that is, the tendency for women to be concentrated in certain occupations and industries with the result that the enforced abundance of supply lowers marginal productivity in some areas, whilst maintaining it at a higher level in the male sector through barriers to mobility.[5] There are certain problems in ascertaining how far crowding is a consequence rather than a cause of differences between the sexes and there are alternative explanations for such concentrations of employment, but the data contained in the NES do enable us to test for the significance of this effect.

THE OVERALL EARNINGS DISTRIBUTION

In order to determine the effect of crowding on female earnings we need to ascertain to what extent women are concentrated in low paying occupations and industries. There appear to be three separate hypotheses that can be formulated:

(i) The greater the percentage of women in the labour force, *ceteris paribus*, the lower the level of female earnings;
(ii) the greater the pay of men, *ceteris paribus*, the lower the percentage of women in the labour force, and
(iii) the greater the percentage of women in the labour force, the greater the male/female earnings differential, which is also consistent with Becker's 'tastes' explanation of discrimination.

The results of attempts to test these hypotheses by means of a simple regression model are contained in Tables 2.1, 2.2 and 2.3, using data from the 1976 NES. It should, however, be noted that results are only provided for those occupations and industries represented by at least 100 persons in the sample and for which the estimate of average weekly

TABLE 2.1 Occupational analysis of earnings and female employment distribution

Dependent variable	Constant	Females as a percentage of all employees in each occupational group	R^2	No. in sample
Female				
weekly earnings[a]	51.2	− 3.55	.003	25
Mean	£49.6	0.453		
|t|		(0.26)		
Male				
weekly earnings[a]	64.8	− 3.71	.00003	25
Mean	£64.6	0.453		
|t|		(0.03)		
Weekly male/female				
earnings ratio[c]	.535	− 0.241	.105	25
Mean	.426	0.453		
|t|		(1.64)		
Female				
hourly earnings[b]	107.7	− 0.04	.000	17
Mean	107.7	0.468		
|t|		(0.00)		
Male				
hourly earnings[b]	146.5	− 4.47	.003	17
Mean	144.41	0.468		
|t|		(0.23)		
Hourly male/female				
earnings ratio[d]	.358	− 0.028	.004	17
Mean	.345	.468		
|t|		(0.26)		

NOTES

[a] Excluding those whose pay during the survey period was affected by absence.

[b] Excluding the effect of overtime.

[c] $\dfrac{WEM - WEF}{WEF}$ where WEM = male weekly earnings. WEF = female weekly earnings.

[d] $\dfrac{HEM - HEF}{HEF}$ where HEM = male hourly earnings. HEF = female hourly earnings.

TABLE 2.2 Industrial analysis of earnings and female employment distribution—manual employees

Dependent variable	Constant	Females as a percentage of all manual employees in each industry	R^2	No. in sample
Weekly earnings, female	41.9	−.021	.078	24
Mean	£40.3	.362		
|t|		(0.00)		
Weekly earnings, male	66.6	−16.7	.237	24
Mean	£50.0	.362		
|t|		(0.55)		
$(WE_m - WE_f)/WE_f$	.567	−.187	.079	24
Mean	.499	.362		
|t|		(1.37)		
Hourly earnings, female	105.5	−7.806	.046	24
Mean	101.4	.362		
|t|		(0.14)		
Hourly earnings, male	148.1	−57.9	.190	24
Mean	131.9	.362		
|t|		(0.93)		
$(HE_m - HE_f)/HE_f$	.360	−.149	.080	24
Mean	.360	.362		
|t|		(1.38)		

NOTE
[a] Some of these regressions took a quadratic form (i.e. % Females + % Females^2) to test for a non-linear relationship but this had a negligible influence on the results.

earnings has a percentage standard error of not more than 2.0 per cent. This means that there are certain occupational and industrial groups for which there are no results either for men or for women and this reduces the size of sample over which comparisons can be made. In order to maximise the number of observations the procedure has been to use the narrower occupational groups and minimum list heading rather than industrial order, wherever data are provided for both sexes and, where this is not the case, data on broader occupational group or industrial order are utilised, again as far as possible.[6] This may well introduce bias

TABLE 2.3 Industrial analysis of earnings and female employment distribution—non-manual employees

Dependent variable	Constant	Female as a percentage of all non-manual· employees in each industry	R^2	No. in sample
Weekly earnings, female	41.81	10.43	.0395	21
Mean	£45.78	.380		
$\|t\|$		(0.88)		
Weekly earnings, male	80.79	−.729	.0002	21
Mean	£80.5	.380		
$\|t\|$		(0.06)		
$(WE_m - WE_f)/WE_f$	.901	−.315	.095	21
Mean	.781	.380		
$\|t\|$		(1.41)		
Hourly earnings, female	110.98	36.26	.0352	21
Mean	124.78	.380		
$\|t\|$		(.83)		
Hourly earnings, male	202.2	14.58	.00051	21
Mean	207.7	.380		
$\|t\|$		(0.31)		
$(HE_m - HE_f)/HE_f$	.788	−.248	.0629	21
Mean	.694	.380		
$\|t\|$		(1.13)		

into the results, particularly by excluding occupations and industries where there is marked sex segregation. However, as indicated by the mean employment level for women in Table 2.1, women tend to be over-represented in the samples—that is male rather than female dominated occupations are excluded. Further, this is perhaps a minor problem compared to lack of inclusion of other essential standardising variables. The occupational analysis suggests that females are not unduly concentrated in low paying occupations, excluded from high paying male occupations, or concentrated in occupations where the male earnings differential is particularly high. Although the female employment percentage has the expected sign in the case of both hourly and weekly earnings of men and women the |t| statistic is never remotely significant and in the case of the male/female earnings ratio the sign is perverse. This confirms the results of a similar exercise by Chiplin and Sloane (1976 (b)) and casts doubt on the widely held view that it is in lack of access to higher paid occupations rather than differences in pay that has the major effect in depressing female earnings, although it must be recognised that a certain amount of sex segregation may be hidden within the KOS occupational classification used in the NES.

The results of similar analyses of industrial distributions of female employment are given separately for manual (Table 2.2) and non-manual women (Table 2.3). Again, the explanatory variables are not significant in any of the equations. As far as manual workers are concerned the sign on percentage female employment is negative as expected, both for weekly and hourly earnings, but for non-manual employees the sign is positive in three out of four cases. In all four male/female earnings ratio equations the sign on the percentage female coefficient is again the reverse of that expected. An attempt to test for a non-linear relationship also failed to provide significant results. The results for non-manual employees accord with earlier results using NES data obtained by Chiplin and Sloane (1976(b)). However that study, using a non-parametric test, found a significant negative relationship between male manual earnings and female employment as a percentage of total employment in each industry both in 1971 and 1974. Yet, a considerable difference in the explained variance in the two cases suggested a certain degree of short-run volatility in the earnings rankings of the various industries. Therefore we may conclude that there is little evidence that the distribution of female employment is unfavourable in relation to areas of high earnings or compared to that of men.

It is possible, however, to go further than the question of the existing employment distribution and ask what difference it would make if women were to be distributed in the same way as men in relation to occupation and pay. Estimates by Chiplin and Sloane[7] suggest that inequality of pay is roughly twice as important as inequality of occupational distribution using NES data, but that much of the relative importance of pay can be explained in terms of the concentration of women in low-paying firms and of the use of incremental pay systems.

OCCUPATIONAL ANALYSIS

Female employment tends to be far more homogeneous than that of men with no less than 40 per cent of women in the NES engaged in clerical and related occupations. The concentration of women in non-manual occupations is notable and contrasts with that of men. Thus in the case of women 69 per cent of the sample are non-manual whereas the comparable figure for men is 38 per cent. A ranking of occupations in order of the degree to which females predominate also suggests that the vast bulk of female employees are concentrated in a very small number of occupational groups where the labour force is predominantly female.[8] Barron and Norris (1974) refer to the widely held belief that the characteristics of such occupations are that the work is generally unskilled, repetitive, requiring manual dexterity, lacking in responsibility and poorly paid. To this list may be added the fact that such occupations frequently require the application of skills acquired in the household and thus demand little further training. Frequently also, particularly in the manual sector, there is a limited career hierarchy and an avoidance of contexts in which women are required to supervise men. Occupations with large numbers of female employees which fall into some or all of these categories include primary teaching, social work, nursing, secretarial and clerical activities, catering, cleaning and sewing machining.

Table 2.4 ranks broad occupational groups according to the percentage of women earning less than £40 per week. As might be anticipated the greater proportion of low-paid women are to be found in the less skilled categories, but no less than 44 per cent of women employed in the managerial (excluding general management) group are low paid according to the above definition. Further examination of the narrower occupational breakdown suggests that part of the explanation may be the relative failure of women to advance up the career hierarchy. Thus only 4.1 per cent of women in the clerical and related group are classified as supervisors compared with 11.9 per cent of men. Robinson and Wallace (1977) note that in distribution there is a comparatively high female concentration in 'groceries and provisions', 'clothing and footwear', 'other non-food' and 'general stores' each of which has relatively low earnings. In contrast furniture, carpet and electrical goods shops, where earnings are amongst the highest in retailing together employed three-quarters of men in all household goods trades, and in these three trades women formed only a third of the employed labour force. Therefore there seems to be segregation of the sexes according to earnings levels prevailing within the separate trades, though it is difficult to disentangle cause and effect. Again, in engineering where females account for about one quarter of total employment, one third of full-time women are employed in clerical and related jobs, one half in semi-skilled production work, largely as assemblers and machinists, and a further 10 per cent in unskilled work.[9]

Table 2.4 shows that there is a close relationship between percentage earning less than £40 per week and percentage earning less than 100p per hour ($r = 0.848$). This is also the case for percentage of low paid and the lowest decile female earnings ($r = -.925$ between the lowest decile and percentage earning less than £40). The relationship between percentage low pay for men and for women ($r = .678$) is less close but still significant. It appears, therefore, that certain occupations are low paid for men as well as women, though the differences in the percentage of low paid employees between the sexes is marked. This does not seem to be entirely consistent with dualist interpretations of the operation of the labour market, including the crowding hypothesis.

INDUSTRIAL ANALYSIS

Over half of all female employees are to be found in three major service industries: professional and scientific services, the distribution trades and miscellaneous services (e.g. catering, laundries, etc.), whilst by contrast no single industry accounts for as much as 10 per cent of all male employees. Thus the 1971 Census of Population shows that the female share of all employment varies widely from 4.4 per cent in mining and quarrying to 74.1 per cent in clothing and footwear with a mean employment percentage of 38.5 per cent.[10]

The National Board for Prices and Incomes (1971) surveyed three low-paying industries—laundry and dry cleaning, the National Health Service and contract cleaning—and found that a common factor in all three industries was the low level of skill and the fact that low pay tended to attract employees who were at a competitive disadvantage in the labour market. Workers in those industries, who include a large number of women, were said to be not actively seeking better jobs. However, other factors such as market environment, management organisation and ability, union organisation and collective bargaining arrangements were very different. The implication of these findings was that the means of remedying low pay differed from one industry to

TABLE 2.4 Low pay by occupational group—full-time and part-time women aged 18 and over, whose pay for the survey pay period was not affected by absence

	Occupational group	Percentage with weekly earnings less than £40 %	Percentage with hourly earnings less than 100p %		10% earned less than the amount below per week £
			Full-time	Part-time	
VIII N.M.	Selling	86.6 (13.5)	86.1	93.1	22.8
XIII M.	Making and repairing (excluding metal and electrical)	64.1 (4.7)	61.4	70.1	25.9
XII M.	Material processing (excluding metals)	63.8 (5.3)	63.0	67.0	28.3
X M.	Catering, cleaning, hairdressing and other personal services	61.3 (18.8)	54.4	71.5	24.1
XVIII M.	Miscellaneous	50.9 (9.9)	51.8	n.a.	28.0
XVII M.	Transport operating, materials moving and storing and related	49.3 (6.8)	48.6	65.2	27.0
XV M.	Painting, repetitive assembling, product inspecting, packaging and related	46.7 (3.6)	45.3	55.7	28.3
VII N.M.	Clerical and related	44.0 (6.2)	31.3	50.9	29.1
VI N.M.	Managerial (excluding general management)	44.0 (4.4)	n.a.	n.a.	27.8
XIV M.	Processing, making, repairing and related (metal and electrical)	38.1 (1.6)	37.4	54.6	30.1
IV N.M.	Literary and artistic	35.4 (4.0)	n.a.	n.a.	27.6

TABLE 2.4 (*contd.*)

Occupational group	Percentage with weekly earnings less than £40 %	Percentage with hourly earnings less than 100p % Full-time	Percentage with hourly earnings less than 100p % Part-time	10 % earned less than the amount below per week £
V N.M. Professional and related in science, engineering, technology and similar fields	19.8 (1.5)	14.6[a]	n.a.	35.0
II N.M. Professional and related supporting management and administration	14.2 (2.5)	n.a.	n.a.	37.3
III N.M. Professional and related in education, welfare and health	12.3 (2.4)	22.2[b]	14.6[b]	38.9
IX N.M. Security and protective service	8.1 (2.7)	6.6	n.a.	41.1

NOTES
[a] Laboratory Technicians (scientific, medical only).
[b] Nursing professionals only.

Figures in brackets relate to the percentage of adult men earning less than £40 per week in each occupation group.

another. It must also be borne in mind that some low paying occupations (e.g. clerical) are found in some high paying industries.

As a broad generalisation, as indicated in Tables 2.5 and 2.6, the largest concentration of low pay both for manual and non-manual women tends to be in services. Women do rather better in parts of manufacturing and particularly engineering. Low pay also tends to be more marked in the private than in the public sector. The experience of

TABLE 2.5 Low pay ranked by industry—April 1976—full-time and part-time manual women, aged 18 and over, whose pay for the survey was not affected by absence

Industrial order	Percentage earning less than £40 per week %	Percentage earning less than 100p per hour		10% earned less than the amount below per week Full-time £
		Full-time %	Part-time %	
Distributive trades	78.7 (19.0)	75.1	89.4	24.0
Clothing and footwear	77.7 (17.7)	74.9	81.0	24.5
Miscellaneous services	72.3 (25.0)	71.8	74.5	20.6
Textiles	65.8 (6.6)	64.8	74.5	27.5
Other manufacturing industries	61.4 (4.9)	60.8	71.9	26.7
Professional and scientific services	56.3 (11.3)	42.8	68.1	29.4
Bricks, pottery, glass, cement, etc.	51.2 (2.7)	48.8	n.a.	31.1
Food, drink and tobacco	50.9 (3.7)	51.0	58.9	28.9
Metal goods NES	50.9 (3.8)	47.8	63.5	28.2
Chemicals and allied industries	48.7 (2.4)	44.9	50.4	29.9
Paper, printing and publishing	45.0 (3.3)	45.1	66.0	30.4
Public administration	42.0 (8.6)	41.1	75.6	31.5
Instrument engineering	41.8 (4.5)	40.2	n.a.	28.1
Mechanical engineering	34.5 (1.9)	34.1	n.a.	30.1
Electrical engineering	33.7 (2.7)	31.7	38.7	32.7
Transport and communication	18.2 (1.7)	18.4	35.6	36.0
Vehicles	17.9 (0.6)	17.6	n.a.	36.7

Figures in brackets relate to percentage of male manual workers earning less than £40 per week in each industry.

TABLE 2.6 Low pay ranked by industry—April 1976—full-time and part-time non-manual women, aged 18 and over, whose pay for the survey week was not affected by absence

Industrial order	Percentage earning less than £40 per week %	Percentage earning less than 100p per hour Full-time %	Part-time %	10% earned less than the amount below per week Full-time £
Distributive trades	79.3 (14.2)	74.1	89.4	24.4
Textiles	70.2 (3.3)	56.3	n.a.	28.1
Construction	64.9 (5.1)	52.0	56.6	27.2
Miscellaneous services	49.8 (12.3)	41.5	62.7	26.0
Mechanical engineering	48.0 (1.7)	33.7	50.5	29.8
Food, drink and tobacco	46.2 (2.7)	33.1	60.6	29.2
Insurance, Banking, finance and business services	44.7 (5.6)	30.0	49.9	28.5
Paper, printing and publishing	42.0 (3.6)	29.0	48.5	30.1
Electrical engineering	39.8 (1.4)	28.6	n.a.	32.7
Chemicals and allied industries	36.8 (1.5)	25.1	n.a.	31.3
Gas, electricity and water	28.7 (1.7)	16.6	n.a.	36.3
Metal manufacture	25.5 (0.5)	15.5	n.a.	33.5
Vehicles	23.9 (1.0)	15.3	n.a.	34.6
Transport and communications	20.8 (2.3)	14.0	35.4	34.1
Professional and scientific services	19.2 (4.3)	15.3	22.4	35.3
Public administration	18.7 (1.2)	8.1	16.9	37.4

Figures in brackets relate to percentage of male non-manual workers earning less than £40 per week in each industry.

low pay amongst men bears a close relationship to the female pattern ($r = 0.774$ for manual employees and 0.628 for non-manual employees in relation to percentage earning less than £40 per week) as was found for the occupational analysis.[11]

The relationship between percentage earning less than £40 a week and the lowest decile of earnings is given by $r = -0.916$ for manual women and $r = -0.906$ for non-manual women. Here it is worth pointing out that Marquand (1967) using the 1960 Ministry of Labour

Distribution of Earnings Survey, made a test of the similarity of shape of the weekly earnings distribution by comparing the ranking of the 128 industries in the survey by the level of earnings at the lowest decile with the corresponding ranking at the lower quartile. The shape of the lower end of the earnings distribution was found not to differ significantly from industry to industry. Though no similar test has been performed here in relation to NES data, the evidence from Tables 2.5 and 2.6, and in other tables, suggests that misleading answers are not likely to be obtained by concentrating on a particular point within the earnings distribution.

It has been suggested elsewhere that women suffer low earnings because they tend to be concentrated more than proportionately in small firms, which in turn tend to pay lower wages than large.[12] Unfortunately no data are available on employment by sex by size of establishment. However, using data on proportions employed in small establishments and average size of establishment from the 1968 Census of Production we can examine whether there is any relationship between these variables and the percentage of weekly low pay by industry as defined above (though it does not necessarily follow that women are concentrated in the small establishments within each industry). Equations 1 and 2 in Table 2.7 show a highly significant negative relationship between mean size of establishment and the percentage of low paid manual women in an industry (whether measured in terms of hourly or weekly pay). This explanatory variable can account for over 40 per cent of the variance in the low paid percentage. Equations 3 and 4 suggest that the relationship between percentage weekly low paid workers and employment in small establishments as a proportion of total employment is less marked. Whilst the sign on the coefficient is as expected in the case of both manual and non-manual women, the independent variable is only significant for the latter group.[13] Thus it definitely seems that industries with small units of production tend to have low average pay.[14] However, the extent to which this is a factor causing women's low pay (i.e. whether women are concentrated within such industries) cannot yet be precisely determined.

PART-TIME WOMEN

The growth of part-time employment, particularly among married women has been a major feature of the post-war British labour market.

Table 2.7 Low pay and size of establishment

Dependent variable	Constant	Mean employment size of establishment	R^2	No. in sample
Percentage of manual women earning less than £40 per week				
Coefficient	73.019	−0.125	.404	17
Mean 57.782		121.824		
|t|		(−3.19)		
Percentage of manual women earning less than 100p per hour				
Coefficient	71.254	−0.126	0.434	17
Mean 55.947		121.824		
|t|		(13.39)		
Percentage of manual women earning less than £40 per week		Employment in Small establishments as percentage of Total Employment		
Coefficient	40.414	0.924	0.122	14
Mean 47.979		8.186		
|t|		(1.29)		
Percentage of non-manual women earning less than £40 per week				
Coefficient	38.762	1.305	0.338	15
Mean 50.720		9.167		
|t|		(2.57)		

[a] defined as establishments with less than 25 employees.

According to the 1971 Census of Population, 33.5 per cent of all female employees were engaged on a part-time basis, defined as working not more than 30 hours a week. No less than two-thirds of female part-timers are to be found in three service industries (professional and scientific services, the distributive trades and miscellaneous services). It should be noted that since 1975 the NES has covered only employees who are members of PAYE schemes, which has the effect of excluding some lower paid employees, mainly part-timers. Further some of those part-timers included in the Survey may have more than one job and could conceivably appear twice in the results. That is, information relating to different jobs is not combined to obtain total earnings of the employee. Tables 2.4, 2.5 and 2.6 enable us to compare the percentage of part-timers relative to full-timers earning less than 100p per hour. It can be seen that in every occupation but one and in every industry where data are available a higher percentage of part-timers than full-timers are low paid according to this criterion. It would seem, therefore, that part-time women, in particular, might require special attention. There is no easy solution, however, since a move to increase part-timers' pay, unless accompanied by an increase in their skills, is likely to cause unemployment. Those occupations and industries with high proportions of low paid full-timers also tend to be those with high proportions of low paid part-timers, which indicates a common factor in the kinds of skills required by occupation/industry. An exception may be noted, however: one of the highest concentrations of low paid manual part-timers, but not manual full-timers, is to be found in public administration (Table 2.5).

Adopting an identical approach as in tables 2.1, 2.2 and 2.3 it is possible to test whether females are unfavourably distributed in terms of levels of pay and employment on a part-time basis. Tables 2.8, 2.9 and 2.10, contrasting with the results for full-time employees, do in fact provide some evidence to suggest this is the case. Table 2.8 shows a highly significant negative relationship between part-time female employment by occupation and both male weekly and hourly earnings. The relationship between part-time female employment distribution and areas of low female earnings is, however, less marked, only being significant with respect to weekly earnings, whilst there is no relationship between the part-time female occupational distribution and the male/female earnings differential. The industrial distribution follows a similar pattern as far as manual women are concerned with a significant inverse relationship between part-time female employment and male earnings, but no relationship with female earnings. However, in this case there is a significant inverse relationship between the part-time female employment distribution and the male/female earnings differential. As with full-time females there is no relationship with any of the earnings variables as far as non-manual employees are concerned. That there are not many part-time workers in industries where male or female earnings are high need not necessarily mean that part-time workers are 'disadvantaged'. It may well mean that these are high skill industries with too high a specified capital investment per worker to make part-time hirings worthwhile.

TABLE 2.8 Occupational analysis of earnings and part-time female employment

Dependent variable	Constant	Part-time women as a percentage of all employees in each occupational group	R^2	No. in sample
Male weekly earnings				
Coefficient	63.827	−0.200	0.543	14
Mean 59.907		17.786		
|t|		(3.78)		
Male hourly earnings				
Coefficient	148.004	−0.482	0.554	14
Mean 139.429		17.786		
|t|		(3.86)		
Female weekly earnings				
Coefficient	42.095	−0.118	0.338	14
Mean 40.000		17.786		
|t|		(2.48)		
Female hourly earnings				
Coefficient	108.256	−0.249	0.184	14
Mean 103.821		17.786		
|t|		(1.65)		
$(WE_m - WE_f)/WE_f$				
Coefficient	0.519	−0.001	0.019	14
Mean 0.503		17.786		
|t|		(0.48)		
$(HE_m - HE_f)/HE_f$				
Coefficient	0.371	−0.001	0.054	14
Mean 0.348		17.786		
|t|		(0.83)		

Therefore it would appear that there is a weight of evidence to suggest that part-time, particularly manual, females are low paid[15] relatively to men[16] and to full-time women. How far this reflects their relatively low level of unionisation or simply a willingness to accept work at lower pay because the hours are better fitted to their personal preferences remains, however, to be determined.

Table 2.9   Industrial analysis of earnings and part-time female manual employment

Dependent variable	Constant	Part-time women as a percentage of all employees in each occupational group	R^2	No. in sample
Male weekly earnings				
Coefficient	63.449	−0.240	0.328	15
Mean 58.793		19.440		
|t|		(2.52)		
Male hourly earnings				
Coefficient	138.009	−0.471	0.332	15
Mean 128.860		19.440		
|t|		(2.54)		
Female weekly earnings				
Coefficient	39.418	−0.040	0.026	15
Mean 38.633		19.440		
|t|		(0.59)		
Female hourly earnings				
Coefficient	97.638	0.034	0.003	15
Mean 98.293		19.440		
|t|		(0.20)		
$(WE_m - WE_f)/WE_f$				
Coefficient	0.614	−0.005	0.331	15
Mean 0.527		19.440		
|t|		(2.53)		
$(HE_f - HE_f)/HE_f$				
Coefficient	0.413	−0.005	0.533	15
Mean 0.316		19.440		
|t|		(3.85)		

AGE PROFILES

Human capital theory suggests that earnings will be related to age (which can be viewed as a proxy for experience) and this is borne out by the figures from the NES. Thus Table 2.11 shows that for male manual employees earnings rise with age until the 30 to 39 age group and decline thereafter. Similarly for women earnings rise with age but peak earlier

TABLE 2.10   Industrial analysis of earnings and part-time female non-manual employment

Dependent variable	Constant	Part-time women as a percentage of all employees in each occupational group	R^2	No. in sample
Male weekly earnings				
Coefficient	84.183	−0.422	0.135	13
Mean 79.923		10.085		
|t|		(1.31)		
Male hourly earnings				
Coefficient	223.942	−1.648	0.125	13
Mean 207.323		10.085		
|t|		(1.25)		
Female weekly earnings				
Coefficient	48.059	−0.198	0.024	13
Mean 46.062		10.085		
|t|		(0.52)		
Female hourly earnings				
Coefficient	134.961	−0.822	0.029	13
Mean 126.677		10.085		
|t|		(0.58)		
$(WE_m - WE_f)/WE_f$				
Coefficient	0.789	−0.002	0.004	13
Mean 0.774		10.085		
|t|		(0.21)		
$(HE_m - HE_f)/HE_f$				
Coefficient	0.702	−0.002	0.010	13
Mean 0.680		10.085		
|t|		(0.33)		

in the 25 to 29 age range. Unfortunately, a distinction between married and single women is not possible. Mean earnings in the age ranges under 18 to 24 and 60 to 64 fall below the definition of low pay (£40 per week). Whilst the percentage of men earning less than £40 per week declines sharply with age to reach a minimum of 4 per cent in the 30 to 39 age range and rises thereafter to reach 22.2 per cent in the 65 and over category, that for women falls less dramatically with age to a minimum of 51.6 per cent in the 25 to 29 age group and rises to 75.8 per cent in the 65 and over category. The percentage with low hourly earnings follows a very similar pattern.

In the case of non-manual employees women tend to fare better

TABLE 2.11 Analysis by age group—full-time males and females, whose pay for the survey period was not affected by absence

Manual employees

Age group at 1 January 1976	Average gross weekly earnings £			Percentage with weekly earnings less than £40 %		Percentage with hourly earnings less than 100p %	
	Men	Women	Women as % of men	Men	Women	Men	Women
Under 18	28.8	27.0	93.8	90.0	93.4	93.0	94.2
18–20	45.5	35.6	78.2	38.8	67.8	47.2	66.1
21–24	59.4	38.9	65.5	9.5	56.3	12.9	55.1
25–29	65.6	40.5	61.7	5.1	51.6	7.3	49.9
30–39	68.9	40.4	58.6	4.0	53.1	5.9	48.9
40–49	67.8	40.1	59.1	4.0	54.0	6.1	49.8
50–59	64.0	40.0	62.5	5.3	54.5	7.7	49.8
60–64	59.0	37.6	63.7	9.5	63.3	12.3	59.1
65 and over	52.7	n.a.	n.a.	22.2	75.8	26.6	76.1
All ages	62.8	38.8	61.8	10.4	57.8	13.1	54.4

TABLE 2.11 (contd.)

Non-manual employees

	Men	Women	Women as % of men	Men	Women	Men	Women
Under 18	25.6	25.7	100.4	96.5	96.2	95.6	93.7
18–20	39.2	34.5	88.0	59.3	76.8	51.6	66.1
21–24	55.5	44.6	80.4	13.3	38.1	10.3	27.1
25–29	71.1	51.8	72.9	4.0	25.5	3.3	19.1
30–39	86.3	53.2	61.6	2.4	30.7	2.2	22.5
40–49	91.6	53.4	58.3	2.8	31.3	2.4	25.0
50–59	87.4	53.4	61.1	3.9	31.2	3.4	24.4
60–64	76.6	n.a.	n.a.	8.2	36.9	6.2	33.1
65 and over	n.a.	n.a.	n.a.	22.9	50.4	21.5	41.9
All ages	78.9	47.6	60.3	8.4	41.3	7.6	33.8

relatively to men in the younger age groups actually earning more in the under 18 age group, and from the age of 21 fewer women fall into the category of low paid, reaching a minimum of 25.5 per cent on a weekly basis and 19.1 per cent on an hourly basis in the 25 to 29 range. Why women should fare worse relative to men in the middle years both for non-manual and manual employees can be illustrated by the following diagram (Fig. 2.1). This is consistent with a situation in which married women leave the labour force to raise a family in the early years and return later with less labour market experience than primary workers, thereby depressing the overall average level pay of women relative to men in the middle age ranges.

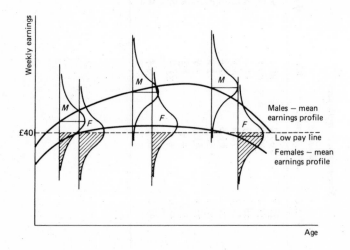

FIG. 2.1 The cross-hatched areas show the proportion of a given age group's earnings distribution which falls below the low pay line. The flatter earnings profile for women means that a much smaller proportion of them escape the low earnings level in the middle age range than do men.

Allowance should be made for the fact that no consideration is given in Table 2.11 to differences in occupational distribution, industrial distribution or other features of employment. The NES does, however, allow us to correct for occupation. In Table 2.12 data are provided for seven occupations in which detailed information is provided for both sexes classified by age. In all, these seven occupations contain some 90 per cent of these full-time women in the sample whose pay was not affected by absence. In five of the seven occupations average female

Table 2.12   Gross weekly earnings and age in selected occupations

Occupation and age group	Lowest decile			Median		
	Men £	Women £	Female earnings as % of male %	Men £	Women £	Female earnings as % of male %
Professional and related supporting management and adminis-tration						
21–24	34.9	35.7	102.3	55.3	53.2	96.2
25–29	52.0	40.3	77.5	75.6	67.3	89.0
30–39	61.7	43.1	69.9	92.3	70.3	76.2
40–49	64.5	38.8	60.2	97.6	68.0	69.7
50–59	60.9	36.4	59.8	95.1	76.7	80.7
All ages	52.7	36.9	70.0	85.8	64.0	74.6
Professional and related in education, welfare and health						
21–24	42.1	39.6	94.1	56.2	52.1	92.7
25–29	52.0	43.4	83.5	71.7	63.9	89.1
30–39	63.0	40.3	64.0	92.3	70.2	76.1
40–49	63.8	43.3	67.9	101.1	77.3	76.5
50–59	56.9	41.3	72.6	100.4	78.2	77.9
60–64	53.9	38.8	72.0	93.7	77.8	83.0
All ages	52.0	38.3	73.7	86.6	61.9	71.5
Clerical and related						
Under 18	19.8	18.3	92.4	27.3	25.7	94.1
18–20	28.5	25.1	88.1	38.0	33.6	88.4
21–24	38.1	30.3	79.5	50.1	40.9	81.6
25–29	44.7	32.0	71.6	59.3	44.7	75.4
30–39	46.8	30.7	65.6	63.1	43.7	69.3
40–49	47.2	30.5	64.6	62.9	43.9	69.8
50–59	44.6	31.4	70.4	60.9	45.1	74.1
60–64	39.6	27.3	68.9	54.8	44.4	81.0
All ages	37.9	27.4	72.3	56.9	40.8	71.7

TABLE 2.12   *(contd.)*

Occupation and age group	Lowest decile			Median		
	Men £	Women £	Female earnings as % of male %	Men £	Women £	Female earnings as % of male %
Selling						
Under 18	18.0	18.0	100.0	21.8	21.7	99.5
18–20	24.2	21.1	87.2	34.4	27.0	78.5
21–24	30.9	24.5	79.3	47.3	31.0	65.5
25–29	38.9	24.4	62.7	58.7	30.8	52.5
30–39	43.0	24.1	56.0	64.5	31.2	48.4
40–49	40.5	22.6	55.8	64.4	30.1	46.7
50–59	35.5	23.1	65.1	57.5	30.0	52.2
All ages	32.1	20.8	64.8	56.8	29.0	51.1
Catering, clean- ing, hair- dressing and other per- sonal services						
18–20	25.0	19.5	78.0	42.4	29.9	70.5
21–24	31.0	23.7	76.5	47.5	35.9	75.6
25–29	32.1	23.0	71.7	55.1	38.0	69.0
30–39	36.5	24.8	67.9	55.4	36.6	66.1
40–49	36.5	25.5	69.9	53.8	37.0	68.8
50–59	36.9	27.4	74.3	51.0	37.8	74.1
60–64	34.6	23.3	67.3	49.2	36.2	73.6
All ages	33.4	23.4	70.1	51.1	36.4	71.2
Making and re pairing						
Under 18	18.7	19.6	104.8	26.0	25.9	99.6
18–20	28.1	25.9	92.2	43.4	35.7	82.3
21–24	40.0	25.1	62.8	35.1	55.1	35.6
25–29	44.8	26.3	58.7	62.1	37.5	60.4
30–39	46.3	25.3	54.6	65.0	37.7	58.0
40–49	46.7	27.1	58.0	63.6	37.0	58.2
50–59	44.9	26.8	59.7	58.1	35.8	61.6
All ages	38.8	24.6	63.4	58.3	35.5	60.9

TABLE 2.12 (*contd.*)

Occupation and age group	Lowest decile			Median		
	Men £	Women £	Female earnings as % of male %	Men £	Women £	Female earnings as % of male %
Painting, repetitive assembly, product inspecting, packaging and related						
Under 18	20.1	20.8	103.5	28.3	29.2	103.2
18–20	30.8	28.1	91.2	44.8	39.1	87.3
21–24	41.7	29.9	71.7	56.0	41.5	74.1
25–29	46.7	29.5	63.2	62.9	41.3	65.7
30–39	47.1	27.5	58.4	64.8	45.9	64.7
40–49	47.5	29.1	61.3	64.0	41.7	65.2
50–59	46.1	27.8	60.3	61.1	40.5	66.3
All ages	42.4	27.3	64.4	60.4	40.3	66.7

earnings relative to male are well in excess of the figure over all occupations. Only in selling are they appreciably worse. This, however, is simply a result of the fact that the 61 per cent overall figure (Table 2.11) is a weighted average—and selling has a very high weight. The tendency for the male earnings differential to decline with age, but eventually to rise again, is confirmed by the analysis of individual occupations. Further, the lowest decile for men and women appears to behave in the same way as the median earnings level, so that comparisons between men and women in terms of the median do not give a misleading picture of what is happening at the lower end of the earnings distribution. The only exception here is selling, where women fare considerably better at the lowest decile relative to men than at the median.

Nickell (1974) includes in his regressions separately for manual men and for manual women a variable measuring the percentage of men (or women) aged 21 to 24 and that aged 25 to 54. For males the young age coefficient is negative (though not quite significant), whilst the prime age coefficient is significantly positive, demonstrating that even when corrected for skill mix there is a strong tendency for average hourly earnings to rise with age. For females, in contrast, the young age coefficient is strongly positive and the prime age coefficient non-significant. Thus he takes to imply a lack of training opportunities for the female labour force in the manufacturing sector.

THE MAKE-UP OF PAY

Overtime and shiftwork are normally paid at premium rates and can thus make a significant contribution to weekly earnings. Likewise payment-by-results enables the employee to increase his income in line with measured increases in productivity. NES data show that these three pay components contributed jointly in 1976, 24.6 per cent of weekly earnings for manual men, 13.9 per cent for manual women, 5.6 per cent for non-manual men and 2.1 per cent for non-manual women. Therefore they favoured in particular manual men. It is not possible to determine how far these differences reflect demand side factors (e.g. offers of overtime) and how far they are influenced by supply side variables (e.g. willingness to work overtime and shiftwork or to work more intensively, and Factory Act limitations on women's shiftwork). Data are, however, available on percentages of employees in receipt of such payments. For manual workers these reveal that 54.5 per cent of men compared to 14.3 per cent of women received overtime pay; 37.9 per cent of men as opposed to 31.0 per cent of women received payment-by-results income and 23.3 per cent of men compared with 11.2 per cent of women received shift payments. In the case of non-manual employees 17.4 per cent of men and 8.5 per cent of women received overtime pay: 7.6 per cent of men and 3.2 per cent of women received payment-by-results income and 5.7 per cent of men and 8.6 per cent of women received shift pay. In general it would appear, therefore, that men's earnings are increased relative to those of women by two factors—the fact that relatively more men receive these forms of payment and the fact that the size of such payments is generally higher for men.

As far as low pay is concerned it has been suggested that low paid workers tend to work more overtime in order to increase weekly earnings.[17] Thus we might expect to find an inverse relationship between the percentage of low paid workers and percentage receiving overtime pay to the extent that overtime pay is a means of escaping from the low paid section of the labour force. Similarly payment-by-results

TABLE 2.13 Low pay and the make-up of pay

Dependent variable % with weekly earnings < £40	Constant	Overtime pay	Percentage of employees who received		R²	No. in sample
			PBR etc. payments	Shift etc. premium payments		
INDUSTRIAL ANALYSIS						
Full-time manual women						
Coefficient	103.85	−1.109	−.724	−.713	.537	40
Mean 58.79		14.19	33.54	7.92		
|t|		(2.54)	(4.41)	(2.62)		
Full-time non-manual women						
Coefficient	33.78	1.238	3.545	−2.818	.322	53
Mean 47.75		4.98	3.52	1.66		
|t|		(1.49)	(3.38)	(2.72)		
OCCUPATIONAL ANALYSIS						
Full-time manual women						
Coefficient	97.912	−0.641	−0.755	−0.814	0.463	20
Mean 57.47		13.305	29.890	11.505		
|t|		(0.84)	(3.08)	(3.07)		
Full-time non-manual women						
Coefficient	25.063	0.092	3.157	0.028	0.293	35
Mean 39.36		10.563	4.134	10.011		
|t|		(0.19)	(3.52)	(0.11)		

and shift-payments would raise the weekly earnings of employees who otherwise would be low paid. Table 2.13 clearly supports these hypotheses when employees are classified by industry since all three variables are significant with the expected sign and over 50 per cent of the variance in percentage low paid is explained. In the case of non-manual women, however, the coefficients on overtime and payment-by-results have positive signs and the latter is significant. This could be rationalised by pointing out that overtime and payment-by-results may denote lower status in the non-manual case and the lower basic rates for such workers more than offset the higher income from overtime and additional effort. In this respect it would have been interesting to have been able to hold human capital factors such as education constant here. It is noticeable that when the data are classified by occupation, the payment-by-results variable retains its significance and positive sign for non-manual women, the coefficient on overtime declines with a $|t|$ value close to zero and the shiftwork premium loses its significance. In the case of manual women the payment-by-results and shiftwork variables are little changed but the overtime variable is insignificant though of negative sign. The make-up of pay thus seems an important factor in the low pay of women.[18]

The question of the make-up of pay also brings into focus the relationship between wage rates and earnings and their relative movement over time (i.e. wage drift). Thus, whilst between March 1970 and March 1975 the index of manual men's basic rates rose by 113 per cent, that of women rose by 147 per cent (the respective figures for manufacturing industries being 102 and 148 per cent). The effect on earnings was, however, less marked. As Addison (1976) has pointed out, the assumption that basic pay in the NES is broadly synonymous with nationally negotiated wage rates is invalid since basic pay itself includes a wage gap component. Elaborating on this theme, Robinson and Wallace (1977) point out that NES data are inadequate for analysing the components of 'all other pay' (i.e. total earnings minus overtime, payment-by-results and shift payments) which includes service increments, personal allowances, merit, payments for higher graded jobs and other variables. The Equal Pay Act 1970 implies common minimum rates but not necessarily equal higher rates. Thus they find that 'differentials in male and female earnings in retail co-operative societies stem not only from men's higher overtime, payment-by-results and shift pay but increasingly from their greater reliance on pay components which are unspecified in NES data, but are included with negotiated rates to make up "all other pay". By contrast, women's earnings have become increasingly dependent on the negotiated rate for the lowest grade of general distributive worker.' The above points seems to reinforce the need to concentrate on earnings as opposed to wage rates in analysing the low pay of women.

COLLECTIVE BARGAINING ARRANGEMENTS

The 1976 NES provides data on employees subject to three types of collective bargaining arrangement—national agreements in the private sector, national agreements in the public sector, and wage boards and councils. Table 2.14 shows that these types of bargaining structure occur together with sharp differences in concentrations of low paid female workers, with the wages councils having over 80 per cent of their employees below the £40 per week earnings level compared with 59.6 per cent in the private sector and 24.9 per cent in the public sector. The smaller preponderance of low pay in the public sector is even more marked when attention is focused on hourly pay, reflecting the relatively favourable hours in that sector. This can be related to the 41 per cent (8 per cent) of manual (non-manual) workers in public administration who are low hourly paid (Tables 2.5 and 2.6).

The data provided in the 1976 Survey on collective bargaining' arrangements are, however, inferior to those provided in the 1973 Survey, which distinguishes four categories of agreement coverage—national plus supplementary agreements, national agreements only, company/district/local agreement only, and no agreement. It also provides data analysed in terms of the percentage of full-time adults reported to be affected by various types of collective agreement. An analysis of specially prepared data from the 1973 Survey by Thomson, Mulvey and Farbman (1977) reveals that whereas only 16.8 per cent of manual men are not covered by a collective agreement, the figure for manual women is 28.3 per cent. In contrast rather more non-manual men than non-manual women (39.6 per cent compared with 35.2 per cent) are not so covered. Collective bargaining coverage is greater in the public as opposed to the private sector for all groups. They hypothesise that there will be a positive earnings differential for groups covered by collective agreements over those not covered and additionally find as they hypothesise that the earnings differential for those covered by agreements relative to those not covered is consistently greater for women than comparable men. That is, manual females covered by one of the three types of agreement earn 18.6 per cent more than women not

TABLE 2.14   Low pay by type of collective agreement, 1976 full-time women, aged 18 and over whose pay was not affected by absence

	Percentage with weekly earnings < £40	*Percentage with hourly earnings < 100p*
NATIONAL AGREEMENTS IN THE PRIVATE SECTOR		
Engineering, etc.: Manual workers (UK)	26.6	25.2
Clerical workers (UK)	35.7	21.5
Textiles, clothing		
and footwear: Clothing manufacture (GB)	78.0	77.4
Cotton & man-made fibres etc.	71.7	69.5
Knitting industry NJIC	61.8	61.7
Footwear manufacture (UK)	55.6	54.3
Paper and		
printing General printing & bookbinding	46.8	48.2
Retail and		
wholesale		
distribution Retail Co-op Societies (GB)	92.2	91.5
Retail multiple grocery etc.	88.9	89.3
Other Banking JNC	38.8	23.2
Unweighted average	59.6	56.2
NATIONAL AGREEMENTS IN THE PUBLIC SECTOR		
Gas, electricity		
and water: Gas supply NJC—admin. & clerical	21.8	8.8
Electricity supply NJC—admin.		
& clerical	36.2	26.6
Local authorities		
(England &		
Wales): Admin., professional and technical		
staff	19.0	9.1
General and clerical division	34.2	15.5
Manual workers NJC	48.8	41.2
School meals service NJC	80.8	56.0
Local authorities		
(Scotland): Admin., professional and technical		
staff	28.2	16.8
General and clerical division	41.0	na.
Manual workers NJC	57.4	55.2
National		
government: Admin. group—middle and higher		
grades	1.4	0.3
Admin. group—clerical grades	17.0	5.8

TABLE 2.14   *(contd.)*

		Percentage with weekly earnings < £40	*Percentage with hourly earnings < 100p*
NATIONAL AGREEMENTS IN THE PUBLIC SECTOR			
National government:	Secretarial, typing and machine grades	10.9	5.8
	Government industrial establishments JCC	39.5	43.9
National Health service:	Admin. & clerical staff—Whitley Council	18.6	9.8
	Nurses and midwives—Whitley Council	20.5	17.5
	Ancillary staff—Whitley Council	34.4	27.4
Post Office:	Clerical and executive grades	5.6	3.5
	Manipulative grades	5.2	2.2
Teaching (England & Wales):	Teachers in primary and secondary schools	1.3	0.4
	Teachers in FE establishments	0.7	n.a.
Teaching (Scotland):	Teachers in primary and secondary schools	0.6	0.0
	Unweighted average	24.9	18.2
WAGES BOARDS AND COUNCILS			
Catering:	Industrial and staff canteens (GB)	72.7	67.6
	Licensed residential establishments and restaurants (GB)	89.6	93.3
Manufacturing textiles/ clothing:	Dressmaking and women's light clothing	84.0	81.4
	Made-up textiles (GB)	69.9	67.9
	Ready-made and bespoke tailoring	81.0	79.0
Retail and wholesale distribution:	Retail drapery, outfitting and footwear (GB)	77.1	70.9
	Retail food trades	88.6	88.9

TABLE 2.14   (*contd.*)

		Percentage with weekly earnings < £40	Percentage with hourly earnings < 100p
WAGES BOARDS AND COUNCILS			
Retail and wholesale distribution:	Retail furnishing and allied trades (GB)	82.8	80.4
Others	Hairdressing, undertaking (GB)	90.9	88.5
	Unweighted average	81.8	79.8

subject to a collective agreement (the comparable figure for manual men being 12.2 per cent), whilst for non-manual employees the female differential is 28.1 per cent (and that of men negative, −4.7 per cent). Explanations for the more sizeable effect in the case of women may include spillover effects for women who are a small proportion of the workforce in male dominated, organised establishments, the fact that unorganised women are concentrated in small establishments and the possibility that exploitation is greater in the case of unorganised women. In manufacturing, however, the differential for non-manual women subject to a collective agreement over those subject to no agreement is (slightly) negative. Thomson *et al* also hypothesise that the differential for those covered by a collective agreement over those not so covered will be lower when a high proportion of the total group is covered than when a low proportion is covered, since the spillover effect is likely to be greater in such a case.

In Table 2.15 the 1973 NES collective bargaining coverage data are used to explain the extent of low pay. In the case of manual employees it can be seen that all three types of coverage have a negative sign on the coefficient and that 'national and local agreements' and 'national agreements only' are highly significant. (The other independent variable, female employment percentage, proved to be insignificant in the case of both groups of worker.)[19] In the case of non-manual women, by contrast, only 'national only' agreements appear to be related to the incidence of low pay. This is interesting, since the extent of collective bargaining coverage can be seen to be not much different between manuals and non-manuals in the case of 'local only' (as also for

TABLE 2.15 Regression results for low pay and collective bargaining arrangements

	Constant	Non-manual females as % of all non-manuals	Percentage covered by agreements:			R^2
			National + local	National only	Local only	
Dependent variable – non-manual women % earning < £40 per week N = 16						
Coefficient	60.2	.42	-.392	-.634	-.664	.568
Mean		35.10	14.47	31.85	12.17	
|t|		(-1.02)	(-1.06)	(-2.97)	(-0.88)	
Coefficient	76.1		-.578	-.579	-.668	.527
Mean			14.47	31.85	12.17	
|t|			(-1.79)	(-2.80)	(-0.89)	
Dependent variable – manual women % earning < £40 per week N = 19						
Coefficient	88.5	.41	-.902	-.481	-.495	.773
Mean		21.8	29.0	33.9	11.2	
|t|		(-2.64)	(-4.71)	(-2.67)	(-0.95)	
Coefficient	112.4		-1.110	-.619	-.886	.660
Mean			29.0	33.9	11.2	
|t|			(-5.35)	(-3.03)	(-1.51)	

'national only') agreements. American results similarly imply that white collar unionisation has a smaller impact on pay than does blue collar.[20] This seems to support the following contention of Thomson *et al*:

> If nothing else, it indicates the need for more research on the factors affecting the earnings of females and non-manuals, especially as these are becoming more important groups both in collective bargaining and unionisation, and in the labour force as a whole.

It has frequently been suggested that the lower degree of unionisation amongst women relative to men explains their inferior bargaining position but union membership is now increasing at a faster rate than that of men, increasing in total by one million between 1964 and 1974, so that in 1974 over 3,174,000 out of a total union membership of 11,755,000 were women. Unfortunately it is not possible to obtain union membership figures by industry by sex to test for any relationship between levels of earnings and degree of unionisation. Nickell (op. cit.) was, however, able to obtain figures on the percentage of the workforce unionised by industry (undifferentiated by sex or manual/non-manual status) and this variable has a significant positive effect on female earnings. (This is in contrast to a non-significant effect on male earnings and a significant negative effect on the male/female earnings differential.) Thus from this analysis it would appear that trade unions have a favourable impact on both the absolute earnings of women and their level relative to that of men.[21] It should be noted, however, that this result is quite compatible with unions unfavourably affecting (via entry barriers) the occupational/industrial representation of women relative to men. Unions could thus widen the overall female-male pay differential even though they narrow it within the firms in which they operate.

The fact that length of service proved to be insignificant in the above regressions should not, however, be taken to imply that length of service has no effect on earnings. The above analysis used length of service classified only by industry and thus includes within each industry diverse occupations and collective bargaining agreements. Further, the 1975 data do not relate length of service to earnings according to individual observations, but simply provide percentage figures of average length of service in each industry. Thus, in Table 2.16 in all nine industries in which complete data are provided for non-manual women in 1976 weekly earnings increase in each successive service group, and the same is true for three out of seven industries where complete data are available for manual women. In seven out of twelve collective

TABLE 2.16   Weekly earnings by length of service by industry group, 1976

Industry group	Full-time manual women aged 18 and over				
	Weekly earnings by length of service £				
	Under 1 year	1 or 2 years	3 or 4 years	5 to 9 years	10 years and over
Food, drink and tobacco	36.9	40.3	40.4	42.3	42.5
Electrical engineering	38.8	40.9	43.5	44.6	46.4
Textiles	35.1	37.6	38.5	38.8	39.2
Clothing and footwear	29.6	33.3	34.4	36.5	36.1
Distributive trades	32.9	33.5	33.1	34.9	34.8
Professional and scientific services	39.3	39.7	39.2	40.0	40.1
Miscellaneous services	31.6	33.3	33.1	37.8	34.9
	Full-time non-manual women aged 18 and over				
Food, drink and tobacco	36.3	39.3	42.4	44.2	53.0
Mechanical engineering	37.4	39.7	41.4	42.7	45.8
Electrical engineering	37.7	39.8	43.2	47.2	48.7
Transport and communication	40.2	45.0	47.5	53.0	57.8
Distributive trades	32.4	32.7	33.0	36.0	39.5
Insurance, banking, finance and business services	38.0	38.8	43.1	49.2	57.4
Professional and scientific services	51.1	55.7	58.1	66.2	76.5
Miscellaneous services	38.2	42.8	43.6	46.7	50.1
Public administration	43.5	45.1	51.2	54.0	63.7

NOTE
Details are given only where observations are provided in the NES for all service classifications.

agreements for which complete service data are provided earnings increase with each successive service group (Table 2.17). Complete service data are only available for eight occupational groups, but in all three non-manual cases and two out of the five manual cases earnings increase in each successive service group. Clearly, therefore length of service, consistent with human capital theory, is an important determinant of earnings.

REGIONAL ANALYSIS AND LOCATIONAL FACTORS

It appears that the variation in the percentage of low paid women

TABLE 2.17 Weekly earnings by length of service by collective agreement (full-time women aged 18 and over)

	Weekly earnings by length of service £				
	Under 1 year	1 or 2 years	3 or 4 years	5 to 9 years	10 years and over
National agreements in the private sector Engineering—manual workers (UK)	39.6	43.8	45.8	46.5	47.2
National agreements in the public sector Local authorities (England & Wales) Admin., professional and technical staff	50.6	50.0	58.2	56.2	63.2
General & clerical division	39.5	41.3	45.0	46.5	49.5
Manual workers NJC	43.9	41.7	42.7	41.8	41.7
National government Admin. group—clerical grades	40.3	43.5	48.8	51.7	55.1
National Health Service Admin. & clerical staff— Whitley Council	47.8	48.0	50.4	54.7	61.0
Nurses & midwives— Whitley Council	45.7	49.5	53.1	60.4	68.9
Ancillary staff— Whitley Council	42.7	44.6	43.8	45.9	44.8
Teaching (England &Wales) Primary and secondary schools	62.2	69.1	73.4	81.9	95.6
Wages boards and councils Retail drapery, outfitting and footwear (GB)	32.0	33.1	33.5	35.9	41.1
Retail food trades (England and Wales)	29.8	30.7	31.8	34.1	33.3
Retail furnishing and allied trades (GB)	32.5	32.1	33.5	34.5	37.8

exceeds the variation in median earnings levels across regions (Table 2.19). For manual women median weekly earnings range from £36.80 in Yorkshire and Humberside to £40.20 in the South East, whilst the percentage with weekly earnings less than £40 ranges from 63.4 per cent

TABLE 2.18   Weekly earnings by length of service by occupational group, 1976

	Full-time women aged 18 and over				
Occupational group	*Weekly earnings by length of service £*				
	Under 1 year	*1 or 2 years*	*3 or 4 years*	*5 to 9 years*	*10 years and over*
Non-manual					
Professional and related in education, welfare and health	54.6	59.6	62.9	71.5	83.8
Clerical and related	37.5	39.5	41.9	46.1	50.5
Selling	30.1	30.7	30.9	33.5	35.2
Manual					
Catering, cleaning, hairdressing and other personal services	35.4	37.5	36.9	39.3	39.9
Materials processing (excluding metals)	36.9	38.3	39.7	39.8	39.3
Making and repairing (excluding metal and electrical)	33.0	36.7	37.5	39.3	39.0
Processing, making, repairing and related (metal and electrical)	36.1	42.5	44.0	44.6	45.0
Painting, repetitive assembling, product inspecting, packaging and related	36.4	40.4	40.8	42.4	43.6

NOTE
Details are given only where observations are provided in the NES for all service classifications.

in Yorkshire and Humberside to 49.3 per cent in the South-East. For non-manual women median weekly earnings range from £41 in East Anglia to £48.30 in the South-East, whilst the percentage with weekly earnings less than £40 ranges from 47.2 per cent in East Anglia to 28.9 per cent in the South-East. For both manual and non-manual women there is again a close relationship between the incidence of low hourly pay and low weekly pay, but the relationship between low pay and average weekly earnings appears to be stronger in the case of female earnings as opposed to male earnings, especially for manual workers, whilst there is no clear relationship between the incidence of low pay and the male/female earnings differential. Thus, it does not appear that

TABLE 2.19   Low pay and distribution by region full-time women aged 18 and over, whose pay for the survey period was not affected by absence

Region	Median earnings Men	Women	Percentage with weekly earnings < £40	Percentage with hourly earnings <100p	$\dfrac{WE_m - WE_f}{WE_f} \times 100$
				MANUAL WOMEN	
Yorkshire and Humberside	62.2	36.8	63.4	61.1	69.0
East-Midlands	60.6	37.0	61.8	59.5	63.8
South-West	57.4	37.4	61.4	58.8	53.5
East Anglia	57.2	37.3	60.6	55.8	53.4
North-West	61.6	37.7	58.4	54.3	63.4
West Midlands	63.1	38.4	68.2	51.8	64.3
North	65.3	38.2	55.6	51.7	70.9
Scotland	62.2	38.7	55.1	53.5	60.7
Wales	63.2	39.2	53.0	50.8	61.2
South East	63.4	40.2	49.3	43.8	57.7
of which Greater London	66.4	43.6	39.8	34.2	52.3
of which Remainder of South-East	61.1	37.8	58.5	53.1	61.6
Great Britain	62.1	38.4	56.0	52.3	61.7
				NON-MANUAL WOMEN	
East Anglia	69.5	41.0	47.2	39.6	69.5
Yorkshire and Humberside	69.2	41.5	45.7	35 3	66.7
South-West	70.7	42.0	44.8	37.3	68.3
East-Midlands	68.9	41.7	44.6	36.1	65.2
North-West	72.3	42.5	43.3	34.9	70.1
Scotland	73.7	42.8	43.3	35.2	72.2
North	71.6	42.9	42.3	34.5	66.9
West-Midlands	70.5	42.5	41.9	33.3	65.5
Wales	71.2	43.5	39.5	33.3	63.7
South-West	78.6	48.3	28.9	21.8	63.1
of which Greater London	82.0	51.8	19.9	13.6	60.0
of which Remainder of South-East	74.3	43.5	40.2	32.2	70.8
Great Britain	73.9	44.2	38.2	30.3	67.2

women suffer from an unfavourable regional distribution relative to men.

To some extent regional earnings differences may be explained by differences in occupational or industrial employment distribution among regions (see Table 2.20). Unfortunately whilst the NES does provide details of average earnings by industry group by region and by occupational group by region, there are a large number of regions for which no data appear for particular industries and occupations. Where observations are available for most regions for separate industries and occupations there is no clear tendency for the earnings spread to be reduced other than for manual occupations for which adequate data are available.

In the Chiplin and Sloane inter-industry study (1976(c)) a regional variable (proportion of the British labour force in the South-East and East and West Midlands) proved to be insignificant in explaining the variance in female earnings, but highly significant in explaining the variance in the absolute male/female earnings differential. In contrast to the above, Nickell found that the percentage employed in the South-East and Midlands was highly significant in explaining the variance in female earnings. The percentage employed in conurbations also had a positive effect on female earnings.[22] One way in which location may influence pay is in relation to the journey to work. Women's job search may be constrained by the location of the husband's job and its subsequent effect on the place of residence. This constraint is likely to be smaller where the husband locates in a conurbation (due to the greater job opportunities for the wife) and consequently women's pay tends to be higher.[23]

EDUCATION

No information on levels of earnings classified according to educational qualifications is available in the NES but information is provided in the General Household Survey, 1973. Table 5.5 of the GHS provides median annual earnings levels for men only by level of school or college last attended full-time and shows a positive relationship between the two. Thus median earnings for those whose educational level was limited to a secondary modern/junior secondary school were £1650 as opposed to a figure of £2700 in the case of a UK University. Table 5.8 reproduced in part below as Table 2.21 does, however, compare earnings of men and women by level of education qualification and shows that a similar relationship holds for women. Although levels of

TABLE 2.20   Average gross weekly earnings by industry group by region Full-time Women, aged 18 and over whose pay was not affected by absence

	South East	Greater London	Remainder of S.E.	East Anglia	South West	West Midlands	East Midlands	Yorks and Humberside	North West	North	Wales	Scotland	Great Britain
MANUAL WOMEN													
Clothing & footwear	32.0	31.7	32.3				34.9	33.2	34.1	37.4	34.6	33.9	34.4
Professional and scientific services	43.8	48.4	39.7		37.2	37.3	38.3	38.2	38.6	37.7	39.2	39.3	39.8
Miscellaneous services	37.5	40.2	34.5		30.1	31.5		32.8	33.0	34.1		33.0	33.9
NON-MANUAL WOMEN													
Transport and communication	54.4	57.3	48.0		49.2	49.1	47.3	46.5	49.2			44.4	50.3
Distributive trade	38.4	42.3	34.8	32.8	31.5	33.3	33.7	33.0	33.6	32.5	31.5	32.4	34.5
Insurance, banking, finance and business services	49.3	53.2	41.5	37.7	39.9	40.7	39.4	39.2	38.4	43.0	40.6	41.2	44.5
Professional and scientific services	62.3	64.1	60.4	57.5	58.8	60.8	60.3	59.3	60.2	62.1	60.5	59.9	60.8
Miscellaneous services	48.9	53.5	40.9		38.0		38.0	40.2	42.8			41.1	43.9
Public administration	56.8	61.2	50.2	46.0	49.3	49.7	46.4	47.2	49.8	47.2	48.2	48.0	51.4

TABLE 2.20 (*contd.*)

	South East	Greater London	Remainder of S.E.	East Anglia	South West	West Midlands	East Midlands	Yorks and Humberside	North West	North	Wales	Scotland	Great Britain
Average gross weekly earnings by occupational group													
ALL FULL-TIME WOMEN													
Professional and related in education, health and welfare	67.2	69.5	65.1	61.5	64.8	65.8	64.0	63.5	64.5	66.9	65.8	64.5	65.5
Clerical and related	46.8	50.4	41.7	38.7	41.1	40.9	40.1	40.2	40.5	41.1	41.1	40.7	43.0
Selling	34.8	38.9	31.6	30.1	39.5	32.0	30.9	31.0	30.4	30.5	30.3	30.7	31.8
Catering, cleaning, hairdressing and other personal services	42.1	45.7	37.9	35.0	34.8	35.2	35.1	36.1	37.1	36.1	36.8	37.3	38.0
Materials processing (excl. metals)	38.2						38.7	38.7	37.2			39.6	38.9
Making and repairing (excluding metal and electrical)	38.5	37.6	39.5			38.4	36.8	36.6	36.9	39.5	37.0	37.0	37.7
Processing, making and repairing and related (metal and electrical)	42.0	43.5	40.7			42.9		42.0	43.0				43.4
Painting, repetitive assembling, product inspecting, packaging and related	41.2	42.9	40.0	40.3	40.7	41.7	40.1	38.7	40.6	42.7	44.0	41.8	41.1

TABLE 2.21 Highest qualification level attained by annual earnings, by sex

Full-time employed[a] aged 16 to 64   Great Britain—1973

Percentage of persons aged 16 to 64 in full-time employment with earnings in or greater than each quoted range

| Gross annual earnings | Highest Qualification Level Attained | | | | | | Total no. in each earnings range[b] |
	Degree or equivalent (1, 2) %	Below-degree higher education (3, 4) %	GCE 'A' level or equivalent (5, 6) %	GCE 'O' level or equivalent/CSE grade 1 (7) %	CSE other grades/commercial/apprenticeship (8, 9) %	No qualifications %	
Males							
less than £250	100	100	100	100	100	100	118
£250 "	99	100	99	97	99	99	118
£500 "	98	99	96	95	97	97	258
£750 "	98	99	94	90	92	396	821
£1000 "	96	97	89	83	92	87	948
£1250 "	95	93	80	73	82	73	2146
£1500 "	92	88	71	65	69	55	1290
£2000 "	80	67	44	42	34	25	629
£2500 "	70	46	24	22	15	10	803
£3000 or more	54	27	12	11	6	5	
Total no. in each level	440	403	512	958	839	4021	7558
median earnings £	3000+	2410	1890	1800	1770	1630	

TABLE 2.21 (contd.)

Full-time employed^a aged 16 to 64   Great Britain—1973
Percentage of persons aged 16 to 64 in full-time employment with earnings in or greater than each quoted range Highest Qualification Level Attained

Gross annual earnings	Degree or equivalent (1, 2) %	Below-degree higher education (3, 4) %	GCE 'A' level or equivalent (5, 6) %	GCE 'O' level or equivalent/CSE grade 1 (7) %	CSE other grades/commercial/apprenticeship (8, 9) %	No qualifications %	Total no. in each earnings range^b
Females	%	%	%	%	%	%	
less than £ 250	100		100		100	100	903
£ 250 ,, £ 500	97		95		96	95	1002
£ 500 ,, £ 750	93		88		88	81	996
£ 750 ,, £1000	92		72		72	61	852
£1000 ,, £1250	80		50		49	31	608
£1250 ,, £1500	67		28		26	11	284
£1500 ,, £2000	53		17		13	4	242
£2000 ,, £2500	31		5		5	1	
£2500 ,, £3000	12		2		2	0	182
£3000 or more	6		1		1	0	
Total no. in each level	302		570		308	1629	5069
Median earnings £	1560		1250		990	840	

NOTES
^a Working 31 hours or more per week (26 hours or more for teachers and lecturers)
^b Including foreign and 'other' qualifications.

SOURCE
General Household Survey, Table 5.8 (HMSO, 1973).

earnings are appreciably higher for men for given educational qualifications, the return to women from continuing their education appears to be higher than that of men at the lower educational levels. Thus, median earnings at the CSE/commercial apprenticeship level are 17.9 per cent above the median earnings at the no qualifications level and a further 26.3 per cent above the former at the GCE 'O' level or equivalent, whilst the corresponding figures for men are 8.6 and 1.7 per cent respectively.[24]

In focusing on the low pay issue, obvious attention should be paid to those employees without any educational qualifications. Here, the NBPI (1971) noted in its analysis of low paid workers that whilst the general level of education was equally low for both sexes in this group, 19 per cent of the men had some further education compared with 8 per cent of the full-time and 6 per cent of the part-time women. A further 39 per cent of the men had received some formal training at work, mostly over three months. Of the women only 16 per cent had received such training and less than 10 per cent of this was of more than three months' duration. Education and training are likely to be major factors in explaining women's low pay. Systematic British research is just beginning, however. The direction it is likely to take and the problems associated with human capital analyses are discussed in the final Chapter.

CONCLUSIONS

As the NBPI observed some six years ago, and this remains so, despite progress in relation to the implementation of equal pay[25] and equal opportunity, the main problem is not so much that some women are paid much less than others but that women as a whole have much lower pay than men. This, as outlined above, arises from a multiplicity of reasons.

As a broad generalisation it can be said that the following combination of factors epitomises a low paid female job—an unskilled manual occupation involving part-time employment in a small establishment in the service sector in a low wage region. There is, also, little opportunity for overtime or shiftwork, a time rate method of payment, a lack of collective bargaining arrangements, or wages council coverage. A low paid women would be typically young (or elderly) with few years experience in the labour market and possessing few educational qualifications.

To ascertain the quantitative significance of each of these factors more precisely than has been possible here would require the use of a detailed multiple regression model, which is dependent on more complete data than are currently available in the New Earnings Survey.

NOTES

1. It does not give data other than employment cross-classified by occupation and industry which could explain in part the considerable spread of earnings within occupations. See the evidence of G. G. C. Routh, ibid., p. 282.
2. Selected Evidence submitted to the Royal Commission for Report no. 1: Initial Report on the Standing Reference, HMSO (1976) p. 263.
3. See for instance, Marquand (1967) and National Board for Prices and Incomes (1971).
4. The differential adult age seems anomalous in view of the fact that the application of such differences in the case of the same or broadly similar work would be a clear breach of the Equal Pay Act. The continued use of the traditional age limits is defended on the grounds that it ensures the exclusion from the adult figures of those not paid at adult rates, whilst maintaining comparability with earlier surveys. Adult rates are increasingly being paid to both males and females under 21, but 'there are still major collective agreements in which the operative age is still 21 for some types of jobs which are mainly done by males' (NES, 1976, part A, p. A39).
5. See Barbara R. Bergmann (1971) for a full discussion of this hypothesis.
6. The fact that data are not available on a consistent basis for several variables means that it is not feasible to use a full scale multiple regression model to explain the variance in published NES earnings data.
7. For a full discussion of these results see ibid., pp. 40–8 and chapter 3.
8. See Chiplin and Sloane, ibid., p. 30.
9. See N. Jones (1976).
10. For a full discussion of this feature of female employment see Department of Employment Survey, *Women and Work* (1974).
11. There is a closer relationship between low weekly and low hourly pay than in the occupational analysis ($r = 0.984$ for both manual and non-manual women).
12. See Chiplin and Sloane (1976(a)). It should be noted that in smaller establishments women may not be directly covered by the Equal Pay Act either because there are no male employees with whom a comparison can be made or because there is no collective agreement or formal pay structure.
13. Two attempts have been made to analyse the relative earnings position of manual women across industry by means of a detailed multiple regression cross section model. First, S. J. Nickell (1974) found that average establishment size had a significant positive effect on female earnings. Secondly, Chiplin and Sloane (1976(c)) found likewise that plant size was significant in explaining the variance in female earnings in most equations

run but the small establishments variable was insignificant in the case of women.

14. Similar tests carried out for men reveal that in the case of manual men mean employment size of establishment is highly significant, as in the case of women, but can explain only 13 to 16 per cent of the variance of low pay compared to 40 to 44 per cent in the case of women. In the case of non-manual men the size of establishment variable is only significant at the 10 per cent level for the weekly low pay percentage. The results for the employment in small establishments variable are similar to those for women, the variable being insignificant for manual workers but significant for non-manual workers, roughly one-third of the variance being explained in the latter case for both sexes.

15. For further evidence, see Chiplin and Sloane (1976(b)).

16. Barron and Norris, (op. cit.), suggest that the high proportion of part-time men who are low paid illustrates the clear difference between the part-time and full-time labour markets. Unfortunately the NES does not provide data for part-time men corresponding to that for part-time women.

17. See Whybrew (1968).

18. Could then the use of gross earnings rather than earnings net of overtime be masking the effects of variables such as occupation or industry? For this to be the case there would need to be significant differences in the variation across industries etc. between gross and net earnings. In fact, for non-manual women mean gross and net earnings are almost perfectly correlated ($r = 0.998$), whilst for manual women there is also a high correlation ($r = 0.819$). Mean gross and net pay are also highly negatively correlated with the percentage of low paid employees by industry: for manual women $r = -0.852$ for the low wage percentage and net earnings and -0.972 for the low wage percentage and gross weekly earnings, whilst for non-manual women the figures are -0.866 and -0.875 respectively. It is doubtful, therefore, whether the procedure adopted is itself masking the effect of other variables such as occupation and industry.

19. Regressions were also run including both total hours worked and length of service but with insignificant results for these variables.

20. Hamermesh (1970/71).

21. In the Chiplin and Sloane inter-industry study (1976(c)), the extent of unionisation (a different measure) was, however, never significant. This study did, however, find a positive significant relationship between 'national and local agreements' coverage and female earnings.

22. These different results may be influenced by the fact that Nickell, unlike Chiplin and Sloane, includes a 'proportion in conurbations' variable in addition to the regional variable. It should, however, be noted that in a later paper, S. J. Nickell, 'Trade Unions and Women in the Wage Structure', *British Journal of Industrial Relations*, July 1977, the regional variable is not significant in the female hourly wage equations for 1972 (as opposed to 1966).

23. The NBPI (1971) in its Social Survey of Low Paid Workers found that journey to work distance was on average longer for men. Despite this journey times were shorter for men because more of them used private transport. In relation to low pay it is also worth noting that whilst for men

the amount of overtime worked was inversely related to time spent on journey to work, no such relationship was observed for women.

24. Strictly speaking these earnings figures should be discounted over time, but the differences in the gross figures are so great that this is unlikely to alter the conclusion.

25. For a discussion of some problems in implementing equal pay, see P. Glucklich, C. R. J. Hall, M. Povall and M. W. Snell (1976). They conclude that 'the extent to which it has been possible to adjust pay structures and jobs to reduce the effects of the Act on women's earnings, while at the same time staying within the Act, is indeed noteworthy'. There is no reason to anticipate that experience under the Sex Discrimination Act will be very different. For an econometric analysis of the effects of equal pay see Chapter 3.

REFERENCES

J. T. Addison, 'The Composition of Manual Worker Earnings', *British Journal of Industrial Relations* (March 1976).

R. D. Barron and G. M. Norris, 'Sexual Divisions and the Dual Labour Market', paper presented to the Conference on Sexual Divisions in Society, British Sociological Association (1974).

B. Bergmann, 'The Effect of White Incomes on Discrimination in Employment', *Journal of Political Economy*, 79 (1971).

B. Chiplin and P. J. Sloane, 'Male/Female Earnings Differences, a Further Analysis', *British Journal of Industrial Relations* (March 1976a).

——, *Sex Discrimination in the Labour Market* (London: Macmillan, 1976(b)).

——, 'Sex Differences and the Inter-Industry Wage Structure for Manual Workers in UK Manufacturing', *Paisley College of Technology Working Paper*, no. 21 (June 1976 c).

Department of Employment, *Women and Work. A Statistical Survey*, Manpower Paper, no. 9 (1974).

P. Glucklich *et al.*, 'Equal Pay Experiences in 25 firms', *Department of Employment Gazette* (December 1976).

D. Hamermesh, 'White-Collar Unions, Blue-Collar Unions, and Wages in Manufacturing', *Industrial and Labour Relations Review* (1970/1).

N. Jones, 'Equal Pay and Pay Structure in Engineering Establishments', SSCR Symposium into Research into Equal Pay and Equality of Opportunity in Labour Markets, Bath University, School of Management (17–18 March 1976).

J. Marquand, 'Which are the Low Paid Workers?' *British Journal of Industrial Relations*, V (1967).

National Board for Prices and Incomes, Report no. 169, *General Problems of Low Pay*, Cmnd., 4648 (April 1971).

S. J. Nickell, 'An Analysis of the Industrial Wage Structure for Both Men and Women', Unpublished manuscript, London School of Economics (August 1974).

O. Robinson and J. Wallace, 'Equal Pay Legislation in a Low Pay Industry', paper presented at an SSRC Symposium into Equal Pay and Equal Opportunity, op. cit.

——, 'National Wage Rates and Earnings Composition: A Note on Potential Sources of Sex Discrimination in Pay', *British Journal of Industrial Relations* (March 1977).

Royal Commission on Income Distribution and Wealth, Selected Evidence Submitted to the Royal Commission, Report no. 1: Initial Report on the Standing Reference, HMSO (1976).

A. J. W. Thomson, C. Mulvey and M. Farbman, 'Bargaining Structure and Relative Earnings in Great Britain', *British Journal of Industrial Relations* (July 1977).

E. G. Whybrew, *Overtime Working in Britain*, Research Paper no. 9, Royal Commission on Trade Unions and Employers Associations (1968).

3 Relative Female Earnings in Great Britain and the Impact of Legislation

B. CHIPLIN, M. M. CURRAN
and C. J. PARSLEY

INTRODUCTION

The purpose of this chapter is to examine the changes that have occurred in the pay position of women relative to men in the last ten years or so. An attempt is made to analyse the causes of such changes and assess the effects of government legislation and policies. The likely future effects of present legislation are considered. Unlike Chapter 2 the emphasis is placed upon the male/female earnings ratio rather than the percentage of low paid workers.

MALE AND FEMALE EARNINGS—THE EXTENT OF THE DIFFERENTIAL

The discussion of earnings below relates, unless otherwise specified, to the gross weekly earnings of full-time workers since, from the viewpoint of the recipient, these appear to be a more valid measure of income than hourly earnings. Hourly earnings, discussed in a later section, may be more relevant to a study of payment than one of income. The number of hours worked per week is normally in the control of the employer rather than the employee, and hence the employee may typically regard the hours worked as only one part of the total job 'package' associated with an agreed level of weekly earnings. From the individual employee's standpoint hours of work only become a variable if he is absent; as in Chapter 2 those whose pay is affected by absence are excluded, so that

58   *Women and Low Pay*

the earnings portrayed represent average income for a full week's work.

In the consideration of income distributions median earnings might be suggested as the appropriate measure of central tendency. However, the mean has been used throughout this study in order to maintain comparability between all variables and employee groups since the median is in many instances not available.

The pay position of women, relative to men, during the last decade is summarised in Table 3.1 by the presentation of female/male (*F/M*) earnings ratios, calculated by expressing female average gross weekly earnings as a percentage of male average gross weekly earnings.

TABLE 3.1   *F/M* weekly earnings ratios—aggregate data

	NES all employees	NES manual all industries	NES manual manufacturing industries	NES manual non-manufacturing industries	NES non-manual all industries	NES non-manual manufacturing industries	NES non-manual non-manufacturing industries	DEG all industries	DEG manual manufacturing industries
1966		–	–	–	–	–	–	49.59	48.44
1967	–	–	–	–	–	–	–	49.39	48.16
1968	–	–	–	–	–	–	–	49.12	47.90
1969	–	–	–	–	–	–	–	48.76	47.40
1970	54.33	50.00	49.12	49.80	49.72	43.05	51.84	49.89	48.36
1971	55.62	52.04	50.48	52.16	50.64	44.33	52.58	51.08	50.40
1972	55.86	52.13	51.30	52.41	51.03	44.52	52.53	51.09	50.66
1973	55.13	51.71	51.38	51.10	51.35	44.76	52.82	51.71	50.94
1974	56.39	54.13	53.45	53.68	52.57	47.34	53.68	55.54	55.07
1975	61.51	57.63	57.24	58.03	57.89	51.53	59.24	57.38	57.30
1976	64.34	60.52	59.79	60.79	59.80	53.28	61.00	–	–

The F/M earnings ratio for the various categories of employees are shown graphically in Figs. 3.1 to 3.4. It is clear from this data that, for all categories of employees, female earnings have increased relative to male over the period under consideration. The Department of Employment Gazette (DEG) data,[1] the only earnings series available before 1970, show that in the nine years from 1966 to 1975 the *F/M* earnings ratio for manual workers in all industries covered by the survey increased by 15.7 per cent (from 49.59 to 57.38) whilst NES aggregate data show an increase of 18.4 per cent in the period 1970 to 1976.

The increase in relative female earnings over the last decade has therefore not been uniform. In fact from 1966 to 1969 the *F/M* earnings

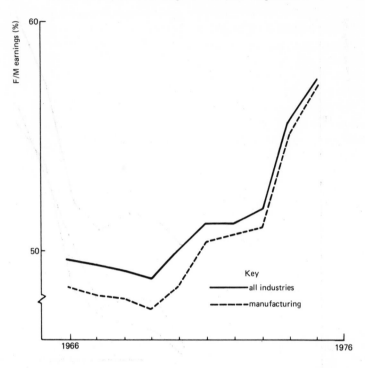

F<small>IG</small>. 3.1 Female/male earnings ratios—manual workers (DEG)

ratio for manual workers was declining (DEG), whilst from 1970 to 1972 all available data show the ratio to be increasing. In 1973 the NES F/M earnings ratio for non-manufacturing manual workers fell below its 1972 level as also, through the influence of this sector, did the 'all workers' and 'all manual workers' ratios. Other sectors showed only marginal increases above their 1972 levels. After 1973 the F/M earnings ratios for all categories of employees displayed a dramatic increase, for example the NES ratio for all employees increased by 16.7 per cent in the three years 1973–6.

The F/M earnings ratio for manufacturing industries was, during the whole period, lower than that for all industries for manual workers (see Fig. 3.1). The difference between manufacturing and non-manufacturing may be seen more clearly from a comparison of Figs. 3.3 and 3.4 and of columns 3, 4, 6 and 7 in Table 3.1 which show that for non-manual employees the F/M earnings ratio in manufacturing was below that in non-manufacturing for the whole period, although the

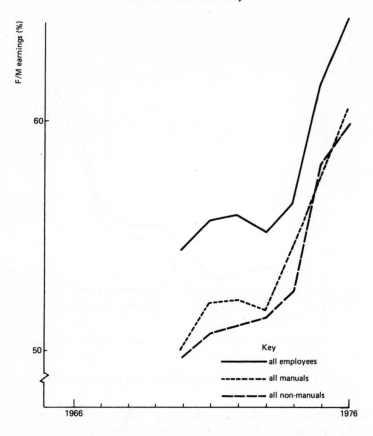

FIG. 3.2 Female/male earnings ratios—(NES) aggregate data

differential between the two was less in 1976 than in 1970. The experience with regard to manual workers is a little less clear cut since, although the ratio in manufacturing was below that in non-manufacturing for most of the period, there was a reversal of this situation for one year in 1973. After this reversal the non-manufacturing ratio again exceeded that in manufacturing but, as noted in the case of non-manual workers, the difference between the two was significantly less than that in 1970.

From Fig. 3.2 it may be seen that F/M earnings ratio for manual employees followed, over the period 1970–6, the same broad pattern as that for all employees, differing only insofar as it maintained a more

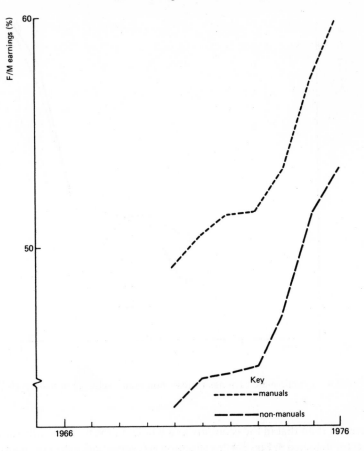

FIG. 3.3 Female/male earnings ratios—manufacturing industries (NES)

steady rate of increase from 1973 to 1976. The ratio for non-manuals experienced a slow steady increase from 1970 to 1973 in contrast to the rise and fall of the manual ratio during this period. The non-manual ratio was generally below that for the manual group, but in 1975 it exceeded the manual as a result of its steeper increase from 1974 to 1975. This increase 'levelled off' in 1975–6, whilst the more steady increase in the manual ratio was maintained leading to its exceeding the non-manual ratio again in 1976.

In manufacturing industries (see Fig. 3.3) the manual ratio clearly exceeded the non-manual throughout the period by a margin much

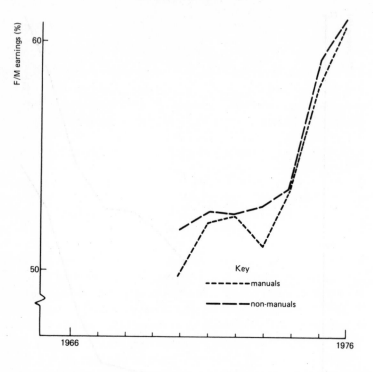

FIG. 3.4 Female/male earnings ratios—non manufacturing industries (NES)

greater than that in the economy as a whole. In the non-manufacturing sector depicted in Fig. 3.4 this situation is reversed since the non-manual ratio did not fall below the manual during the period, although the two were equal in 1974. Thus, the fact that the manual ratio on aggregate exceeds the non-manual is the result of two opposite situations in the manufacturing and non-manufacturing sectors of the economy.

To summarise: it appears that the female/male earnings ratio has in general increased in the period 1969–76, thus reversing its decline for 1966–9. This general increase was experienced by both manual and non-manual employees in manufacturing and non-manufacturing sectors of the economy. In the economy as a whole there was a reversal of this general increase in 1973, an effect experienced most significantly by manual workers in non-manufacturing industries. This setback was followed by a dramatic increase in the ratio for all workers in all sectors in the period 1974–6.

FACTORS AFFECTING THE CHANGE IN RELATIVE EARNINGS

The preceding discussion highlights the trend towards more equality in earnings, reflected by the F/M earnings ratio, particularly since 1973. It now seems appropriate to consider what factors may affect the fluctuations in relative earnings. The F/M hours worked ratio (total female weekly hours expressed as a percentage of male hours worked each week) seems to have had some effect on relative earnings up to 1973 especially for manuals and all workers. Thus a comparison of Tables 3.1 and 3.2 shows that the F/M earnings ratio is always higher for hourly than for weekly earnings.

Generally the F/M hours ratio has remained fairly stable, in the 82–7 per cent range, mainly because absolute hours of work have been relatively constant for males and females, though the trend since 1951 has been downwards. The differences in the F/M hours ratio between various sectors may be due to the amount of overtime worked (see below). In particular the non-manual weekly hours ratio is higher than that for manuals (Fig. 3.6) since men work relatively more overtime than women in the latter, despite overtime hours absolutely being higher for both sexes in the manual sector.

More specifically, the manual hours ratio has shown on upward trend in recent years (Fig. 3.7 and to a lesser extent Fig. 3.6), whilst the non-manuals' hours ratio has remained constant. The main difference in the

TABLE 3.2   F/M hourly earnings ratio – aggregate data (NES)

Year	Hourly earnings ratio excluding overtime			Hourly earnings ratio including overtime		
	Manual	Non manual	All employees	Manual	Non manual	All employees
1970[a]	n.a.	n.a.	n.a.	58.84	52.60	62.97
1971[a]	61.25	53.17	63.70	59.84	53.43	63.71
1972[a]	61.76	53.98	64.53	60.36	54.12	64.38
1973	61.99	54.31	64.35	60.71	54.44	64.16
1974	64.43	55.54	65.86	63.42	55.76	65.80
1975	68.04	60.65	70.57	66.78	60.87	70.41
1976	71.06	62.58	73.47	70.08	62.77	73.50

NOTE
[a] Earnings for 1970, 1971 and 1972 include the earnings of those whose pay was affected by absence. These are excluded from the earnings in later years.

TABLE 3.3 Average weekly hours—aggregate data

	NES all employees	NES manual all inds.	NES manual manuf. industries	NES manual non-manuf. inds.	NES non-manual all inds.	NES non-manual manuf. inds.	NES non-manual non-manuf. inds.	DEG manual all inds.	DEG manual manufac. inds.
1966 M								46.0	45.0
F								38.1	38.0
F/M								82.83	84.44
1967 M								46.2	45.3
F								38.2	38.0
F/M								82.68	83.89
1968 M								46.4	45.8
F								38.3	38.2
F/M								82.54	83.41
1969 M								46.5	45.7
F								38.1	37.9
F/M								81.94	82.93
1970 M	42.9	45.8	45.4	46.3	39.1	39.5	38.8	45.7	44.9
F	37.2	38.4	38.0	39.1	37.1	37.4	37.0	37.9	37.7
F/M	86.71	83.84	83.70	84.44	94.88	94.68	95.36	82.93	83.96
1971 M	43.6	45.0	44.4	45.8	38.7	38.9	38.6	44.7	43.6
F	38.0	38.4	38.0	39.1	36.9	37.2	36.8	37.7	37.5

TABLE 3.3 (*contd.*)

	NES all employees	NES manual all inds.	NES manual manuf. industries	NES manual non-manuf. inds.	NES non-manual all inds.	NES non-manual manuf. inds.	NES non-manual non-manuf. inds.	DEG manual all inds.	DEG manual manufac. inds.
F/M	87.15	85.33	85.58	85.37	95.34	95.62	95.33	84.34	86.00
1972 M	43.4	44.9	44.3	45.6	38.6	38.8	38.5	45.0	44.1
F	37.8	38.6	38.3	39.2	36.6	37.1	36.5	37.9	37.7
F/M	87.09	85.96	86.45	85.96	94.81	95.61	94.80	84.22	85.48
1973 M	43.8	46.7	46.4	46.9	38.8	39.2	38.5	45.6	44.7
F	37.8	39.9	40.0	39.7	36.8	37.3	36.7	37.7	37.5
F/M	86.30	85.43	86.20	84.64	94.84	95.15	95.32	82.67	83.89
1974 M	43.7	46.5	46.2	46.9	38.8	39.1	38.6	45.1	44.0
F	37.8	39.8	39.9	39.8	36.8	37.3	36.7	37.4	37.2
F/M	86.49	85.59	86.36	84.86	94.84	95.39	95.07	82.92	84.54
1975 M	43.0	45.5	45.0	46.1	38.7	39.2	38.5	43.6	42.7
F	37.4	39.4	39.5	39.2	36.6	37.1	36.5	37.0	36.8
F/M	86.97	86.59	87.77	85.03	94.57	94.64	94.80	84.86	86.18
1976 M	42.7	45.3	45.1	45.5	38.5	39.1	38.2		
F	37.3	39.3	39.6	38.9	36.5	37.1	36.4		
F/M	87.35	86.75	87.80	85.49	94.80	94.88	95.28		

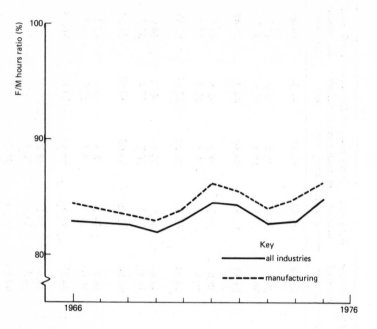

FIG 3.5 Female/male ratio of hours worked manual workers (DEG)

hours ratios is between the manual (where males are more concentrated) and non-manual sectors and not between manufacturing and
non-manufacturing as already indicated.

A comparison of Figs. 3.1, 3.2, 3.3, 3.4 with Figs. 3.5, 3.6, 3.7, 3.8
respectively illustrates that hours and earnings ratios followed a similar
pattern until 1973 for manual and all workers. There appeared no such
patterns for non-manual workers over this period. After 1973 the F/M
weekly hours ratios for manual and all workers seems to have little
effect on the respective relative earnings, thus indicating the presence of
other forces working to increase the F/M earnings ratio.

The factors which have been at work to increase the F/M ratio
including the possible impact of Government policy will be discussed in
detail in a later section. But in describing the general trends it is worth
noting that overtime is clearly one factor which can exert a significant
influence on the F/M earnings ratio. Generally females work fewer
overtime hours than men. This is more noticeable with respect to
manuals than non-manuals since there is a higher concentration of

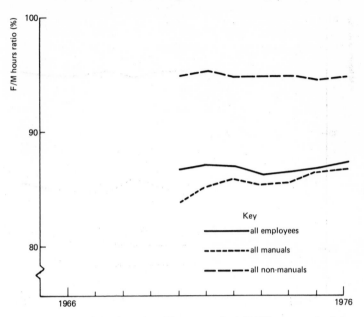

FIG. 3.6 Female/male ratio of hours worked (NES) aggregate data

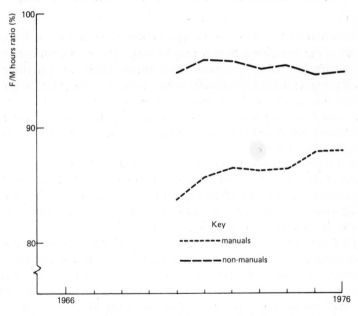

FIG. 3.7 Female/male ratio of hours worked: manufacturing

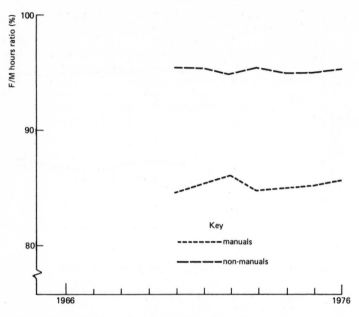

F<small>IG</small>. 3.8 Female/male ratio of hours worked: non-manufacturing

women in the latter. Also interestingly the decline in overtime hours as a result of the recession is born mainly by males absolutely, but overtime by females has fallen by a greater proportion (Table 3.4). Overtime is slightly higher in the non-manufacturing sector than the manufacturing sector for females and for males. The F/M overtime ratio (female overtime hours expressed as a percentage of male overtime hours) is oscillatory and as such does not correspond to the movement of relative earnings over time.

A further factor which could affect the earnings of females relative to males is the various payment systems adopted, i.e. remuneration on a payment-by-results basis (PBR payments) and payments for shift work. Insufficient data proved a problem in both cases: NES figures were available from only 1973 onwards.

PBR payments are much higher in the manual sector, especially in the non-manufacturing manual sector where there is greater equality of payments for female relative to male workers. This may be one of many reasons why the F/M earnings ratio is considerably higher for manuals as opposed to non-manuals in manufacturing (Fig. 3.3). In non-manufacturing both manual and non-manual males receive higher PBR

TABLE 3.4   Average weekly overtime hours—aggregate data (NES)

		All employ-ees	*Manual all indus-tries*	*Manual manuf-acturing inds.*	*Manual non-manuf. inds.*	*Non-manual all inds.*	*Non-manual manuf. inds.*	*Non-manual non-manuf. inds.*
1970	*M*							
	F							
	F/M							
1971	*M*	4.3	5.9	5.6	6.3			
	F	0.6	1.0	0.8	1.3			
	F/M	13.95	16.94	14.28	20.63			
1972	*M*	4.1	5.8	5.5	6.1			
	F	0.5	1.0	0.9	1.2			
	F/M	12.19	17.24	16.36	19.67			
1973	*M*	4.6	6.5	6.3	6.7			
	F	0.6	1.2	1.1	1.1			
	F/M	13.04	18.46	17.46	16.41			
1974	*M*	4.7	6.5	6.3	6.8	1.4	1.4	1.4
	F	0.6	1.2	1.0	1.5	0.4	0.4	0.4
	F/M	12.76	18.46	15.87	22.05	28.57	28.57	28.57
1975	*M*	4.0	5.6	5.1	6.1	1.4	1.4	1.4
	F	0.5	0.9	0.6	1.2	0.4	0.3	0.4
	F/M	12.50	16.07	11.76	19.67	28.57	21.42	28.57
1976	*M*	3.8	5.4	5.2	5.5	1.3	1.4	1.2
	F	0.4	0.8	0.7	1.0	0.3	0.3	0.3
	F/M	10.52	14.81	13.46	18.18	23.07	21.42	25.00

payments than women. On the other hand, shift payments for manual workers are higher than for non-manual workers and are greater for males than for females. In the non-manufacturing sectors, however, average shift payments are fairly similar between the sexes for both manual and non-manual workers, and this may explain why the *F/M* earnings ratios are close together (Fig. 3.4).

Table 3.5 Average weekly PBR and shift payments—aggregate data (NES)
payment-by-results payment (£ p.w.)

		All employ-ees	Manual all indus-tries	Manual manuf-acturing inds.	Manual non-manuf. inds.	Non-manual all inds.	Non-manual manuf. inds.	Non-manual non-manuf. inds.
1973	M	2.8	3.6	4.6	2.7	1.3	1.2	1.4
	F	0.9	2.4	3.7	0.5	0.2	0.2	0.2
	F/M	32.14	66.66	80.43	18.51	15.38	16.66	14.28
1974	M	3.2	4.3	5.0	3.4	1.5	1.2	1.6
	F	1.1	3.0	4.4	0.7	0.2	0.2	0.1
	F/M	34.37	69.76	88.0	20.58	13.33	16.66	6.25
1975	M	5.6	4.7	5.4	4.0	1.4	1.3	1.4
	F	2.7	3.1	4.6	0.9	0.2	0.3	0.2
	F/M	48.21	65.95	85.18	22.50	14.28	23.07	14.28
1976	M	3.8	5.2	6.0	4.5	1.8	1.5	1.9
	F	1.2	3.7	5.8	1.0	0.2	0.4	0.2
	F/M	31.57	71.15	96.66	22.22	11.11	26.66	10.52

Shift premium payments (£ p.w.)

		All employ-ees	Manual all indus-tries	Manual manuf-acturing inds.	Manual non-manuf. inds.	Non-manual all inds.	Non-manual manuf. inds.	Non-manual non-manuf. inds.
1973	M	0.7	1.0	1.4	0.6	0.2	0.2	0.2
	F	0.2	0.3	0.2	0.4	0.1	–	0.2
	F/M	28.57	25.00	14.28	66.66	50.00	–	100.0
1974	M	0.8	1.2	1.6	0.7	0.2	0.3	0.2
	F	0.2	0.3	0.2	0.5	0.1	–	0.2
	F/M	25.00	25.00	12.50	71.42	50.00	–	100.0
1975	M	1.9	1.7	2.2	1.2	0.4	0.4	0.4
	F	0.9	0.5	0.3	0.9	0.3	0.1	0.3
	F/M	47.36	29.41	13.63	75.00	75.00	25.00	75.00
1976	M	1.4	2.1	2.7	1.5	0.5	0.4	0.5
	F	0.4	0.8	0.4	1.2	0.3	0.1	0.4
	F/M	28.57	38.09	14.81	80.00	60.00	25.00	80.00

INDUSTRIAL DATA

The industrial figures in Tables 3.6 to 3.15 generally reflect the conclusions outlined above. The main concern here is to illustrate inter-industry earnings differences and possible influences upon them.

In the manual sector the industries with consistently high relative earnings ratios are Transport and Communications and Public Administration. The high earnings ratio in Transport and Communications may be due to high ratios of weekly hours, shift payments and overtime—particularly the latter, since the F/M overtime ratio is consistently much higher than in other industries. In Public Administration the F/M ratios are above the average for total hours, overtime hours and shift payments. The Bricks, Pottery, Glass, etc. industry has a low F/M earnings ratio, coupled with a low female/male ratio for weekly hours and overtime, so that these various factors could exert some influence on the earnings in the different industries, though to what precise degree is uncertain. It is, of course, not suggested that the influence of weekly hours, overtime, shift and PBR payments provide a complete explanation of the earnings of females relative to males, as pointed out in the first section, though they appear to have some influence. The region in which a person works, for example could affect his or her relative earnings position since relative earnings are higher in some areas (e.g. South East) than in others (e.g. Yorkshire and Humberside) for all workers.

Turning now to the non-manual sector the Professional and Scientific industry has a high earnings ratio along with higher than average ratios in weekly hours, overtime and shift payments. The relatively high F/M earnings ratio for Miscellaneous Services in 1976 corresponds with fairly high F/M ratios for overtime and shift payments. Construction, an industry with a relatively low F/M earnings ratio, also has a low ratio for weekly hours and overtime. One problem that makes such *ad hoc* interpretation even more bizarre is insufficient data, particularly for shift and PBR payments and non-manual overtime hours where the lack of figures could indicate that these activities are not prominent or that there are insufficient females to ensure a significant sample.[2] Simply because there are no figures for some industries does not mean that the activities are not present and one cannot assume this to be a cause of a low F/M earnings ratio.

Having said that, it is apparent that total hours worked, overtime, shift and PBR payments do have some influence on the relative earnings

TABLE 3.6   F/M earnings ratios for manual workers—industry data (DEG)

Industry	1969	1970	1971	1972	1973	1974	1975
I Agriculture, forestry &fishing	—	—	50.40	—	—	—	—
II Mining & quarrying	43.31	45.20	52.69	54.27	56.36	59.93	61.83
III Food, drink & tobacco	49.30	51.21	52.12	52.60	60.67	55.09	61.53
IV Coal and petroleum products	49.07	49.56	50.14	50.45	51.97	56.01	59.27
V Chemicals & allied industries	47.36	48.87	47.93	49.51	48.07	52.90	56.66
VI Metal manufacture	47.77	45.47	57.57	58.82	58.06	61.91	66.16
VII Mechanical engineering	51.91	53.86	55.48	55.95	58.24	60.63	66.50
VIII Instrument engineering	52.65	54.39	54.95	56.03	57.13	61.09	64.06
IX Electrical engineering	51.32	52.57	52.01	52.29	57.91	55.57	58.03
X Shipbuilding, marine engineering	44.08	47.89	55.95	57.19	57.24	63.49	67.71
XI Vehicles	51.22	52.62	51.43	52.73	53.00	57.04	61.30
XII Metal goods n.e.c.	47.63	48.12	53.85	53.92	54.12	58.34	59.20
XIII Textiles	51.97	52.99	51.35	51.31	51.95	54.07	55.42
XIV Leather, leather goods and fur	50.38	49.84	55.88	56.23	56.14	59.55	59.59
XV Clothing and footwear	53.64	54.53	48.95	49.18	49.68	54.64	57.64
XVI Bricks, pottery, glass, cement etc.	47.94	48.31	58.32	57.78	58.26	63.27	65.86
XVII Timber, furniture etc.	55.20	55.35	47.45	48.19	46.81	54.75	59.09
XVIII Paper, printing and publishing	42.91	46.04	48.55	48.97	49.91	54.47	56.73
XIX Other manufacturing industries	46.74	46.32	44.57	41.54	45.79	49.07	50.43
XX Construction	46.56	47.76	54.91	55.51	57.92	62.65	64.12
XXI Gas, electricity and water	56.55	55.54	66.17	65.71	66.59	66.38	69.06
XXII Transport and communications	65.21	65.02	—	—	—	—	—
XXIII Distributive trades	—	—	—	—	—	—	—
XXIV Insurance, banking, finance and business services	—	—	—	—	—	—	—

TABLE 3.6 *(contd.)*

	1969	1970	1971	1972	1973	1974	1975
XXV Professional and scientific services	–	–	–	–	–	–	–
XXVI Miscellaneous services	49.16	48.52	47.39	48.46	49.08	52.13	52.43
XXVII Public administration	64.27	71.22	71.68	68.77	74.62	77.05	77.47
All manufacturing industries	47.40	48.36	50.40	50.66	50.94	55.07	57.30
All non-manufacturing industries	–	–	–	–	–	–	–
All industries and services	48.76	49.89	51.08	51.09	51.71	55.54	57.38

TABLE 3.7　F/M earnings ratios for manual workers—industry data (NES)

Industry	$\dfrac{F}{M}$ earnings						
	1970	1971	1972	1973	1974	1975	1976
I Agriculture, forestry, fishing	–	–	–	–	–	–	–
II Mining—quarrying	–	–	–	–	–	–	–
III Food, drink & tobacco	50.18	53.00	54.33	54.90	55.94	59.96	61.23
IV Coal & petrol products	–	–	–	–	–	–	–
V Chemicals & allied industries	48.96	50.64	51.85	52.02	53.29	56.61	59.38
VI Metal manufacture	–	–	–	–	–	–	–
VII Mechanical engineering	51.04	53.25	55.99	55.50	58.20	62.43	65.32
VIII Instrument engineering	54.45	56.45	56.87	56.63	57.97	–	67.58
IX Electrical engineering	52.90	54.18	56.16	55.87	59.11	62.80	66.92
X Shipbuilding & marine engineering	–	–	–	–	–	–	–
XI Vehicles	54.29	54.44	56.30	56.56	62.16	–	70.31
XII Metal goods n.e.c.	48.06	50.17	51.07	50.78	51.45	60.04	63.61
XIII Textiles	54.84	55.47	55.52	56.25	56.23	61.74	62.40
XIV Leather, leather goods and fur	–	–	–	–	–	–	–
XV Clothing & footwear	57.38	58.30	57.24	56.76	58.20	64.30	65.15
XVI Bricks, pottery, glass, cement etc.	49.64	51.76	54.05	49.38	52.04	57.59	59.97
XVII Timber, furniture etc.	–	–	–	–	–	–	–
XVIII Paper, printing & publishing	43.81	45.75	46.50	47.62	50.41	56.85	60.71
XIX Other manufacturing industries	47.14	49.67	49.42	50.77	52.71	57.06	59.14
XX Construction	–	–	–	–	–	–	–
XXI Gas, electricity & water	–	–	–	–	–	–	–
XXII Transport & communication	69.12	66.99	67.42	68.16	67.77	71.22	73.16
XXIII Distributive trades	52.42	52.73	53.02	53.42	56.60	58.42	62.71

Table 3.7 (contd.)

	1970	1971	1972	1973	1974	1975	1976
XXIV Insurance, banking, finance & business services	—	—	—	—	—	—	—
XXV Professional & scientific services	54.46	58.00	60.89	60.93	67.23	67.13	69.46
XXVI Miscellaneous services	50.68	54.20	53.99	55.45	56.94	62.16	66.47
XXVII Public administration	62.15	66.12	69.89	70.10	71.23	74.48	76.58
All manufacturing industries	49.12	50.48	51.30	51.38	53.45	57.24	59.79
All non manufacturing industries	49.80	52.16	52.41	51.10	53.68	58.03	60.79
All industries & services	50.00	52.04	52.13	51.71	54.13	57.63	60.52

TABLE 3.8 F/M earnings ratios for non-manual workers—industry data (NES)

Industry	1970	1971	1972	1973	1974	1975	1976
I Agriculture, forestry, fishing	—	—	—	—	—	—	—
II Mining & quarrying	—	—	—	—	—	—	—
III Food, drink & tobacco	—	—	—	46.53	49.80	53.56	55.02
IV Coal & petrol products	—	—	—	—	—	—	—
V Chemicals & allied industries	41.77	44.75	43.90	44.07	48.20	49.93	50.71
VI Metal manufacture	—	44.84	44.52	46.92	49.43	54.12	57.25
VII Mechanical engineering	43.63	44.33	—	44.78	45.90	52.82	52.68
VIII Instrument engineering	—	—	—	—	—	—	—
IX Electrical engineering	42.12	—	45.29	44.62	48.56	51.52	54.84
X Shipbuilding—marine engineering	—	—	—	—	—	—	—
XI Vehicles	44.85	46.89	47.04	47.2	49.37	54.99	58.02
XII Metal goods n.e.c.	—	—	—	43.92	47.15	50.92	—
XIII Textiles	—	—	—	—	—	—	—
XIV Leather, leather goods and fur	—	—	—	—	—	—	—
XV Clothing & footwear	—	—	—	—	—	—	—
XVI Bricks, pottery, glass, cement, etc.	—	—	—	—	—	—	—
XVII Timber, furniture etc.	—	—	—	—	—	—	—
XVIII Paper, printing & publishing	—	—	47.8	47.66	49.30	—	55.86
XIX Other manufacturing industries	—	—	—	—	—	—	—
XX Construction	—	41.81	42.53	43.42	43.30	47.00	48.97
XXI Gas, electricity & water	49.45	51.16	50.76	53.36	53.37	55.97	54.29
XXII Transport & communications	52.15	51.52	53.35	52.76	54.56	56.38	59.11
XXIII Distributive trades	42.34	44.24	43.84	45.25	46.88	50.71	51.77

TABLE 3.8 (contd.)

	1970	1971	1972	1973	1974	1975	1976
XXIV Insurance, banking, finance & business services	44.35	45.98	45.02	45.09	46.89	50.21	50.57
XXV Professional & scientific services	59.03	58.68	59.87	59.60	59.25	68.19	69.17
XXVI Miscellaneous services	49.07	52.69	51.64	53.72	56.56	–	62.98
XXVII Public administration	57.56	56.69	58.26	56.17	59.57	59.33	60.26
All manufacturing industries	43.05	44.33	44.52	44.76	47.34	51.53	53.28
All non manufacturing industries	51.84	52.58	52.53	52.82	53.68	59.24	61.00
All industries & services	49.72	50.64	51.03	51.35	52.57	57.89	59.80

TABLE 3.9 Average weekly hours—industry data (DEG) for manual workers

	1969 M	1969 F	1969 F/M	1970 M	1970 F	1970 F/M	1971 M	1971 F	1971 F/M	1972 M	1972 F	1972 F/M	1973 M	1973 F	1973 F/M	1974 M	1974 F	1974 F/M	1975 M	1975 F	1975 F/M
Agric. forestry. fishing																					
Mining & quarrying	51.5	37.5	72.81	51.8	37.6	72.58	49.3	37.9	76.87	49.0	38.2	—	48.8	38.6	—	48.0	—	—	47.2	—	—
FDT	47.6	38.6	81.09	46.8	38.5	82.26	46.4	38.2	82.32	46.4	38.2	82.32	47.1	38.6	81.95	46.6	38.0	81.54	46.2	37.7	81.60
Coal/petroleum	44.3	39.9	90.06	44.0	39.2	89.09	43.6	39.3	90.13	42.9	38.6	89.97	42.3	38.6	91.25	43.8	38.8	88.58	42.6	38.6	90.61
Chemical & allied	46.1	38.9	84.38	44.9	38.7	86.19	44.0	38.4	87.27	44.2	38.7	87.55	44.6	38.5	86.32	44.2	38.4	86.87	42.7	37.9	88.75
Metal manuf.	45.8	38.0	82.96	45.1	37.4	82.92	43.3	37.3	86.14	44.6	38.3	85.87	45.1	37.7	83.59	44.8	37.5	83.70	41.9	36.7	87.59
Mech. eng.	45.9	38.4	83.66	44.9	38.1	84.85	43.0	37.9	88.13	43.5	38.4	88.27	44.6	38.1	85.42	44.2	38.0	85.97	42.6	37.5	88.02
Instrument eng.	44.1	37.9	85.94	44.1	38.2	86.62	42.8	38.2	89.25	43.4	38.2	88.01	43.9	38.2	87.01	43.7	38.0	86.72	42.0	37.4	89.04
Elect. eng.	45.2	38.0	84.07	44.4	37.7	84.90	43.4	37.7	86.86	43.5	37.8	87.09	44.0	37.4	85.00	43.4	37.9	85.71	42.2	37.1	87.99
Shipbuilding E.M.E.	45.3	37.2	82.11	45.3	38.4	84.76	43.8	37.7	85.84	43.5	38.2	87.81	44.0	40.0	90.90	43.5	37.2	84.36	43.9	37.0	84.28
Vehicles	43.6	38.1	87.38	42.4	37.9	89.38	41.2	37.7	91.50	42.3	38.2	90.30	43.0	37.7	87.67	42.3	37.9	89.59	41.4	37.5	90.57
Metal goods n.e.s.	46.0	37.6	81.73	45.2	37.4	82.74	43.2	37.1	85.87	43.9	37.7	85.87	44.7	37.3	83.44	43.7	37.1	84.89	42.1	36.8	87.41
Textiles	45.8	37.7	82.31	44.7	37.3	83.44	44.1	37.3	84.58	44.7	37.6	84.11	44.9	37.3	83.07	43.6	37.2	85.32	42.4	36.1	85.14
Leather, fur.	45.1	37.2	82.48	45.0	37.3	82.88	44.5	37.0	83.14	44.2	37.5	84.84	44.5	36.7	82.47	44.2	36.1	81.67	43.7	36.5	83.52
Clothing & footwear	41.9	37.0	88.30	41.5	37.2	89.63	41.2	36.8	89.32	41.5	36.7	88.43	42.0	36.4	86.66	41.1	36.1	87.83	40.5	35.5	87.65
Bricks, pottery, glass etc.	47.8	37.2	77.82	46.9	36.9	78.67	46.3	36.5	78.83	46.5	36.8	79.13	47.1	36.5	77.49	46.1	36.3	78.74	44.5	35.9	80.67
Timber, furniture	45.8	37.5	81.88	45.6	37.4	82.01	44.7	37.7	84.34	45.0	38.1	84.66	45.1	37.5	83.14	43.8	37.7	86.07	43.1	37.0	85.84
Paper, printing, publ.	46.1	37.9	82.21	44.3	38.0	85.87	44.4	38.7	87.16	44.7	38.3	85.58	45.1	38.6	85.58	43.9	38.7	88.15	43.3	38.7	89.38
Other manuf.	46.2	38.6	83.55	45.5	37.8	83.07	44.2	37.6	85.06	44.4	37.8	85.13	44.9	37.7	83.96	43.9	37.5	85.42	42.5	37.3	87.76
Construction	48.2	38.0	78.84	47.5	38.1	80.21	47.2	37.1	78.60	47.0	36.8	78.29	47.2	37.2	78.81	46.8	38.1	81.41	45.2	37.5	82.96
Gas, elec, water	44.1	37.6	85.26	44.0	36.1	82.04	43.7	35.9	82.15	43.1	37.1	86.07	43.8	37.3	85.15	44.0	36.7	83.40	42.3	35.4	83.68
Transport & comm.	50.9	44.2	86.83	49.2	42.8	86.99	48.0	43.3	90.20	48.5	42.8	88.24	49.6	43.0	86.69	49.5	42.4	85.65	47.3	41.5	87.73
Distributive trades																					
Insurance, banking																					
Professional & scientific																					
Miscellaneous services	44.6	39.0	87.44	44.4	38.5	86.71	43.9	38.5	87.69	43.6	38.5	88.30	44.1	38.4	87.07	43.8	38.7	88.35	43.2	38.3	88.66
Public admin.	43.8	40.1	91.55	43.7	39.7	90.84	43.5	39.6	91.03	43.5	40.0	91.95	43.9	40.3	91.79	43.7	39.5	90.38	43.2	40.3	93.28

TABLE 3.10 Average weekly hours for manual workers—industry data (NES)

	1970[a]			1971[a]			1972[a]			1973			1974			1975			1976		
	M	F	M/F	M	F	M/F	M	F	M/F	M	F	M/F	M	F	M/F	M	F	M/F	M	F	M/F
Agri., forestry fishing	47.3			47.3						47.7			48.9			45.7			45.5		
Mining & quarrying	41.2			41.9						43.6			42.5			42.7			43.3		
FDT	47.7	39.1	81.97	47.1	39.5	83.86	46.7	39.3	84.15	48.4	40.7	84.09	48.7	40.7	83.57	47.6	40.3	84.66	48.0	40.1	83.54
Coal & petroleum products	46.6			43.8			43.6			44.4			44.8			44.7			44.6		
Chemical & allied	45.5	38.6	84.83	44.2	38.6	87.33	44.4	39.2	88.28	45.2	39.8	88.05	45.5	39.9	87.69	41.1	39.3	89.11	44.9	39.2	87.30
Metal manuf.	45.0			43.6			43.4			46.0			46.1			44.7			44.5		
Mech. eng.	46.0	38.7	84.13	44.6	38.0	85.20	44.2	38.7	87.55	46.8	40.5	86.53	46.5	40.4	86.88	45.6	40.3	88.37	45.1	40.1	88.91
Instrument eng.	44.1	37.8	85.71	44.1	38.1	86.39	43.5	38.7	88.96	45.3	40.1	88.52	44.9	40.3	89.75	43.7			43.9	39.5	89.97
Elec. eng.	45.3	38.2	84.32	44.1	38.2	86.62	43.8	38.2	87.21	45.6	40.3	88.37	45.3	40.4	89.18	44.1	39.7	90.02	44.2	39.8	90.04
Shipbuilding/marine eng.	45.2			45.8			45.2			47.8			48.3			47.8			48.2		
Vehicles	42.8	38.6	90.18	42.7	38.1	89.22	42.2	38.5	91.23	44.5	40.6	91.23	44.3	40.4	91.19	43.7			44.4	40.4	90.99
Metal goods nes	46.0	38.1	82.32	44.4	38.0	85.58	44.4	38.2	86.03	46.8	40.3	86.11	46.9	39.6	84.43	44.8	39.6	88.39	44.9	39.5	87.97
Textiles	44.8	37.5	83.70	43.5	37.2	85.51	44.4	38.1	85.81	45.9	39.8	86.71	46.2	39.6	85.71	44.2	39.3	88.91	44.7	39.6	88.59
Leather, goods & fur																					
Clothing and footwear	41.9	37.0	88.30	41.7	37.3	89.44	41.8	37.0	88.51	43.0	38.9	90.46	43.2	38.7	89.58	42.5	38.5	90.58	42.2	38.5	91.23
Bricks, pottery, glass, etc.	48.2	37.6	78.0	47.3	37.5	79.28	47.3	38.0	80.33	49.3	40.0	81.13	49.1	39.4	80.24	47.1	39.3	83.43	47.6	39.2	82.35
Timber, furniture	45.0			44.4			45.0			46.6			45.4			44.8			44.5		
Paper, printing, publishing	46.1	39.0	84.59	44.3	38.8	87.58	44.9	39.7	88.41	46.9	40.8	86.99	46.1	40.7	88.28	44.4	39.9	89.86	44.3	40.0	90.29
Other manuf.	45.6	38.1	83.55	43.9	37.6	85.64	45.5	38.4	84.39	47.0	40.4	85.95	46.5	40.2	86.45	44.1	39.8	90.24	45.2	40.1	88.71
Construction	48.0			46.7			47.4			48.7			48.2			46.7			46.3		
Gas, electricity water	44.3			44.2			43.8			44.3			44.5			44.7			43.5		
Transport & comm.	49.0	42.6	86.93	48.0	43.0	89.58	47.4	42.2	89.02	48.9	44.1	90.18	49.4	44.2	89.47	48.5	42.9	88.45	47.3	42.8	90.48
Distributive trades	45.5	38.8	85.27	45.4	38.7	85.24	45.0	38.8	86.22	45.9	39.0	84.96	45.5	39.4	86.59	44.9	38.7	86.19	44.6	38.7	86.77
Insurance, banking	44.5			44.7			44.6			44.0			45.1			44.6			43.8		
Professional & scientific	45.0	38.1	84.66	44.7	38.1	85.23	44.3	38.2	86.23	44.9	38.5	85.74	44.8	38.5	85.93	45.0	38.0	84.44	44.7	37.6	84.11
Miscellaneous services	45.8	40.0	87.33	45.2	40.1	88.71	45.1	39.8	88.24	45.8	40.4	88.20	45.0	40.2	89.33	44.6	39.8	89.23	44.0	38.5	89.77
Public admin.	44.1	38.0	86.16	44.1	38.9	88.20	43.9	39.4	89.74	44.9	39.9	88.86	44.9	40.2	89.53	44.4	40.6	91.44	43.8	40.1	91.55

NOTE
[a] 1970, 1971, 1972 include people whoose pay was affected by absence

TABLE 3.11   Average weekly hours for non-manual workers—industry data (NES)

	1970ᵃ			1971ᵃ			1972ᵃ			1973			1974			1975			1976		
	M	F	F/M	M	F	F/M	M	F	F/M	M	F	F/M	M	F	F/M	M	F	F/M	M	F	F/M
Agric. forestry, fishing																					
Mining & quarrying																39.5	37.4	94.68	40.2		
FDT		37.6		38.4	37.3		38.3	37.0		38.7	37.4	96.64	39.5	37.5	94.94	38.5	37.0	96.10	38.5	36.9	95.84
Coal & Petroleum products																					
Chemical & allied	38.5	37.5	97.40	38.0	37.3	98.16	37.9	—	95.56	38.3	37.3	97.38	38.4	37.4	97.40	38.5	37.2	96.62	38.1	37.2	97.64
Metal manufacture				38.8	36.5	94.07	38.3	36.6	95.86	38.4	36.4	94.79	38.4	36.4	94.79	38.7	36.4	94.06	38.1	36.4	95.54
Mechanical engineering	40.0	37.5	93.75	39.0	37.1	95.12	38.7	37.1	—	39.3	37.3	94.91	39.2	37.2	94.90	39.4	37.4	94.92	39.2	37.3	95.15
Instrument engineering																					
Electrical engineering	39.8	38.0	95.47	39.1	37.7	96.41	39.0	37.7	96.66	39.6	38.0	95.95	39.4	38.0	96.45	39.3	37.7	95.93	39.6	37.6	94.95
Shipbuild/marine eng.																					
Vehicles	40.3	37.9	94.04	39.2	37.7	98.17	39.6	37.5	94.69	40.4	37.8	93.56	40.0	37.7	94.25	39.9	37.7	94.49	40.2	37.7	93.78
Metal goods n.e.s.					36.9	—		36.8	—	39.0	37.0	94.87	39.0	37.2	95.38	39.7	37.0	93.20			
Textiles					37.0	—		36.7			37.1			37.1			36.8			37.0	
Leather, leather goods/fur																					
Clothing and footwear																					
Bricks, pottery, glass etc.																					
Timber, furniture																					
Paper, printing, publishing	38.3			38.3			38.2	36.5	95.54	38.7	36.8	95.09	38.4	36.7	95.57		36.5	—	38.5	36.4	94.55
Other manufacturing					37.4			37.2			37.3			37.5							
Construction	40.8			40.0	37.0	92.50	39.7	37.0	93.19	39.7	37.2	93.70	39.8	37.2	93.47	39.9	36.8	92.23	39.9	36.8	92.23
Gas, electricity/water	39.2	38.4	97.95	39.0	38.1	97.69	39.0	38.3	98.20	39.2	38.5	98.21	39.4	38.4	97.46	39.1	38.2	97.70	38.6	37.7	97.67
Transport & comm.	42.1	38.1	90.49	41.9	38.0	90.69	41.3	37.6	91.04	41.2	37.8	91.74	41.4	37.8	91.30	41.3	37.6	91.04	40.4	37.4	92.57
Distributive trades	40.7	38.9	95.57	40.3	38.6	95.78	40.3	38.4	95.28	40.5	38.9	96.04	40.2	38.5	95.77	40.3	38.4	95.29	39.9	38.2	95.74
Insurance, banking	37.0	36.3	98.10	36.9	36.1	97.83	36.8	35.9	97.55	36.7	36.0	98.09	36.6	35.9	98.09	36.9	35.9	97.29	36.8	35.8	97.28
Professional & scientific	34.2	35.4	103.5	34.0	35.1	103.23	34.0	34.5	101.47	34.2	34.8	101.75	34.6	34.9	100.87	34.4	34.5	100.29	34.4	34.6	100.58
Miscellaneous services	42.1	38.6	91.68	40.7	38.1	93.61	41.2	38.3	92.96	41.0	38.4	93.65	40.8	38.2	93.63		38.0	—		38.0	—
Public administration	39.7	37.4	94.20	40.1	37.6	93.76	40.3	37.5	93.05	40.0	37.2	93.00	39.8	37.2	93.47	39.7	37.4	94.21	39.1	37.1	94.88

NOTE
ᵃ 1970, 1971, 1972 include those whose hours are affected by absence

TABLE 3.12 Average weekly overtime hours for manual workers—industry data (NES)

INDUSTRIAL DATA MANUALS Overtime—weekly average, unaffected by absence (NES)

	1971			1972			1973			1974			1975			1976		
	M	F	F/M	M	F	F/M	M	F	F/M	M	F	F/M	M	F	F/M	M	F	F/M
Agric, forestry, fishing	5.1	·	—	5.6	—	—	8.0	—	—	8.0	—	—	5.1	—	—	4.8	—	—
Mining & quarrying	6.2	—	—	6.0	—	—	5.0	—	—	5.0	—	—	5.2	—	—	5.7	—	—
F.D.T.	7.3	1.4	19.18	7.0	1.5	21.43	8.2	1.6	19.51	8.6	1.5	17.44	7.5	1.2	16.00	8.0	1.0	12.50
Coal & petroleum products	4.3	—	—	4.0	—	—	4.8	—	—	5.1	—	—	5.0	—	—	4.9	—	—
Chemical & allied	4.7	0.8	17.02	4.7	1.0	21.28	5.2	0.8	15.38	5.4	0.8	14.81	4.1	0.3	7.32	4.9	0.4	8.16
Metal manufacture	5.3	—	—	5.1	—	—	6.1	—	—	6.3	—	—	4.8	—	—	4.7	—	—
Mechanical engineering	6.2	0.9	14.52	5.5	1.1	20.00	6.8	1.4	20.59	6.6	1.5	22.73	5.8	1.2	20.69	5.2	0.8	15.38
Instrument engineering	4.8	1.1	22.92	4.5	1.1	24.44	5.5	1.1	20.00	5.2	1.2	23.08	4.0	—	—	4.1	0.6	14.63
Electrical engineering	5.3	0.6	11.32	5.1	1.0	19.61	5.8	1.0	17.24	5.5	1.0	18.18	4.4	0.5	11.36	4.4	0.6	13.64
Shipbuilding/marine eng.	7.6	—	—	6.9	—	—	7.7	—	—	8.2	—	—	7.8	—	—	8.2	—	—
Vehicles	4.1	0.9	21.95	4.2	0.7	16.67	4.6	1.1	23.91	4.5	1.0	22.22	3.8	—	—	4.5	0.9	20.00
Metal goods n.e.s.	6.1	0.9	14.75	5.7	0.9	15.79	6.8	1.3	19.12	7.0	0.9	12.86	5.0	0.5	10.00	5.1	0.5	9.80
Textiles	4.8	0.6	12.50	5.4	0.8	14.81	6.0	0.9	15.00	4.4	0.7	11.11	4.4	0.5	11.36	4.9	0.6	12.24
Leather, leather goods/fur	—	—	—	—	—	—	—	—	—	—	—	—	—	—	—	—	—	—
Clothing & footwear	2.6	0.5	19.23	2.5	0.4	16.00	3.0	0.6	20.00	3.2	0.4	12.50	2.6	0.3	11.54	2.2	0.3	13.64

TABLE 3.12 (*contd.*)

INDUSTRIAL DATA MANUALS Overtime—weekly average, unaffected by absence (NES)

	1971			1972			1973			1974			1975			1976		
	M	F	F/M	M	F	F/M	M	F	F/M	M	F	F/M	M	F	F/M	M	F	F/M
Bricks, pottery, glass etc.	7.9	0.6	7.59	7.7	1.0	12.99	8.5	0.8	9.41	8.5	0.8	9.41	6.5	0.4	6.15	6.9	0.4	5.80
Timber, furniture	5.3		–	5.5		–	6.2		–	5.0		–	4.4		–	4.1		–
Paper, printing, publishing	5.2	0.9	17.31	5.8	1.4	24.14	7.0	1.7	24.29	6.3	1.5	23.81	4.6	0.7	15.22	4.6	0.9	19.57
Other manufacture	5.4	0.8	14.81	6.5	1.0	15.38	7.0	1.3	18.57	6.6	1.2	18.18	4.3	0.6	13.95	5.5	0.9	16.36
Construction	7.2		–	7.5		–	7.9		–	7.5		–	6.2		–	5.8		–
Gas, electricity/water	4.6		–	4.3		–	4.2		–	4.6		–	4.8		–	3.7		–
Transport and comm.	8.6	4.3	50.00	8.1	3.9	48.15	9.0	4.6	51.11	9.4	5.1	54.26	8.5	3.8	44.71	7.5	3.6	48.00
Distributive trades	5.1	1.1	21.57	4.8	0.9	18.75	5.4	0.7	12.96	5.2	1.1	21.15	4.7	0.5	10.64	4.5	0.4	8.89
Insurance, banking	5.1		–	5.0		–	4.5		–	5.9		–	5.6		–	5.0		–
Professional & scientific	4.8	1.0	20.83	4.4	0.9	20.45	4.8	0.9	18.75	4.8	1.0	20.83	5.1	0.8	15.69	4.8	0.6	12.50
Miscellaneous services	4.0	1.1	27.50	4.1	1.1	26.83	4.6	1.2	26.09	4.1	1.3	31.71	4.0	1.3	32.50	3.5	1.1	31.43
Public administration	4.7	1.3	27.66	4.5	1.3	28.89	5.1	1.5	29.41	4.7	1.8	34.62	4.7	1.9	40.43	4.2	1.9	45.24

TABLE 3.13   Average weekly overtime hours for non-manual workers –
industry data (NES)

	1974			1975			1976		
	M	*F*	*F/M*	*M*	*F*	*F/M*	*M*	*F*	*F/M*
Agric, forestry, fishing		−							
Mining & quarrying			−	1.8	0.2	11.11	2.5	−	−
FDT	1.1	0.5	45.45	0.8	0.3	37.50	0.8	0.3	37.50
Coal & Petroleum prods.									
Chemical & allied	0.8	0.2	25.00	0.9	0.2	22.22	0.7	0.2	28.57
Metal manufacture	1.3	0.3	23.08	1.7	0.2	11.76	1.1	0.3	27.27
Mechanical engineering	1.4	0.3	21.43	1.5	0.5	33.33	1.4	0.4	28.57
Instrument engineering									
Electrical engineering	1.7	0.6	35.29	1.6	0.4	25.00	1.8	0.3	16.67
Shipbuilding and ME.									
Vehicles	2.1	0.5	23.81	1.9	0.4	21.05	2.3	0.5	21.74
Metal goods n.e.s.	1.1	0.4	36.36	1.4	0.3	21.43	−	−	
Textiles		0.3			0.3			0.2	
Leather, leather goods, fur									
Clothing & footwear									
Bricks, pottery, glass etc									
Timber, furniture									
Paper, publishing, printing	1.1	0.4	36.36	−	0.3	−	1.2	0.2	16.67
Other manuf.		0.4			−			−	
Construction	1.1	0.3	27.27	1.1	0.1	9.09	1.2	0.2	16.67
Gas, elec, water	1.3	0.5	38.46	1.1	0.4	36.36	0.9	0.3	33.33
Transport & comm.	3.5	0.8	22.86	3.0	0.8	26.67	2.4	0.6	25.00
Distributive trades	1.0	0.4	40.00	0.9	0.3	33.33	0.8	0.3	37.50
Insurance, banking	0.8	0.4	50.00	0.9	0.5	55.56	0.8	0.4	50.00
Professional & scientific	0.5	0.2	40.00	0.6	0.2	33.33	0.7	0.1	14.29
Miscellaneous services	1.3	0.5	38.46	−	0.6	−	1.3	0.7	53.85
Public administration	1.9	0.4	21.05	2.1	0.4	19.05	1.8	0.3	16.67

TABLE 3.14 Average weekly PBR payments for manual and non-manual workers—industry data (NES)

	1973 M	F	F/M	1974 M	F	F/M	1975 M	F	F/M	1976 M	F	F/M	1973 M	F	F/M	1974 M	F	F/M	1975 M	F	F/M	1976 M	F	F/M
Agric., forestry, fish.	1.0	0.2	20.00	1.6	0.2	12.50	0.7			1.3	0.1	7.69	1.7			3.6			2.8			3.0		
Mining & quarrying													1.0			0.6			3.3			1.2		
EDT	1.6	0.2	12.50	1.3	0.3	23.08	1.3	0.2	15.38				2.4	1.2	50.00	2.6	1.2	46.15	2.8	1.0	35.71	3.1	1.2	38.71
Coal & petrol. prods.	0.3	0.1	33.33	0.7	0.2	28.57	1.4	0.4	28.57				1.3			0.8			1.3			1.6		
Chem. & allied	1.3	0.1	7.69	1.4			0.7	0.2	28.57	2.4	0.3	12.50	1.8	1.4	77.78	2.0	2.0	100.00	1.9	2.4	126.32	1.9	2.2	115.79
Metal manuf.							1.4	0.2	14.29	0.5	0.1	20.00	6.9			8.1			8.7			9.7		
Mech. eng.										1.9	0.3	15.79	4.3	2.7	62.79	5.3	4.3	81.13	5.7	4.7	82.46	6.2	5.3	85.48
Instrument eng.													2.5	3.2	128.00	2.4	2.8	116.67	2.6			2.4	4.3	179.17
Elec. eng.	1.1	0.1	9.09	1.0	0.3	30.00	1.1	0.4	36.36	1.3	0.3	23.08	3.4	2.9	85.29	3.4	2.9	85.29	4.1	4.1	100.00	4.5	4.4	97.78
Shipbuilding & marine eng.													4.3			4.6			6.9			6.5		
Vehicles	0.4	0.1	25.00	0.4	0.1	25.00	0.4	0.2	50.00	0.4	0.3	75.00	5.9	4.1	69.49	5.2	4.5	86.54	5.3			5.8	6.0	103.45
Metal goods n.e.s.	1.3	0.2	15.38	1.6	0.2	12.50	1.1	0.1	9.09				6.2	4.0	64.52	6.6	4.3	65.15	5.9	4.9	83.05	7.4	6.4	86.49
Textiles	0.1			0.3			0.1			0.1			4.8	6.1	127.08	5.1	7.3	143.14	5.1	6.4	125.49	6.2	9.9	159.68
Leather, leather goods fur																								
Clothing & footwear	1.8	0.1	5.56	1.9	0.3	15.79	0.5			1.8	0.8	44.44	6.1	5.6	91.80	7.8	7.8	100.00	8.7	7.9	90.80	9.7	9.8	101.03
Bricks, pottery, glass	0.1			0.1									6.6			7.7	4.6	59.74	8.9	6.1	68.54	10.6	6.4	60.38
Timber & furniture													5.3			6.3			7.6			8.3		
Paper, printing, publ.							0.9	0.1	11.11	1.1	0.2	18.18	3.1	1.6	51.61	3.7	2.2	59.46	3.4	2.4	70.59	3.7	3.9	105.41
Other manufacture							2.1	0.9	42.86	2.1	0.8	38.10	4.9	2.8	57.14	5.2	3.8	73.08	6.4	4.2	65.63	8.4	4.4	52.38
Construction	0.4			0.7			0.6						5.0			6.6			7.3			9.1		
Gas, elec., water	1.3	0.4	30.77	1.5	0.5	33.33				0.8	0.1	12.50	6.1			7.4			9.6			9.3		
Transport & commun.	0.2			0.4									1.9	1.0	52.63	2.3	1.3	56.52	2.1	1.3	61.90	2.4	1.1	45.83
Distributive trades	2.5	0.3	12.00	2.6	0.4	15.38	2.7	0.4	14.81	3.3	0.5	15.15	0.8			2.3	1.1	47.83	2.3	0.6	26.09	2.6	1.5	57.69
Insurance, banking	5.0	0.4	8.00	5.4	0.2	3.70	4.9	0.4	8.16	6.5	0.4	6.15	1.0	0.3	30.00	1.0			1.1			1.8		
Professional & scientific	0.2			0.3			0.2			0.3	0.1	33.33	1.6	0.5	31.25	1.3	0.6	46.15	2.1	0.8	38.10	2.4	1.0	41.67
Miscellaneous services	2.5	0.2	8.00	3.1	0.1	3.23	0.2			3.3	0.2	6.06	2.7	0.4	14.81	2.1	0.6	28.57	2.2	0.7	31.82	2.3	0.7	30.43
Public admin.	0.1			0.1						0.1	0.0					3.2	0.6	18.75	5.6	1.1	19.64	6.5	1.3	20.00

TABLE 3.15 Average weekly shift premium payments for manual and non-manual workers—industry data (NES)

Non-manual

	1973 M	1973 F	1973 F/M	1974 M	1974 F	1974 F/M	1975 M	1975 F	1975 F/M	1976 M	1976 F	1976 F/M
Agric, forestry, fishing												
Mining & quarrying	0.2	0.1	50.00	0.3	0.1	33.33	1.1	0.0	—	0.5	0.1	20.00
F.D.T.												
Coal/Petroleum												
Chemical & allied	0.4			0.4	0.1	25.00	0.6	0.1	16.67	0.7	0.1	14.29
Metal Manuf.	0.7			0.9			1.5	0.2	13.33	1.5	0.2	13.33
Mechanical engineering	0.1			0.1			0.1	—		0.1	0.0	—
Instrument engineering												
Electrical engineering	0.2			0.2			0.4	—		0.3	0.0	—
Shipbuilding & M.E.												
Vehicles	0.3			0.5	0.1	20.00	0.5	0.1	20.00	0.6	0.1	16.67
Metal goods n.e.s.				0.1			0.2	—		0.0		—
Textiles												
Leather, fur												
Clothing, footwear								0.0				
Bricks, pottery, glass etc												
Timber, furniture												
Paper, printing, publish.	0.2	0.0		0.3						0.3	0.0	—
Other manuf.												
Construction				—	0.0					0.1	0.0	—
Gas, elec, water	0.3			0.4			0.1	0.0	16.67	0.8	0.1	12.50
Transport & comm.	0.6	0.2	33.33	0.7	0.2	28.57	0.6	0.1	16.67	1.2	0.4	33.33
Distributive trades	0.1			0.1			1.3	0.3	23.08	0.3	0.1	33.33
Insurance, banking	0.1			0.1			0.2	0.1	50.00	0.1	0.0	—
Professional & scientific	0.2	0.4	200.00	0.2	0.4	200.00	0.2	0.1	50.00	0.4	0.8	200.00
Miscellaneous services	0.2	0.1	50.00	0.1	0.1	100.00	0.3	0.6	200.00	0.4	0.2	50.00
Public administration	0.1			0.2	0.1	50.00	0.4	0.1	25.00	0.5	0.2	40.00

Manual

	1973 M	1973 F	1973 F/M	1974 M	1974 F	1974 F/M	1976 M	1976 F	1976 F/M
Agric, forestry, fishing				—			0.1		
Mining & quarrying	1.4			2.3			2.4		
F.D.T.	1.5	0.5	33.33	2.2	0.7	31.82	2.8	0.9	32.14
Coal/Petroleum	3.6			4.1			5.2		
Chemical & allied	1.6	0.2	12.50	3.2	0.1	3.13	3.7	0.2	5.41
Metal Manuf.	3.4			5.1			6.1		
Mechanical engineering	1.0	0.1	10.00	1.3	0.4	30.77	1.5	0.2	13.33
Instrument engineering	0.7	0.1	14.29	1.3	—		1.2	0.1	8.33
Electrical engineering	1.4	0.2	14.29	1.6	0.2	12.50	1.7	0.2	11.76
Shipbuilding & M.E.	0.6			1.2			1.2		
Vehicles	2.4			2.8	—		3.9	0.8	20.51
Metal goods n.e.s.	1.2	0.3	25.00	1.5	0.4	26.67	1.7	0.7	41.18
Textiles	1.6	0.2	12.50	2.1	0.2	9.52	2.8	0.2	7.14
Leather, fur				—			—		
Clothing, footwear	0.1	0.2	200.00	0.2	—		0.1	0.0	—
Bricks, pottery, glass etc	1.6	0.6	37.50	1.9	0.5	26.32	2.4	0.9	37.50
Timber, furniture	0.2			0.1			0.2		
Paper, printing, publish.	1.6	0.3	18.75	1.9	0.4	21.05	2.5	0.7	28.00
Other manuf.	2.1	0.2	9.52	2.7	0.4	14.81	3.2	0.5	15.63
Construction	0.2			2.3			0.3		
Gas, elec, water	1.9						2.2		
Transport & comm.	1.3	1.1	84.62	2.5	2.1	84.00	3.1	2.5	80.65
Distributive trades	0.4	—		0.3	0.1	33.33	0.8	0.2	25.00
Insurance, banking	0.2			0.6			0.6		
Professional & scientific	1.1	0.9	81.82	1.9	1.3	68.42	2.2	1.5	68.18
Miscellaneous services	0.2	0.2	100.00	0.5	0.6	120.00	0.4	1.2	300.00
Public administration	0.4	0.3	75.00	0.6	0.5	83.33	0.8	0.9	112.50

of the two sexes, but that these influences can vary in both character and magnitude between the different industries. Their influence may be small, however, in comparison to the sex differential in earnings within industries, where the major differences occur. In 1976 female average gross weekly earnings were £46.20. Suppose one granted females the average male wage in that industry, then their earnings would rise by £28.89 to £75.09. But if one now redistributed females so that the proportion of females in an industry was the same as the ratio of females to males in total (and granted them the average male wage in each industry), this would only raise female weekly earnings by a further £2.18 to £77.07. This does not correct for age and hours of work but such a calculation is unlikely to alter the conclusions. It would thus appear that earnings differences are greater within industries rather than between them.

There is, of course, no reason why this cross-section result should necessarily hold over time. Thus, changes in the industrial distribution of the male and female working population over the period could have significantly affected the F/M ratio. Using NES data, much of which is reproduced in the appended tables, it is possible to eliminate the effects of changes in the industrial distribution over time. For manual workers there is full information available for fifteen SIC orders for each of the years between 1970 and 1976. The corresponding number for non-manual employees is eight.

A weighted average F/M earnings ratio is constructed for each year using current weights, i.e.

$$R_t = \sum_{i=1}^{i=n} (r_{ti})(W_{ti})$$

where $W_{ti} = \dfrac{m_i + f_i}{M_t + F_t}$

and $R_t = F/M$ ratio of all employees in all industries in year t

$F_{ti} = F/M$ ratio in industry i in year t

W_{ti} = the industrial weighting in year t for the ith industry

m_i = the number of males in industry i in year t

f_i = the number of females in industry i in year t[3]

M_t/F_t = the total number of males and females respectively in the industries for year t.

To eliminate the effect of changes in the industrial distribution a base-weighted average (base = 1970) can be constructed showing what would have occurred had the industrial distribution remained stable, i.e.

$$R = \sum_{i=1}^{i=n} (r_{ti})(W_{1970i})$$

$$\text{where } W_{1970i} = \frac{m_{1970i} + f_{1970i}}{M_{1970} + F_{1970}}$$

The results are shown in Table 3.16 and suggest that changes in the industrial distribution of males and females have had an insignificant effect on the F/M earnings ratio between 1970 and 1976. Thus, for manual employees the F/M ratio increased by 11.68 percentage points, of which only 0.15 percentage points are due to the changing industrial composition of the work force.

T ABLE 3.16   The effect of the industrial distribution on relative earnings

	1970	1971	1972	1973	1974	1975	1976
Manuals							
F/M ratio with actual industrial distribution	54.57	55.97	57.17	57.36	58.99	63.53	66.25
F/M ratio with un-changed (1970) in-dustrial distribution	–	56.10	57.31	57.51	59.31	63.45	66.10
Non-manuals							
F/M ratio with actual industrial distribution	51.18	52.15	52.68	52.42	53.46	58.56	59.69
F/M ratio with un-changed (1970) in-dustrial distribution	–	51.67	52.21	52.16	53.45	58.04	59.05

OCCUPATIONAL DATA

As with the industrial data, the occupational statistics reinforce the general conclusions from the aggregate data: that weekly hours are generally higher among manuals, particularly males, which is partly due to higher overtime in both cases and also PBR and shift payments are higher for males and for manuals. The examination of inter-occupational relative earnings differences is more difficult than for industries due mainly to the lack of data.

The two occupations with the highest F/M earnings ratio are Professional and Related Supporting Management and

Administration, and Professional and Related in Education, Welfare and Health, in which the *F/M* ratios for hours worked and shift or overtime payments are above average. These influences would, tend to increase the female/male earnings ratio although they may not be the whole explanation.

As referred to in Chapter 2, an attempt has been made using 1974 NES data to assess the broad contributions of differences in age, hours of work, occupational distribution and earnings within occupations towards 'explaining' the observed differences in average earnings between males and females. This showed that for broad occupational groups the gross differential was £18.90 of which £2.50 (13.2 per cent) was accounted for by differences in hours, £15 (79.4 per cent) by earnings differences within occupational groups excluding hours and £1.40 (7.4 per cent) by occupational distribution. Unfortunately the data do not allow for simultaneous control of both hours and age, but for those occupational age categories where both male and female earnings are given, the gross difference was £18.50 of which earnings differences (including hours) amounted to £12.50 (67.6 per cent), occupational distribution £4.60 (24.9 per cent) and age £1.40 (7.6 per cent).

These figures suggest that differences in earnings within each occupation are the most important single contributory factor and that differences in hours of work and age are relatively minor in comparison. The occupational distribution is similarly relatively insignificant, even though the method of redistribution adopted is the most favourable towards women. Thus, it seems that intra-occupational differences are the major factor in the male/female earnings differential.

As in the case of the industrial data there is no reason for this conclusion to hold over time. However, comparisons over time are complicated by the change in the occupational classification in 1973. Thus comparison is only possible for the years 1973–6. The inconvenience is lessened since these were precisely the years when the *F/M* ratio was rising at its fastest. Full data for each year are only available for ten occupational groups (see Table 3.17). Similar weighted averages are calculated as in the case of industrial data discussed earlier and the results shown in Table 3.20.

As in the case of industrial data, the results indicate that the change in the occupational distribution has had only a marginal effect on the *F/M* ratio. Thus of the 7.78 percentage points change between 1973 and 1976 only some 0.23 percentage points can be accounted for by any changes in the occupational distribution.

TABLE 3.17   *F/M* earnings ratios for all workers—occupation data (NES)

		1973	1974	1975	1976
	Occupation				
I	Managerial occupations (general management)	–	–	–	–
II	Professional & related supporting mgt & admin.	–	65.71	71.36	71.32
III	Professional & related in education, welfare, health	61.69	61.47	71.47	71.74
IV	Literary artistic & sports	–	–	–	–
V	Professional & related in science, eng., technology etc.	–	–	64.78	64.62
VI	Managerial occupations (excl. gen. mgt)	54.93	55.37	56.87	57.71
VII	Clerical & related occupations	63.82	64.96	67.37	68.91
VIII	Selling occupations	44.24	45.96	49.63	49.76
IX	Security & protective service occupations	–	–	–	–
X	Catering, cleaning, hairdressing + other personal services	59.93	63.07	67.16	69.98
XI	Farming & fishing and related	–	–	–	–
XII	Materials processing (excluding metal)	53.30	53.88	58.26	60.12
XIII	Making-repairing (excl. metal & electrical)	48.89	52.32	55.80	58.54
XIV	Processing, making & repairing (metal & electrical)	52.90	54.60	58.63	62.09
XV	Painting, repetitive assembling, prod. inspec., packaging etc.	54.07	56.78	60.67	63.92
XVI	Construction, mining and related	–	–	–	–
XVII	Transport operating, materials moving and storing	59.89	62.08	64.62	66.72
XVIII	Miscellaneous occupations	–	–	–	–
All manual occupations		51.71	54.13	57.63	60.52
All non-manual occupations		51.35	52.57	57.89	59.80
All occupations		55.13	56.39	61.51	64.34

TABLE 3.18 Average weekly hours and average overtime hours—occupation data (NES)

		1973			1974			1975			1976		
		M	F	F/M	M	F	F/M	M	F	F/M	M	F	F/M
Average weekly hours													
Non-manual													
P & r supporting management & admin	II	–	–	–	37.6	36.8	97.87	37.5	36.7	97.87	37.5	36.8	98.13
P & r education, welfare, health	III	–	–	–	33.1	34.6	104.53	33.0	34.2	103.64	33.2	34.3	103.31
P & r in science, engineering, technology etc	V	–	–	–	38.8	–	–	38.9	37.6	96.66	38.7	37.6	97.16
Managerial	VI	–	–	–	40.2	38.9	96.77	40.2	38.9	96.77	39.9	38.9	97.49
Clerical	VII	40.5	37.2	91.85	40.8	37.1	90.93	40.6	37.0	91.13	40.0	36.8	92.00
Selling	VIII	40.5	39.5	97.53	40.6	39.0	96.06	40.3	38.7	96.03	40.0	38.6	96.50
Security and protection	IX	46.8	–	–	46.2	–	–	45.3	–	–	45.0	–	–
Literary, artistic, sports	IV							39.0	–	–	39.0	–	–
Manual													
Catering, cleaning, hairdressing	X	46.4	39.4	84.91	46.5	39.5	84.95	46.2	39.0	84.42	45.6	38.7	84.87
Farming, fishing	XI	45.8	–	–	46.6	–	–	46.6	–	–	44.4	–	–
Materials processing	XII	47.1	40.3	85.56	47.1	40.3	85.56	44.9	39.8	88.64	45.5	40.0	87.91
Making and repairing	XIII	46.0	39.4	85.65	45.1	39.1	86.70	44.1	38.9	88.21	43.8	38.9	88.81
Processing, making, repairing, (metal & elec.)	XIV	46.1	40.5	87.85	45.9	40.3	87.80	45.0	40.1	89.11	44.9	39.9	88.86
Painting, repetitive assembly etc.	XV	45.1	40.2	89.14	44.9	40.1	89.31	43.9	39.7	90.43	43.9	39.7	90.43
Construction, mining	XVI	46.5	–	–	46.1	–	–	45.2	–	–	44.9	–	–
Transport operating, materials moving	XVII	48.4	41.8	86.36	48.5	42.2	87.01	47.6	41.1	86.34	47.2	41.2	87.29
Miscellaneous	XVIII	46.9	–	–	46.7	–	–	45.7	–	–	45.4	–	–

TABLE 3.18 (*contd.*)

		1973 M	1973 F	1973 F/M	1974 M	1974 F	1974 F/M	1975 M	1975 F	1975 F/M	1976 M	1976 F	1976 F/M
Average overtime hours													
Non-manual													
P & r supporting mgmt and administration	II				0.6	0.3	50.00	0.5	0.2	40.00	0.6	0.3	50.00
P & r education, welfare, health	III				0.5	0.2	40.00	0.5	0.2	40.00	0.7	0.2	28.57
P & r in science, engineering, technology etc	V				1.2	–	–	1.2	0.4	33.33	1.2	0.3	25.00
Managerial	VI				1.2	0.4	33.33	1.4	0.5	35.71	1.2	0.5	41.67
Clerical	VII	3.2	0.4	12.50	3.4	0.4	11.76	3.2	0.4	12.50	2.7	0.3	11.11
Selling	VIII	1.6	0.7	43.75	1.7	0.4	23.53	1.6	0.3	18.75	1.4	0.3	21.43
Security and protective	IX	4.9		–	5.3		–	5.5		–	5.4		–
Manual													
Catering	X	5.9	1.2	20.34	6.2	1.4	22.53	6.0	1.1	18.33	5.6	1.0	17.86
Farming	XI	4.5		–	6.1		–	4.3		–	4.0		–
Materials processing	XII	6.8	1.3	19.12	7.0	1.1	15.71	4.8	0.7	14.58	5.4	0.9	16.67
Making/repairing	XIII	5.9	0.8	13.56	5.1	0.6	11.76	4.1	0.3	7.32	3.8	0.4	10.53
Processing, making (metal & elec).	XIV	6.2	1.3	20.97	6.0	1.1	18.33	5.2	0.8	15.38	5.0	0.7	14.00
Painting	XV	5.1	1.0	19.61	5.1	1.0	19.61	4.1	0.6	14.63	4.1	0.7	17.07
Construction	XVI	6.5		–	6.2		–	5.4		–	5.2		–
Transport operations	XVII	8.1	2.4	29.63	8.3	2.9	34.94	7.4	2.0	27.03	7.1	1.9	26.76
Miscellaneous	XVIII	8.8		–	6.8		–	5.8		–	5.5		–

TABLE 3.19 Average weekly PBR and shift premium payments—occupation data (NES)

	No.	1973			1974			1975			1976		
		M	F	F/M	M	F	F/M	M	F	F/M	M	F	F/M
PBR payments Non-manual													
P & r supporting management & administration	II	1.5		—	1.7	0.5	29.41	1.0	0.3	30.00	1.4	0.3	21.43
P & r education, welfare, health	III	0.1		—	0.1		—	0.1		—	0.1	0.0	—
P & r in science, engineering, technology etc	V	0.4		—	0.4		—	0.5	0.1	20.00	0.5	0.2	40.00
Managerial	VI	1.2	0.7	58.33	1.2	0.6	50.00	1.4	1.0	71.43	1.7	0.9	52.94
Clerical	VII	0.4	0.1	25.00	0.4	0.1	25.00	0.5	0.1	20.00	0.5	0.2	40.00
Selling	VIII	6.5	0.5	7.69	7.3	0.5	6.85	8.1	0.6	7.41	10.4	0.8	7.69
Security & protection	IX	0.3		—	0.4		—	0.4		—	0.4		—
Literary/artistic	IV	1.0		—	0.3		—	0.7		—	0.7		—
Manual													
Catering, cleaning, hairdressing	X	1.2	0.4	33.33	1.6	0.7	43.75	1.9	0.9	47.37	2.2	1.0	45.45
Farming, fishing	XI	1.7		—	3.1		—	3.0		—	3.4		—
Materials processing	XII	4.0	4.2	105.00	4.3	4.9	113.95	4.2	4.7	111.90	5.1	6.3	123.53
Making and repairing	XIII	5.6	5.1	91.07	6.5	6.6	101.54	7.3	6.5	89.04	8.1	8.4	103.70
Processing, making repairing (metal and elec. etc)	XIV	4.5	4.2	93.33	5.0	4.6	92.00	5.3	5.6	105.66	5.8	6.6	113.79
Painting, repetitive assembly etc.	XV	4.0	2.6	65.00	4.3	2.8	65.12	4.9	3.2	65.31	5.2	3.9	75.00
Construction, mining	XVI	4.2		—	5.4		—	6.5		—	7.6		—
Transport operating, materials moving	XVII	2.8	1.1	39.29	3.4	1.0	29.41	3.9	1.4	35.90	4.3	1.8	41.86
Miscellaneous	XVIII	2.6		—	3.2		—	4.0		—	4.1		—

TABLE 3.19 (*contd.*)

	1973 M	F	F/M	1974 M	F	F/M	1975 M	F	F/M	1976 M	F	F/M
Shift payments												
Non-manual												
II P & r supporting management and administration	0.1			0.1			0.1	0.1	100.00	0.2	0.1	50.00
III P & r education, welfare, health	0.2	0.5	250.00	0.2	0.5	250.00	0.4	0.8	200.00	0.5	1.0	200.00
V P & r in science, engineering, technology etc.	0.2			0.3			0.5	0.3	60.00	0.5	0.4	80.00
VI Managerial	0.2	0.1	50.00	0.3	0.1	33.33	0.4	0.1	25.00	0.4	0.1	25.00
VII Clerical	0.4			0.5			1.0	0.1	10.00	1.4	0.1	7.14
VIII Selling	0.1			0.2	0.1	50.00	0.2	0.1	50.00	0.3	0.2	66.67
IX Security and protective	0.5			0.8			1.4		–	1.7	–	–
Manual												
X Catering	0.9	0.4	44.44	1.0	0.5	50.00	1.6	0.9	56.25	2.1	1.3	61.90
XI Farming	0.1			0.2			0.1		–	0.2	–	–
XII Materials processing	1.8	0.2	11.11	2.1	0.3	14.29	3.0	0.4	13.33	3.7	0.5	13.51
XIII Making/repairing	0.8	0.1	12.50	1.0	0.1	10.00	1.1	0.1	9.09	1.4	0.2	14.29
XIV Processing, making (metal and electric etc)	1.2	0.2	16.67	1.4	0.2	14.29	1.9	0.3	15.79	2.2	0.4	18.18
XV Painting	1.0	0.2	20.00	1.2	0.3	25.00	1.6	0.4	25.00	2.1	0.5	23.81
XVI Construction	0.2			0.6			0.8			0.9	–	–
XVII Transport operating	0.9	0.5	55.56	1.1	0.6	54.55	1.8	1.2	66.67	2.1	1.0	47.62
XVIII Miscellaneous	1.2			1.4			2.0		–	2.5	–	–

TABLE 3.20 The effect of the occupational distribution on relative earnings

	1973	1974	1975	1976
F/M ratio with actual occupational distribution	56.84	58.44	62.51	64.62
F/M ratio with unchanged occupational distribution (1973)	–	58.48	62.34	64.39

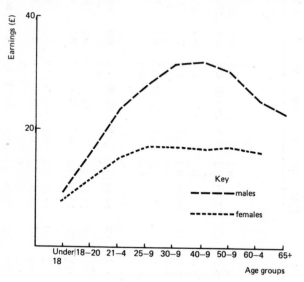

FIG. 3.9 Age-earnings profiles: all workers 1970

AGE-EARNINGS PROFILES

Figs. 3.9 to 3.14 show separately male and female age-earnings profiles for the years 1970, which was the earliest available, and 1976. Table 3.21 shows the absolute difference in earnings by age group along with the F/M earnings ratio for each age group.

Certain conclusions emerge quite clearly, confirming the findings of Chapter 4: women reach their earnings peak earlier than men, generally in the age group 25 to 29 years, after which many women leave the labour force to have children. Subsequently, their earnings remain stable, whereas earnings of males rise faster than females and peak in the 40 to 49 age group (30 to 39 in the case of manuals) with a fall in earnings thereafter, though still remaining well above women of the same age.

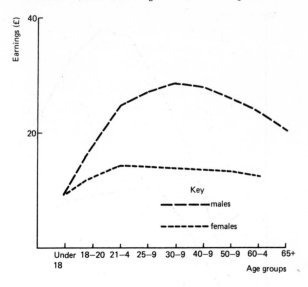

FIG. 3.10   Age earnings profiles: manual workers 1970

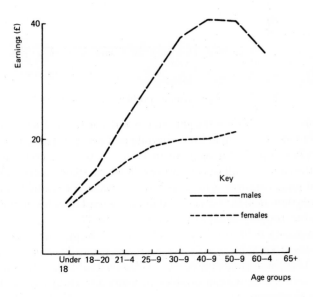

FIG. 3.11   Age earnings profiles: non-manual workers 1970

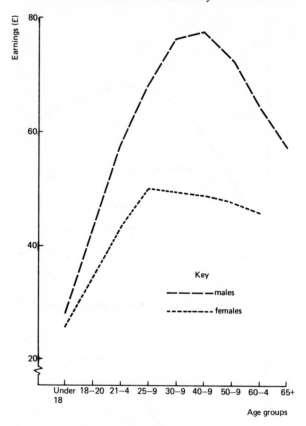

Fɪɢ. 3.12   Age-earnings profiles: all workers 1976

Table 3.21 shows how the gap widens with age to reach a maximum in the 40 to 49 age group in both absolute and percentage terms for 1970 and 1976 (30 to 39 for manuals in 1976). In this age group for 1976 female earnings for all workers were £28.60 less than males or 63.09 per cent of male earnings. Similar differences occur for manuals and non-manuals though in the latter case differences tend to be less in the earlier years, but roughly equal at the ages of 40 to 49.

Comparing 1970 to 1976 illustrates how, although the *F/M* earnings ratio has risen substantially for each age group (except the manual under 18s), the absolute difference has nearly doubled in the 18 to 24 age range and has more than doubled in many age groups above this.

As a final comment on age earnings profiles it is noted that they reflect the occupational structure of the labour force. Occupational choice is

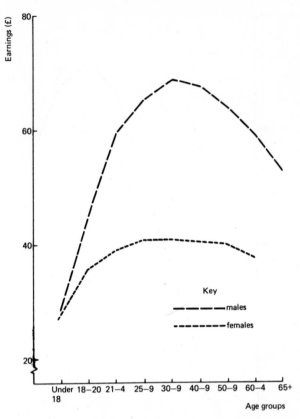

FIG. 3.13 Age-earnings profiles: manual workers 1976

based on personal and family circumstances together with expectations about the future. For women the decision as to whether and when to have children with the associated child-care problems can have a marked impact on occupational choice. In so far as human capital acquisition (or even learning by doing) is important, the expectation of intermittent labour force participation will reduce the expected return from such activities. Furthermore, if earnings are related to experience as demonstrated by recent empirical work, those returning to the labour force after a period of non-participation might be expected to receive lower earnings than those with continuous work histories. If depreciation of human capital occurs, it might be expected that those facing intermittent labour force participation will select occupations where depreciation rates are low. All these factors tend to make

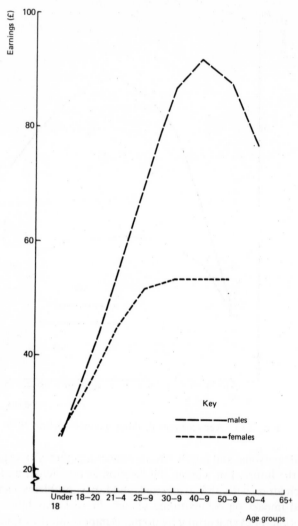

FIG. 3.14   Age-earnings profiles: non-manual workers 1976

substantial changes in occupation difficult in the short run and the effect of equal pay and equal opportunities legislation on career choices, human capital investment decisions etc., which are closely linked to the divisions of labour within the family, can only be expected to influence age-earnings profiles to any marked extent in the long run. But without substantial changes within the household it is likely that even the long

TABLE 3.21 *F/M earnings ratios-distribution by age group—1970 and 1976 (NES)*

Age groups	Full time manual				Full time non-manual				All full time workers			
	M	F	M-F	F/M	M	F	M-F	F/M	M	F	M-F	F/M
1970												
<18 years	9.5	9.2	(0.3)	96.84	9.1	8.1	(1.0)	89.01	9.4	8.4	(1.0)	89.36
18 to 20	17.7	12.3	(5.4)	69.49	14.6	12.0	(2.6)	82.19	16.7	12.0	(4.7)	71.85
21 to 4	24.8	14.2	(10.6)	57.25	22.9	16.0	(6.9)	69.86	24.0	15.7	(8.3)	65.41
25 to 9	27.2	14.3	(12.9)	52.57	29.9	18.7	(11.2)	62.54	28.3	17.7	(12.6)	62.54
30 to 9	28.6	13.8	(14.8)	48.25	37.6	19.7	(17.9)	52.39	32.0	17.6	(14.4)	55.00
40 to 9	28.0	13.5	(14.5)	48.21	40.5	19.7	(20.8)	48.64	32.5	17.1	(15.4)	52.61
50 to 9	25.9	13.2	(12.7)	50.96	40.3	21.0	(19.3)	52.10	30.7	17.2	(13.5)	56.02
60 to 4	23.7	12.4	(11.3)	52.32	34.8	—	—	—	26.8	16.6	(10.2)	61.94
65 + years	20.5	—	—	—	—	—			23.3	—	—	—
Maximum Earnings	28.6	14.3	(14.3)	50.00	40.5	21.0	(19.50)	51.85	32.5	17.7	(14.80)	54.40
1976												
<18 years	28.8	27.0	(1.8)	93.75	25.6	25.7	(−0.1)	100.39	28.1	26.0	(2.1)	92.52
13 to 20	45.5	35.6	(9.9)	78.24	39.2	34.5	(4.7)	88.01	43.5	34.8	(8.7)	80.00
21 to 4	59.4	38.9	(20.5)	65.48	55.5	44.6	(10.9)	80.36	57.8	43.7	(14.1)	75.60
25 to 9	65.6	40.5	(25.1)	61.73	71.1	51.8	(19.3)	72.85	68.2	50.1	(18.1)	73.46
30 to 9	68.9	40.4	(28.5)	58.63	86.3	53.2	(33.1)	61.64	76.4	49.5	(26.9)	64.79
40 to 9	67.8	40.1	(27.7)	59.14	91.6	53.4	(38.2)	58.29	77.5	48.9	(28.6)	63.09
50 to 9	64.0	40.0	(24.0)	62.50	87.4	53.4	(34.0)	61.09	72.5	47.9	(24.6)	66.06
60 to 4	59.0	37.6	(21.4)	63.72	76.6	—	—	—	64.5	46.0	(18.5)	71.31
65 + years	52.7	—			79.7	—			57.4	—		
Maximum Earnings	68.9	40.5	(28.4)	58.78	91.6	53.4	(38.2)	58.29	77.5	50.1	(27.4)	64.64

run impact of such legislation could be small.

Changes in the age distribution of the working population over time may well affect the F/M earnings ratio. Again NES data enable some account to be taken of these movements. The actual F/M earnings ratio in 1976 was 62.25 and that in 1970, 54.54. If the same age distribution had held in 1976 as in 1970 the ratio would have been 64.41. Thus the F/M earnings ratio increased by 10.71 percentage points, of which changes in the age distribution seem to account for 0.84 percentage points; or, in other words, changes in the age distribution account for 7.8 per cent of the change in the ratio. It seems fair to say, therefore, that the age distribution has had more effect than either the industrial or the occupational distribution, but there still remains a large proportion of the change in relative earnings to be explained.

In conclusion, changes in hours of work, and the industrial, occupational and age distributions seem to explain only a small proportion of the increase in the F/M earnings ratio in recent years.

PART-TIME WORKERS

As noted in Chapter 2, very little comparable data are available concerning the earnings of male and female part-time workers as a result of the relatively small numbers of males in the category. For example, the 1976 NES survey sample included 21,549 part-time adult (>18) female workers and only 3649 part-time adult (>21) male workers. The only comparable data which are available concern average gross hourly earnings and are presented below. The comparison of part-time workers earnings must be considered on an hourly basis since the number of hours worked varies widely within the official definition of a part-time worker as one who works fewer than 30 hours per week. In 1976 the average total weekly hours worked for male part-time workers was 18.0, whilst part-time manual female workers worked 20.8 hours on average with non-manual part-time females working an average of 21.0 hours per week. It should be noted that since these figures relate to hourly earnings they are not comparable with the weekly earnings data for full-time workers presented in detail below.

However, if these figures are compared with the average hourly earnings of full-time workers (Table 3.22) it is clear that the F/M hourly earnings ratio for part-time workers has, since 1971, exceeded that for full-time workers. It may be suggested that this is the result of an essential non-comparability between male and female workers since

TABLE 3.22 Average gross hourly earnings of part-time workers

Year	Male (p)	Female (p)	F/M
1970	54.5[a]	33.5[a]	61.47
1971	56.4[a]	38.3[a]	67.91
1972	61.8[a]	42.9[a]	69.42
1973	64.6	43.1	76.01
1974	72.2	57.5	79.64
1975	93.9	81.3	86.58
1976	122.2	99.2	81.18

NOTE
[a] The figures for 1970, 1971 and 1972 include those whose pay was affected by absence.

part-time work may be a long-term arrangement for females of prime working age, whilst many of the males engaging in part-time work may do so only on a temporary or semi-retirement basis. However, in the absence of a data set giving a detailed age, occupational and industrial breakdown of male and female part-time workers, this explanation of the relatively high F/M hourly earnings ratio for part-time workers must remain in the realm of casual empiricism and supposition.

THE DISTRIBUTION OF MALE AND FEMALE EARNINGS

The discussion above has focused on the mean levels of gross weekly earnings for the various categories of employees, thus giving no indication of the dispersion of earnings around these means. In the context of a study of income distribution and low pay, however, the dispersion around the mean and in particular the lower 'tail' of the distribution may be of greater significance than the level of the mean itself. The distributions of weekly earnings for males and females in 1970 and 1976 are shown in Tables 3.23 and 3.24; Figs. 3.15 and 3.16 show graphically the 1976 distribution.

It may be suggested that the observed differences between the pay positions of women and men might derive not only from the difference in their mean pay levels but also from differences in the dispersion of male and female earnings around their respective means; a distinction which may have important policy implications. Hence it may be useful

Women and Low Pay

TABLE 3.23   Distribution of average gross weekly earnings April 1970 (NES)

Earnings Range (£)	Percentage of males	Cumulative % of males	Percentage of females	Cumulative % of females
Less than 5	0.01	0.01	0.13	0.13
5–10	0.21	0.22	11.76	11.89
10–15	2.82	3.04	41.18	53.07
15–20	14.61	17.65	26.55	79.62
20–24	17.64	35.29	9.06	88.68
24–30	25.86	61.15	6.00	94.68
31–31	15.23	76.38	2.43	97.11
35–40	9.34	89.12	1.47	98.58
40–45	5.28	91.00	0.59	99.17
45–50	3.15	94.15	0.40	99.57
50–60	2.85	97.01	0.29	99.86
60–70	1.22	98.23	0.06	99.92
70–80	0.64	98.87	0.05	99.97
80–100	0.59	99.46	0.02	99.99
100 +	0.52	99.98	0.02	100.01

NOTES
£15–£20 indicates a range≥15,< 20. Percentages may not sum to 100 because of rounding.

to compare the male and female distributions with regard to their dispersion, and deviation from equality.

Casual observation of Figs. 3.15 & 3.16 might suggest that there are differences in the degree of dispersion between the male and female earnings distributions; however, the two can only meaningfully be compared by the use of a statistic which takes account of the differences between their means. The coefficient of variation given for male and female distributions from 1970 and 1976 in Table 3.25 is such a measure of relative dispersion. It is clear from Table 3.25 that the measured dispersion of the male earnings distribution has exceeded that of the female distribution for each of the years under consideration, although the difference between the two has been relatively small. It should, however, be noted that there has been considerable fluctuation in the coefficient of variation within each sex over time; this may in part be attributed to the small sample size of the NES, a reservation to be considered in the interpretation of all NES data on income distribution. Hence the evidence for a slightly greater dispersion of male than of female earnings should not be regarded as conclusive.

Table 3.25 also shows the coefficients of skewness for male and female earnings distributions from 1970 to 1976. These, like the coefficients of

TABLE 3.24   Distribution of average gross weekly earnings April 1976 (NES)

Earnings range (£)	Percentage of males	Cumulative % of males	Percentage of females	Cumulative % of females
< 20	0.1	0.1	1.2	1.2
20– 30	0.8	0.9	13.2	14.4
30– 40	4.3	5.2	28.8	43.2
40– 50	13.1	18.3	25.7	68.9
50– 60	20.0	38.3	14.5	83.4
60– 70	19.0	57.3	6.5	89.9
70– 80	14.5	71.8	4.1	94.0
80– 90	9.6	81.4	2.9	96.9
90–100	6.1	87.5	1.3	98.2
100–110	4.2	91.7	0.8	99.0
110–120	2.7	94.4	0.4	99.4
120–130	1.6	96.0	0.2	99.6
130–140	1.0	97.0	0.1	99.7
140–150	0.8	97.8	0.1	99.8
150–170	0.9	98.7	0.1	99.9
170–200	0.6	99.3	–	–
200–250	0.4	99.7	–	–
250–300	0.1	99.8	–	–
300 +	0.1	99.9	–	–

£20–£30 indicates a range ⩾ £20, < £30.
Percentages may not sum to 100 because of rounding.

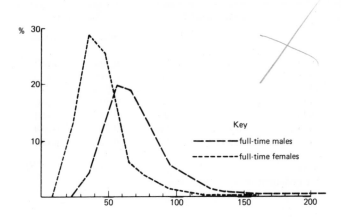

FIG. 3.15   Frequency distribution of average gross weekly earnings 1976 (NES)

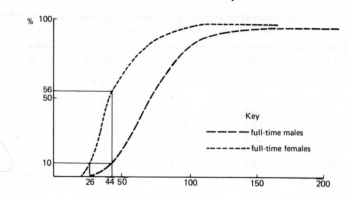

Fig. 3.16 Cumulative frequency distribution of average gross weekly
earnings, 1976 (NES)

variation, exhibit some fluctuation over time within each sex, thus
casting some doubt on the reliability of small sample data. For the entire
period, however, both male and female distributions exhibit some
positive skewness, reflecting distributions which peak in the lower

TABLE 3.25 Distribution of average weekly earnings—
descriptive statistics (NES)

| | Coefficient of Variation[a] | | Skewness[b] | |
	Male	Female	Male	Female
1970	0.488	0.457	0.574	0.685
1971	0.546	0.414	0.518	0.673
1972	0.496	0.378	0.544	0.735
1973	0.425	0.413	0.590	0.692
1974	0.419	0.408	0.585	0.601
1975	0.419	0.387	0.577	0.684
1976	0.447	0.411	0.561	0.601

NOTES

[a] Coefficient of Variation $= \dfrac{S}{X}$

[b] Pearsons second coefficient of skewness $= \dfrac{3(\overline{X} - \text{median})}{S}$

income ranges, a feature which in all cases is more marked in the female distribution.

The Lorenz Curve and its summary statistic the Gini Coefficient may be used to measure deviations from the perfect equality of income since the percentage of employees in given earnings bands is plotted against the percentage of income from employment which is earned by individuals in these bands. Attempts were made to draw male and female Lorenz Curves for 1970 and for 1976 but since it was found that the male and female curves for each year were for all practical purposes indistinguishable they are not presented here.

Atkinson (1970) has noted that, if the Lorenz Curves for two distributions do not intersect, the distribution closer to the diagonal is more equal than the other and the summary statistics such as the coefficient of variation and the Gini Coefficient will reflect this ranking. If, however, the Lorenz Curves intersect, the rankings given by the various summary measures may differ since they embody different implicit values about a desirable distribution of income. In this situation a choice of inequality measure can only be made if the social welfare function is clearly specified. Hence Atkinson suggests that the conventional measures should be rejected in favour of a more direct consideration of the social welfare function.

In the context of the present study the close similarity of the male and female Lorenz Curves, which would almost certainly cross at least at one point casts some doubt on the interpretation of the male and female coefficients of variation but the differences are so small that the practical effect is likely to be negligible. In the absence of superior measures and of a fully specified social welfare function one can only suggest that the fact that the imperfect conventional measures of equality and dispersion did not reveal substantial differences between the male and female distributions should be interpreted as general evidence in favour of the assumption that the male and female distributions are broadly similar. The only clear evidence to induce amendment of this assumption is the recognition that the female distribution may be slightly more asymmetrical (positively skewed) than the male.

Thus, in general, one may suggest that the poor pay position of women relative to men owes more to the position of the female earnings distribution to the left of the male than to differences in 'shape' between the two distributions; this is consistent with the view expressed above that a redistribution of females to accord with the male occupational distribution is much less effective than granting women equal earnings with men in their existing occupations.

Hence redistributive policies which are directed towards the lower 'tails' of the male and female distributions, without attempting to shift the whole female distribution closer to the male, will have little effect on the F/M earnings ratio. For example, a policy which adopted the definition of low pay suggested by the National Board for Prices and Incomes (1971) and raised the pay of the lowest decile to the low pay cut off level (i.e. £44 for males and £26 for females in 1976) would in the short term simply eliminate the sections of the cumulative frequency distributions below the 10 per cent line in Fig. 3.16 without affecting the relative positions of the male and female curves. In the long term if differentials were re-established both the male and female curves would simply be translated to the right, retaining their original form. If the social welfare function included, in addition to a preference for the elimination of low pay, a preference for the narrowing of F/M earnings ratios (in order to eliminate the situation whereby low pay equals female pay), a more optimal policy would be one which included some shift to the right in the female earnings distribution, in order that it might approach the male distribution.

THE EFFECTS OF GOVERNMENT POLICY

The previous sections have traced in considerable detail the movements in relative female earnings over recent years. The purpose of this section is to review the possible impact of Government policy in this area. There are two main strands of policy which should be considered in this context: first, general monetary and fiscal policy which in so far as it affects the cyclical behaviour of the economy may have an impact on the movement of relative earnings; and second, specific policies directed towards the low paid and women in particular. In this connection the most pertinent legislation is the Equal Pay Act of 1970, although the future potential of the Sex Discrimination Act 1975 also needs to be considered.

A significant feature of the Equal Pay Act was that its terms did not become fully operative until the 29 December 1975, also the date of the implementation of the Sex Discrimination Act. This lag of five and a half years was designed to give firms and organisations sufficient time to plan and implement equal pay without major disruptive consequences and implicitly recognised the fact that females are employed in very diverse circumstances such that some organisations would be virtually untouched by the legislation (at least directly), whilst in other cases it would represent a profound economic change.

The Act is designed to prevent discrimination as regards terms and conditions of employment between men and women and this is to be achieved in two main ways:

(i) by requiring that employers grant equal treatment as regards terms and conditions of employment to men and women where
   (a) they are employed on the same or broadly similar work, or
   (b) where, with respect to different jobs, a woman's job has been rated as equivalent to that of a male employee by means of a job evaluation exercise;
(ii) by providing for the Industrial Court (reformulated as the Industrial Arbitration Board under the Industrial Relations Act 1971 and amended to become the Central Arbitration Committee under the Employment Protection Act 1975) to remove discrimination in collective agreements, employers' pay structures and statutory wage orders which contain any provisions applying specifically to men only or women only and which have been referred to the court.

There are many complex issues of interpretation which have been left to be resolved by the industrial tribunals (set up under Section 12 of the Industrial Training Act 1964) and ultimately on points of law by the Employment Appeal Tribunal. This is not the place to review decisions which have been reached since full implementation of the Act but many of the early decisions reflected a narrow interpretation although the Appeal Tribunal has appeared rather more favourably disposed towards the claimants.

In examining the general effects of the Equal Pay Act on relative female earnings it is necessary to consider it on an economy-wide basis. There are severe data and econometric problems underlying any attempt to isolate the impact of the Act. An estimate of the 'alternative position' is required i.e. an estimate of what would have been the level of relative female earnings in the absence of the Act. This estimate could then be compared with the actual outcome. Since the principles of the Act are intended to apply across all employers in the UK there is no control group to assist in this procedure.[4] In the absence of such a control group the approach adopted is to use time series data on relative earnings in general to provide at least some broad indication of the likely order of magnitude of the Equal Pay Act effects.

The basic model essentially follows that proposed by Ashenfelter (1970) in relation to non-white/white relative income in the US. A similar, though less rigorously specified model, was independently used by Rasmussen (1970) and has subsequently been applied in both the US and Canada.[5]

The basic approach adopted here is to estimate an equation for relative female earnings during the period prior to the passing of the Act in order to predict what might have occurred in the absence of legislation. The difficulties inherent in such an approach are outlined in detail below.

Following the basic analysis of discrimination developed by Becker (1971) it is assumed that the typical employer has a taste for discrimination and treats the cost of employing a female worker in period t as if it were $W_f(t)[1 + d(t)]$ with $d_i(t) \geqslant 0$ where $W_f(t)$ is the female wage and $d_i(t)$ is a discrimination coefficient for the ith employer reflecting his tastes for discrimination. It is further assumed that there is no nepotism in favour of men so that the cost of employing males is regarded as being equal to the male wage rate $W_m(t)$. In this model differences in wage rates must occur if employment of females is to take place. In this case the typical net-cost-minimising employer will employ women only if

$$\frac{W_f(t)}{MP_f(t)}[1 + d_i(t)] = \frac{W_m(t)}{MP_m(t)}$$

where MP_m and MP_f are the marginal products of male and female workers respectively. As Ashenfelter has shown, the average extent of discrimination in equilibrium, $\bar{d}(t)$, will be such that

$$\frac{W_f(t)}{MP_f(t)}[1 + \bar{d}(t)] = \frac{W_m(t)}{MP_m(t)}$$

which on re-arranging gives

$$\frac{W_f(t)}{W_m(t)} = [1 + \bar{d}(t)]^{-1}\frac{MP_f(t)}{MP_m(t)} \qquad (1)$$

with $0 \leqslant [1 + \bar{d}(t)]^{-1} \leqslant 1$.

In obtaining an operational form for equation (1) there are several difficulties. The theoretical left hand variable is the ratio of female to male hourly wage rates but published time series data on wage rates are in index number form only and more importantly relate to male and female workers combined. Further, the published data in suitable form refer to hourly earnings including overtime and to manual workers only. It is possible to use a crude method[6] to remove the effects of overtime from the average hourly earnings data but this has become even more unreliable as successive incomes policies have precluded the consolidation of flat rate awards into basic rates. An alternative (or additional) procedure is to incorporate an explanatory variable which reflects the relative utilisation of female and male labour. This is the procedure followed by Ashenfelter, and for the UK the most appropriate variable is the ratio of actual female hours worked to actual male hours worked $(H_f(t)/H_m(t))$.

The second problem is to specify the functional forms of observable proxies for $MP_f(t)/MP_m(t)$ and $[1 + \bar{d}_i(t)]^{-1}$. Following Ashenfelter it may be assumed that a typical production function is as follows:

$$Q(t) = [b_f(t)L_f(t) + b_m(t)L_m(t); K(t)] \qquad (2)$$

where Q stands for output; $b_f(t)$ and $b_m(t)$ represent indexes of the efficiency of female and male labour; L_f and L_m are the amounts of female and male labour employed; and K stands for all other inputs. Thus $MP_f(t)/MP_m(t) = b_f(t)/b_m(t)$. On the assumption that both b_f and b_m shift smoothly over time this can be written as

$$\frac{MP_f(t)}{MP_m(t)} = \frac{\beta_f e^{ft}}{\beta_{me} mt} \qquad (3)$$

As for the discrimination term, $[1 + d(t)]^{-1}$, Becker argued that this will depend on the distribution of the $d_i(t)$ and on the size of the minority group in employment. Specifically, an increase in the average of the distribution of the $d_i(t)$ or a reduction in the dispersion would raise $\bar{d}(t)$; and the greater the proportion of women in employment the larger $\bar{d}(t)$.

The proportion of women in total employment has changed substantially over the years. However, most of the increase has taken place in the non-manual occupational groups. Thus, as Table 3.26 shows, between 1911 and 1961 the figure of female manual workers as a proportion of all manual workers generally fell with each census. It rose in 1966 but subsequently fell slightly in 1971. The available earnings data in a suitable form refer only to manual workers and as far as this group is concerned the underlying theory would suggest that it is the proportion of females to males which is the relevant variable. Unfortunately data on this are not available on an annual basis for any length of time. However, given the facts in Table 3.26 it might not be too unreasonable to regard the proportion of females to total employment in manual occupations as constant since the relatively small shifts observed may not change the market discrimination coefficient to any great extent.[7] The more important effects, therefore, are presumed to derive from changes in the

TABLE 3.26   Females in manual employment

	Total manual workers	Percentage females	Number of females
1911	13,685	30.5	4,174
1921	13,920	27.9	3,883
1931	14,776	28.8	4,255
1951	14,450	26.1	3,771
1961	14,022	26.0	3,646
1966	14,393	29.0	4,173
1971	13,343	28.6	3,816

SOURCE
R. Price and G. S. Bain, 'Union Growth Revisited; 1948–1974 in perspective', *British Journal of Industrial Relations* (November 1976). The results are derived from the Census of Population.

distribution of the d_i. As Ashenfelter argues, it is likely that $\bar{d}$ will change gradually over time. Hence $[1 + \bar{d}(t)]^{-1}$ is a smooth function of time.

Other factors are also expected to operate on d in particular those relating to cyclical demand factors. The cyclical pattern of overall demand can affect the female/male earnings ratio in a number of ways. First, the discrimination component in the ratio might be expected to decline as labour markets tighten. This can arise, for instance, through adaptation of screening processes as suitably qualified males become scarce and the employer might begin hiring females.[8] Such an argument may have more force in relation to race rather than sex since, in the latter case, the effects may be dissipated by the high degree of job segregation by sex and the particular labour force role of women which is marked in general by intermittent labour force participation. Secondly, as labour markets become tight the perceived costs of discriminating against qualified women increase because of the general scarcity of labour. Thirdly, as Ashenfelter points out, a tight labour market provides a better environment for dissolving the restrictive practices in some crafts and unions.

The overall unemployment rate is selected as indicating labour market pressures despite its many well known weaknesses.[9] Thus the following relationship is postulated between the extent of discrimination, time and unemployment $(U(t))$:

$$1 + \bar{d}(t)^{-1} = d_o e^{\lambda t} g(U(t)) \tag{4}$$

where d_o is the average discrimination in year o. In addition it is presumed that the effects of unemployment and relative hours of work on W_f/W_m may be represented by $\alpha_0 \exp\left[\alpha_1 \dfrac{H_f(t)}{H_m(t)} + \alpha_2 U(t)\right]$. Combining (1), (3) and (4) and taking logs produces the following estimating equation:

$$Ln\frac{W_f(t)}{W_m(t)} = a + (\lambda + f - m)t + \left[\alpha_1 \frac{H_f(t)}{H_m(t)}\right] + \alpha_2 U(t) + \Sigma(t) \qquad (5)$$

where $\Sigma(t)$ is the error term and $a = L_n\beta_f - L_n\beta_m + L_n d_o + Ln\alpha_o$. Equation (5) is tested for the period 1949 to 1969 with the results shown in Table 3.27.[10]

TABLE 3.27.   Regression results 1949–69

Dependent variables $L_n W_f(t)/W_m(t)$							
	a	$\dfrac{H_f}{H_m}$	$U(t)$	t	R^2	$D.W.$	F
(5a) Hourly earnings including overtime	−.331	−.17 (.31)	+.007[c] (.004)	−.0033[a] (.0011)	.93	2.02	75.5[a]
(5b) Hourly earnings excluding overtime	.149	+.69 (.43)	+.01[c] (.006)	−.0033[b] (.0016)	.41	1.2	4.0[b]

NOTES
Degree of Freedom 4, 17
Figures in parentheses are standard errors
[a] significant at the 1 per cent level
[b] significant at the 5 per cent level
[c] significant at the 10 per cent level

In these and all subsequent regressions the R^2 is re-computed in terms of the original units of the variables.

Several comments on these results are in order: (5a) is quite successful in explaining the variance in the ratio of male and female earnings although only the time trend is highly significant. The coefficient on $U(t)$ is just significant at the 10 per cent level but has a positive sign—the opposite of that postulated above.[11] This suggests that relative female earnings do not improve as labour markets tighten although evidence for the US suggests that black relative incomes do improve in such circumstances. This is perhaps indicative of the dangers involved in applying arguments primarily derived in terms of race to the case of sex. The highly significant negative time trend indicates clearly that relative female earnings were worsening over time although only at a slow rate (0.3 per cent per annum). This fact does not seem to have been generally appreciated. Equation (5b) is much less successful and overall is only significant at the 5 per cent level. The time trend is still negative, significant and of the same value as in (5a). Unemployment is just significant at the 10 per cent level and again is positive in sign. Although, if accurately measured, the dependent variable is more appropriate in this case, the crude attempts to remove the effects of overtime may well have introduced considerable distortions, particularly given the small variation over time in the underlying earnings ratio.

The relative hours variable is not significant in either equation but it is highly correlated with time ($R = -0.97$). This multicollinearity suggests a possible re-specification of equation (5). Thus it might be postulated that the relationship between relative hours worked and time can be represented by $H_o e^{ht}$ where H_o is the relative hours worked in period O. In this case equation (5) becomes

$$L_n W_f(t)/W_m(t) = a + (\lambda + f - m + h)t + \alpha_1 U(t) + \Sigma(t) \qquad (6)$$

where $a = L_n\beta_f - L_n\beta_m + L_n d_o + L_n\alpha_0 + L_n H_o$

It might be expected that the introduction of the Equal Pay Act in 1970 would have some effect on relative earnings during the transition period. Thus equation (6) is estimated with the introduction of a dummy variable (value 0 before 1970 and 1 thereafter) and an incremental time trend ($D \times T$). This yielded the following relationship for the period 1949–75 for hourly earnings including overtime:

$$L_n W_f(t)/W_m(t) = -0.48 + 0.0098 U(t) + 0.45 D^x + 0.021 \, D \times T^x - 0.003t^x$$
$$\qquad\qquad (0.006) \qquad (0.09) \qquad (0.004) \qquad\qquad (0.0006)$$

$$\tag{6a}$$

$$R^2 = 0.81 \qquad D.W. = 2.7 \qquad F = 25.1 \qquad D.F = 5.21$$

Equation (6a) explains 81 per cent of the variance in relative earnings and the dummy, incremental time trend and time are all highly significant. Unemployment is insignificant but remains positive in sign. The positive sign on the incremental time trend indicates a substantial improvement since 1970 as compared with the decline in the ratio up to that year. Again it would be theoretically superior to estimate the relationship with overtime excluded but the introduction of flat rate increases not consolidated into basic rates is likely to make a crude calculation of the overtime component highly misleading.

Assuming that the coefficient on unemployment remained the same, equation (6a) can be used to predict what would have been the female/male earnings ratio in each year after 1970 had the previous relationship held during the later period. This can be compared with the predicted value on the basis of the post 1970 relationship. The results are shown in Table 3.28.

TABLE 3.28   Predicted F/M hourly earnings ratio (including overtime) 1970–75

	Pre-1970 relationship	*Post-1970 relationship*	*Net change*
1970	0.593	0.605	+0.012
1971	0.598	0.622	+0.024
1972	0.596	0.633	+0.049
1973	0.587	0.636	+0.049
1974	0.586	0.652	+0.066
1975	0.598	0.677	+0.079

NOTE
Estimated from Equation (6a). Data as in Appendix 2.

These results suggest that in October 1975 the female/male hourly earnings ratio was some eight percentage points higher than it would have been but for the change in the underlying relationship. The necessary simplicity of the estimating equation together with the lack of any data to attempt to decompose the time coefficient into its various constituent parts[12] precludes any assignment to causes. Thus the Equal Pay Act is not the only possible cause of change in the labour market since 1970. The lack of any control group has left time series data as the only means of assessing any overall change in the ratio since 1970. There is a further problem relating to equation (6a): the coefficient on unemployment has been constrained to be the same in both time periods, but there seems no *a priori* reason to presume that this would have been unaffected by the Equal Pay Act or other changes in the labour market. There are, however, insufficient observations in the post 1970 period to allow for this possibility.[13] One possible alternative to the estimates in Table 3.28 would be to use equation (5a) to predict the value of the female/male ratio over the years 1970–5 on the basis of the estimated relationship for the period 1949–69. These predictions could be compared with the actual outcome in each year. The results of such an exercise are shown in Table 3.29. Although, as might be expected, the pattern of deviations in each year is somewhat different from the net changes shown in Table 3.28, the ratio in 1975 is more than eight percentage points higher than it otherwise would have been.

TABLE 3.29　Predicted and actual F/M hourly earnings ratio (including overtime) 1970–75

	Predicted value on basis of pre 1970 relationship	Actual ratio	Net change
1970	0.593	0.601	+0.008
1971	0.595	0.649	+0.054
1972	0.593	0.607	+0.014
1973	0.587	0.625	+0.038
1974	0.587	0.67	+0.083
1975	0.592	0.676	+0.084

NOTE
Estimated from equation (5a). Data as in Appendix.

Thus, both methods reveal a similar substantial improvement in the relative earnings position of women by October 1975 which is almost at the end of the transition period allowed under the Equal Pay Act. As noted above, it cannot be presumed that this improvement reflects purely the effects of the Act. The basic model shows that the time trend variable is a combination of various influences. Further, one particularly important factor being picked up by the incremental time trend concerns incomes policies containing flat-rate increases which have been a feature since 1973. These flat-rate changes can be expected to have a marked effect on differentials. It might be possible to attempt to control for this by including a male skill differential variable in the basic equation on the presumption that, holding unemployment constant, these incomes policies have contributed the major part in any change. However, a feature of these policies has been the non-consolidation of the flat-rate awards into basic rates which would seem to rule out the use of basic wage rate data and unfortunately skill differentials in earnings on an annual basis are not available for a sufficient length of time.[14] Since these incomes policies are clearly of substantial importance it is necessary to make at least a crude estimate of their significance for female relative earnings.

The relevant policies and their estimated consequences have been as follows:

(i) Under Stage Two of the Conservative policy pay limits were imposed of £1 per week plus 4 per cent up to a maximum of £250 per annum. According to the Sixth Report of the Pay Board (1974) nearly 17 million workers in firms of over 100 employees were covered by settlements under the policy. Since this represents the bulk of the labour force it seems reasonable to presume that all manual workers received a flat-rate increase of £1 per week.

(ii) Under Stage Three of the policy, the limits were 7 per cent or £2.25 per week with a maximum of £350 per annum. Again, according to the Pay Board (1974) over seven million workers were affected by settlements approved or screened in which the principal element was the flat-rate increase. This suggests that about 32 per cent of the labour force were affected by the flat-rate element or, if the same proportion applies to manual males and females, would imply an average flat-rate increase of 72 pence per week across all manual workers.

(iii) Eleven threshold payments amounting to a total of £4.40 per week became payable under the policy. According to the Department of Employment eight million manual workers were covered by such agreements. Using the proportions revealed in the New Earnings Survey it is calculated that the total manual labour force now amounts to about 12 per cent million which suggests that about 56 per cent of manual employees were covered by thresholds. Assuming men and women were affected in the same proportion this would result in an average threshold payment for all manual workers of £2.46 per week.

(iv) Under the Social Contract it is estimated that most manual workers received awards of £6 per week during the year beginning 1 August 1975. It is impossible to say what proportion of manuals had received this award by the second pay week in October 1975 (the date of the last earnings survey used in the regressions) but as a, probably conservative, estimate it is presumed that it applied to 25 per cent by this date. This gives an average increase of £1.50.

Thus it is calculated that by October 1975 there has been an average flat-rate increase under incomes policies of £5.68 per week for both men and women. This flat-rate increase can be deducted from average weekly earnings in October 1975 and the result divided by hours worked to estimate what the hourly earnings ratio would have been without the flat rate awards. On this basis the estimated ratio is .62 which compares with the actual ratio of .676. The overall change has been estimated above as about eight percentage points and thus it suggests that incomes policies account for in the region of six percentage points which leaves equal pay (and other factors) responsible for around two percentage points of the improvement. However, both Table 3.28 and Table 3.29 show a marked improvement in the relative earnings of women in 1971/72 which is prior to the introduction of flat-rate income policies and may reflect an initial reaction to the Equal Pay Act. But there is little evidence to support the view that the Act had such an immediate impact.[15] There is a further substantial change during 1974/75, a period which marks the end of the transition period together with the introduction of flat-rate .incomes policies. In the present state of knowledge it does not seem possible to disentangle these two effects. Our crude calculations do suggest that incomes policy may have been important, although several authors have recently argued on little substantive evidence that much of the improvement in the relative position of women may be due to the Equal Pay Act.[16] Our interpretation of events would give slightly greater emphasis to the role of incomes policy. This view is perhaps further reinforced by an examination of skill differentials in the engineering industry shown in Table 3.30. Thus the earnings ratios between labourers and semi-skilled labourers and skilled workers remained pretty constant over the period 1963–72 but since 1972 the earnings of labourers relative to skilled workers have improved by eight percentage points and those of labourers to semi-skilled by five percentage points. These changes are almost certainly predominantly the result of successive incomes policies.

All the measures discussed above refer to relative earnings, but the rate of increase in absolute earnings has been somewhat in excess of that suggested by the terms of the incomes policies. The presumption has, therefore, been made that factors leading to increases in earnings greater than those implied by incomes policies have applied equally to both male and female workers. If this is not true, the contribution of incomes policy crudely assessed above will be overstated, but it is impossible to say whether, and to what extent, this is the case.

Even taking the calculations at their face value does not justify the conclusion that flat-rate incomes policies (equivalent in some respects to a minimum wage) are the appropriate means of raising female welfare in

TABLE 3.30 Skill differentials in engineering (hourly earnings excluding overtime): all workers June each year

Labourers	1963	1964	1965	1966	1967	1968	1969	1970	1971	1972	1973	1974	1975	1976
Skilled	0.68	0.67	0.68	0.67	0.67	0.67	0.67	0.68	0.68	0.69	0.71	0.72	0.75	0.77
Semi-skilled	0.75	0.74	0.75	0.75	0.76	0.76	0.76	0.76	0.75	0.77	0.77	0.79	0.81	0.82

SOURCE
DE Gazette

general. In the short run such policies do seem to improve the relative earnings position of those women who remain in employment, but such marked changes in relative earnings create all sorts of problems and pressures in the labour market. In part, a rise in the relative price of female labour might be expected to lead to the substitution of male labour but, perhaps more importantly given the widespread sex segregation in the labour force, to the substitution of capital for female labour. Although some possibility of this latter occurrence exists at the margin in the short run, the most fundamental changes are likely to occur as plant and machinery are replaced and particularly as net investment increases substantially. Unless there is a large rise in the price of capital such new plant is likely to be less labour-intensive. Such adjustments will tend, therefore, to be long run in effect and are not likely to be really seen until the economy recovers from the current recession. When this occurs the problems of female employment are likely to be exacerbated if such incomes policies continue for any length of time. It may well be that we have yet to see the true costs of recent incomes policies for women.

Thus there is evidence of a marked improvement in relative female earnings since 1970 but it may be doubted whether the transition period under the Equal Pay Act has itself made the major contribution to this improvement. Furthermore, the evidence seems to suggest that counter-cyclical policy does not improve the relative earnings of women; indeed it may well worsen it since a fall in the level of unemployment seems to be associated with a worsening of female relative earnings.

The above discussion has related solely to the transition period under the Equal Pay Act; it remains to be seen whether full implementation of the Act together with the Sex Discrimination Act will have any greater effect in the future. It is, however, possible to offer a few speculations about the potential impact.

The Sex Discrimination Act states that a person discriminates against a woman if on the grounds of her sex he treats her less favourably than he treats or would treat a man. This is extended to cover the case where he applied to her a requirement or condition which he applies or would equally apply to a man but:

(i) which is such that the proportion of women who can comply with it is considerably smaller than the proportion of men who can comply with it, and

(ii) which he cannot show to be justifiable irrespective of the sex of the person to whom it is applied, and

(iii) which is to her detriment because she cannot comply with it.

This extension appears to mirror developments in the United States where the definition in legal terms has been transformed from prejudiced treatment to unequal treatment and finally to outlawing employment tests and educational requirements which screen out a greater proportion of whites than blacks.

Leaving many important points of interpretation to be decided by the industrial tribunals, all the available evidence would tend to suggest that such legislation is only likely to have any marked impact on relative earnings in the long run. There are many reasons why male and female earnings and occupational structures are not equal. Many of these relate to decisions taken within the family concerning the division of labour within the household, particularly with respect to child-care. The historical convention, boosted by discrimination, is that it is the female member of the household who undergoes intermittent labour force participation through family circumstances. It is clear, both from theory and practice, that factors such as education, experience and training are important determinants of earnings. Indeed quite a high proportion of the female/male earnings differential can be explained by differences in these and other characteristics.[17] Equal Pay and Equal Opportunities legislation will undoubtedly feed back on to the acquisition of these characteristics which in Spence's terms (1973) are 'signals', subject to manipulation by individuals. Whether there is any marked change in these signals between the sexes may depend to a large extent on whether the division of labour within the family undergoes substantial alteration.

In the short run, at least, one should not expect too much from such legislation. The evidence from the United States tends to suggest that in quantitative terms the significance is relatively minor.[18] The most substantial of these studies relates to the programme based on Executive Orders 11246 (1965) and 11375 (1967). These stipulate that:

(i) federal contractors may not discriminate on the basis of race, creed, colour, sex or national origin in hiring, promotion, pay or training and,

(ii) each federal contractor must institute an affirmative action programme designed to integrate its labour force and to provide more jobs for minorities and women. An enterprise with a federal contract of $10,000 or more that fails to make a 'good faith effort' to correct deficiencies in its utilisation of minorities and women is subject to cancellation or suspension of all or part of its existing governing contracts as well as to disbarment from any future government contracts.

Data collected by the Equal Employment Opportunity Commission does provide a means of testing whether there is any difference between contractor and non-contractor firms. Despite the technical ingenuity of the authors there are many limitations on the analyses and data not least of which concerns the lack of information on wage rates or earnings. Thus the tests are mainly concerned with employment effects. The results of the studies are best summarised by Ashenfelter (1976):

> Together these studies suggest that as a result of the contract compliance program minority employment in firms with government contracts has been significantly increased relative to what otherwise would have been the case. The results are quantitatively small, however, and certainly do not establish the presumption that this government program has been the major force behind the growth in the relative earnings of black workers . . .

As Ashenfelter notes, the results of the research met with incredulity among the top administrators of the Department of Labor. As a consequence the potential quantitative impact that might have been expected from a wildly successful programme was investigated. This study by Robert Flanagan (1976) argued that much of the colour differential was due to factors other than discrimination in the labour market. Thus a comprehensive contract compliance programme that succeeded in equalising opportunity for minorities might directly eliminate about 30–40 per cent of the hourly wage rate differential in each cohort. To allow for non-comprehensive coverage suggests that about 23–4 per cent of the differential is the maximum proportion that could be realised by the contract compliance programme. It is noted that although the potential impact of the programme is lower than generally thought, the actual impact is substantially smaller than this potential which raises questions concerning enforcement.

There is no reason to suspect that women are likely to fare any better in the UK under the legislation. The potential impact of the legislation is likely to be substantially less than the total removal of earnings differences although data are not available to substantiate this on an economy-wide basis.[19] But in the light of these American studies the tentative conclusions reached from the time series data, although far less satisfactory than the cross-section data available in the US, are not surprising. Thus, in the medium term it would not be expected that the Equal Pay Act and the Sex Discrimination Act would result in a substantial narrowing of the sex differential in Britain. Whether more is achieved in the long run is ultimately dependent on substantial changes in attitudes particularly with respect to child care.

APPENDIXES

1 DATA SOURCES AND VARIABLE DEFINITIONS

The data presented in this report are derived from two major sources: the results of the Department of Employment 'October enquiry' as published in the Department of Employment Gazette and the New Earnings Survey. These sources are referred to as DEG and NES respectively.

The Department of Employment October enquiry has been in existence for the whole of the last decade; the period under consideration in this report. The enquiry is conducted at establishment level and returns are obtained from establishments which together employ nearly two thirds of all manual workers, in the industries covered, in the UK. The data concerns full-time manual workers only and excludes males aged under twenty-one years and females aged under eighteen years. Certain employments are excluded from the enquiry: the principal employments excluded are listed below;

agriculture
coal mining
British Rail
London Transport
Shipping service
port transport (dock labour)
distributive trades
catering trades
entertainment industry
commerce
banking
domestic service

The New Earnings Survey data used in this report are based on a 1 per cent sample of all employees in Great Britain in April of each year. A pilot earnings survey, using a 0.5 per cent sample was conducted in September 1968 and followed in April 1970 by the first of the full NES series. Data from the 1968 survey are not presented in this report since there are problems of non-comparability with the later series owing to differences in data presentation.

The NES data presented in this report refer, unless otherwise specified, to full-time adult employees (≥ 21 for males, ≥ 18 for females) whose pay for the survey period was not affected by absence.

EARNINGS

The DEG earnings data in Tables 3.1 and 3.6 *et al* represent the average gross weekly earnings of all those, within each establishment covered, who received some pay in the second pay week in October of each year. It should be noted that those whose pay was affected by absence are therefore included.

The NES earnings figures used in Tables 3.2, 3.7, 3.8 and 3.17 *et al* are the average gross weekly earnings of full time adult (≥ 21 for males, ≥ 18 for females) employees whose pay for the period was not affected by absence.

HOURS

The DEG hours data represent the average total hours worked per week for full-time manual males and females.

The NES hours data represent the average total weekly hours, including overtime, for full-time adult men and women. In 1970, 1971 and 1972 the industrial hours data included those whose pay was affected by absence; for all other hours data presented these employees were excluded.

OVERTIME

The overtime data presented in Tables 3.4, 3.12 and 3.13 refer to hours worked in excess of normal hours regardless of the rates of pay associated with them. Those whose pay was affected by absence are excluded, and those who worked no overtime are included.

PAYMENT BY RESULTS

The figures for payment-by-results in Tables 3.5 and 3.14 represent the average gross weekly value of payments-by-results payments to full-time adult men and women whose pay was not affected by absence.

SHIFT PREMIUM PAYMENTS

The data on shift premium payments represent the average gross weekly value of shift payments to full-time adult men and women whose pay was not affected by absence.

2

The sources of data used in the regressions are as follows:

Earnings: average hourly earnings of manual men and women, October each year, *Department of Employment Gazette*.
Unemployment: Great Britain: Males and females percentage rate, October each year, *Department of Employment Gazette*.
Hours: actual hours of work of manual employees, October each year, *Department of Employment Gazette*.
Time: the time variable takes the value of 1, 2 . . . n; the incremental time trend $(D \times T)$ therefore takes the value 0 before 1970 and 22 . . . 27 thereafter.

The means of the variables are as follows:

1949–75

$$Ln\frac{W_f(t)}{W_m(t)} \quad = -0.488 \text{ (standard deviation} = 0.032)$$

$$U(t) \quad = \quad 2.0 \text{ (standard deviation 0.86)}$$

$$\frac{H_f}{H_m} \quad = \quad 0.85 \text{ (standard deviation 0.019)}$$

1949–69

$$Ln\left(\frac{W_f(t)}{W_m(t)}\right) = -0.499 \text{ (standard deviation 0.015)}$$

$$U(t) \quad = \quad 1.6 \text{ (standard deviation 0.45)}$$

$$\frac{H_f}{H_m} \quad = \quad 0.85 \text{ (standard deviation 0.018)}$$

NOTES

1. Data sources are discussed in the Appendixes.
2. The NES do not publish data where the sample size is less than 100 or the standard error exceeds 2 per cent of the mean.
3. These figures in the case of both occupations and industries are taken from NES data and the numbers used in the example here include those whose pay for the survey period was affected by absence and those for whom hourly earnings were not calculated, but it excludes those who received no pay for the period.
4. If data were available on relative earnings in firms affected and not affected by equal pay it might be possible to make some estimate by comparing the experiences of the two groups. But this is fraught with several obvious difficulties: many firms are likely to be affected by the collective agreement provisions of the Act so the control group may be small; the transition period together with marked occupational differences between firms introduces substantial problems; and there is no readily available source of such data. Attempts have been made in the US to assess the contribution of the affirmative action programme which have been helped by the fact that this applies only to Federal Contractors and hence non-federal contractors provide a suitable control group. The results of these American studies will be summarised below.
5. See Horowitz (1974), Vroman (1974), Masters (1975) and Gunderson (1976).
6. Hourly earnings excluding overtime can be computed as follows (with all data from the *Department of Employment Gazette*): The overtime component of hours is estimated as actual weekly hours minus normal weekly hours. This is multiplied by 1.5 as the assumed overtime premium. The resulting figure is added to normal weekly hours to produce the standard hours equivalent of actual hours worked. This, in turn, is divided into average weekly earnings to produce an estimate of hourly earnings excluding overtime.
7. Thus a change from a proportion of 20 per cent to 30 per cent would alter $\bar{d}(t)$ from the second decile of the distribution of the $d_i(t)$ to the third decile (for a proof see Becker, and Ashenfelter, op. cit.). Whilst the underlying distribution is of paramount importance there seems little alternative but to assume that a change of 2.5 percentage points between 1951 and 1971 (26.1 per cent to 28.6 per cent) has not had a marked effect on $\bar{d}(t)$.
8. See McCall (1972).
9. The rate of growth of GNP at constant prices was also tried as was the lagged unemployment rate but unemployment during the month of the earnings survey appeared to be the most successful in the regressions reported below.
10. For details of the variables and sources see Appendix 2.
11. The alternative cyclical indicators tried all possessed coefficients which were not significantly different from zero.
12. For one possible approach to this given the availability of data see Ashenfelter (op. cit.).

13. The use of bi-annual data (April and October) has been ruled out on grounds of non-comparability between NES and DE data.
14. Thus the data on specific industries e.g. engineering have only been available since 1963.
15. See for instance, Office of Manpower Economics (1972).
16. Dean (1978) and Layard *et al.* (1978).
17. For a summary of the literature (almost exclusively American), see Chiplin and Sloane (1976).
18. George Burman, 'The Economics of Discrimination: the Impact of Public Policy', PhD Dissertation, Graduate School of Business, University of Chicago, 1973; Ashenfelter and Heckman (1976), Goldstein and Smith (1976) and Heckman and Wolpin (1976).
19. For a study relating to one individual firm see Chiplin and Sloane (1976).

REFERENCES

Ashenfelter, O., 'Changes in Labour Market Discrimination Over Time', *Journal of Human Resources*, vol. 5 (Fall, 1970).
Ashenfelter, O., 'Comment', *Industrial and Labor Relations Review* (July 1976).
Ashenfelter, O., and Heckman, J. J., 'Measuring the Effects of an Anti-Discrimination Program', in Ashenfelter, O. and Blum, J. (eds.), *Evaluating the Labour Market Effects of Social Programs* (Princeton University Press, 1976).
Atkinson, A. B., 'On the Measurement of Inequality', *Journal of Economic Theory*, vol. 2 (1970).
Becker, G. S., *The Economics of Discrimination*, 2nd Edition (University of Chicago Press, 1971).
Chiplin, B. and Sloane, P. J., *Sex Discrimination in the Labour Market* (Macmillan, 1976(a)).
——, 'Personal Characteristics and Sex Differentials in Professional Employment', *Economic Journal* (December 1976(b)).
Dean, A. J. H., 'Incomes Policies and Differentials', *National Institute Economic Review* (August 1978).
Flanagan, R., 'Actual Versus Potential Impact of Government Anti-Discrimination Programs', *Industrial and Labor Relations Review* (July 1976).
Goldstein, M. and Smith, R. S., 'The Estimated Impact of the Anti-Discrimination Program Aimed at Federal Contractors', *Industrial and Labor Relations Review* (July 1976).
Gunderson, M., 'Time Patterns of Male-Female Earnings Differentials: Ontario 1946–1971', *Relations Industrielles/Industrial Relations*, 31, no. 1 (1976).
Heckman, J. J. and Wolpin, K. I., 'Does the Contract Compliance Program Work?—An Analysis of Chicago Data', *Industrial and Labor Relations Review* (July 1976).
Horowitz, Ann R., 'The Pattern and Causes of Changes in White—Non-White Income Differences: 1947–72', in Furstenburg, George M. Von, *Discrimination, vol. II: Employment and Income* (D. C. Heath, Lexington Books, 1974).

——, 'Trends in the Distribution of Family Income Within and Between Racial Groups', in Furstenburg, ibid.

Layard, R., Piachaud, D. and Stewart, M., *The Causes of Poverty*, Background Paper no. 5, Royal Commission on the Distribution of Income and Wealth, HMSO (1978).

Masters, Stanley H., *Black-White Income Differentials: Empirical Studies and Policy Implications* (Academic Press, 1975).

McCall, J. J., 'The Simple Mathematics of Information, Job Search and Prejudice', in Pascal, A. H. (ed.), *Racial Discrimination in Economic Life* (D. C. Heath, Lexington Books, 1972).

National Board for Prices and Incomes, *General Problems of Low Pay*, Report no. 169, Cmnd., 4643, HMSO (1971).

Office of Manpower Economics, *Equal Pay*, First Report of the Office of Manpower Economics (HMSO, 1972).

Rasmussen, David, 'A Note on the Relative Income of Non-White Men, 1948–64', *Quarterly Journal of Economics*, vol. 84 (February 1970).

Spence, Michael, 'Job Market Signalling', *Quarterly Journal of Economics* (August 1973).

Vroman, Wayne, 'Changes in Black Workers' Relative Earnings: Evidence from the 1960s', in Furstenburg, op. cit.

4 The Structure of Labour Markets and Low Pay for Women

P. J. SLOANE

INTRODUCTION

Early analyses of discrimination stemming from Gary Becker's *The Economics of Discrimination*, (1957) emphasised discriminatory behaviour as a consequence of the tastes or aversions to particular groups of various parties (including employers, employees and customers). Since many females are employed in areas where contact with the public is important (e. g. retail distribution) it is unlikely that women as a group suffer much from customer discrimination. In examining the extent to which other forms of discrimination depress *the pay* of women relative to men one would place the emphasis on employer rather than employee (or co-worker) discrimination since theory suggests that the latter will give rise to segregation rather than wage differences.[1] However, the 'crowding hypothesis' referred to in Chapter 2 suggests that segregation itself could give rise to wage differences since the enforced abundance of supply of women in certain sectors will lower marginal productivity there and depress the wage rate. Yet employer discrimination or collusion with male employees and their representatives is implied here, for otherwise we would expect demand for labour to increase in the crowded sector which is now cheaper than before. Recent work on the dual labour market (DLM) is particularly relevant in this context.

Of course, differences in pay can arise for reasons other than the discriminatory behaviour on the part of male employers and employees. Thus the human capital approach suggests that differences in pay will be a consequence of differences in the acquisition of skills highly valued in the market. Competition in the labour market may be imperfect

127

(monopsony) and, given that married women in particular have greater limitations on potential mobility than men, female supply curves could be less elastic than those of males and wage differences could arise for this reason. In certain occupations (e.g. those requiring physical strength) men may be more productive than women. Further, the tastes for particular occupations may differ between the sexes with females being willing to contemplate a smaller range of occupations than men, therefore being partly responsible themselves for the crowding alluded to above. Yet very little is known about the work aspiration of women[2] and differences in both occupational choice and the motivation to work, or productivity within occupations, could be themselves influenced by differences in incentives provided for men and women employees or by the presence of discrimination.[3]

In general, however, data are not available to test adequately for the significance of the above factors. Further, recent work on discriminatory behaviour in the labour market has suggested that it is important to analyse the experience of particular groups of employee at the lowest level of aggregation if one is to gain a true understanding of the complex mechanisms through which discrimination or differences in treatment are perpetuated and extended. This partly stems from the fact that in both macro and micro studies discrimination is estimated as a residual after other sources of the male-female wage differential have been held constant, and it is difficult to ensure that adequate allowance has been made for all relevant variables.

This Chapter concentrates on the analysis of the structure of labour markets in the form of internal labour markets (ILMs), dual labour markets (DLMs) and labour market segmentation (LMS) in general in the belief that examination of the institutional framework of the unit of employment can cast considerable light on the above issues. A distinction has been made between neo-classical approaches to sex segregation in the labour market (including Becker's analysis, the overcrowding model, the human capital approach and the monopsony model) and the institutional approach (including ILM and DLM analysis).[4] Yet these approaches are not mutually exclusive. The DLM analysis, for instance, can be regarded as a particular version of the employer discrimination model. Likewise the human capital approach seems highly appropriate to the analysis of the career hierarchy implicit in the ILM. The following sections include an analysis of labour market structures beginning with the concept of the ILM and giving particular emphasis to entry into the ILM and the use of screening devices and to promotion within it viewed from a human capital perspective. There follows an examination of the concept of LMS focusing on DLMs. Finally, an assessment is made of the empirical evidence on structured labour markets and its implications for the relative pay position of women. Most of the work conducted in this area relates to North American experience and focuses on the issue of racial discrimination. However, wherever possible reference is made to available British work and to those studies which have examined the relative position of women in the labour force.

THE ANALYSIS OF LABOUR MARKET STRUCTURES

THE CONCEPT OF THE INTERNAL LABOUR MARKET

In a competitive labour market it is generally assumed that labour is homogeneous and mobile, so that there is a long-run tendency towards equalisation of net advantages and the development of the concept of the ILM may be seen as an attempt to explain how labour market imperfections arising from such factors as the costs of information and of specific training may emerge to modify this result.

In their original analysis Doeringer and Piore (1971) define the ILM as 'an administrative unit within which the pricing and allocation of labour is governed by a set of administrative rules and procedures'. This is distinguished from the external labour market (ELM) where wages are more directly determined by market forces. The two markets are, however, linked at various job levels which constitute ports of entry and exit to and from the ILM, whilst other jobs levels are reached by transfer and promotion of existing employees. The distinction is crucial as far as the disadvantaged worker is concerned because existing employees are likely to be given preferential treatment over outside job applicants.

Examining the concept in more detail and following Kerr (1954) and Alexander (1974) we may consequently adopt a three-way classification of labour markets:

(i) open markets which are unstructured, subject to competitive forces and characterised by lack of skill, low capital/labour ratios and an absence of firm specific training;

(ii) 'guild' or craft markets which are structured horizontally by means of occupational licensing, such that there is considerable mobility of labour between firms but little between industries or crafts—general training is more important than specific training; (iii) 'manorial' or enterprise markets which are structured vertically by means of promotion ladders with relatively little mobility between firms. Training specific to the firm, in part a function of technology, is all important. For manual employees the ILM will generally correspond to the plant but for managerial staff it will be company-wide, whilst other white-collar employees will tend to either pole with clerical workers and technicians being closer to the manual case and the professionally qualified closer to the managerial extreme.

Most of the discussion has centred on the third market category which can be regarded in part as an employer response to the state of the labour market, for if there is abundant labour in the ELM there is little inducement to concentrate on internal recruitment. As Taira (1976) has suggested, there is an incentive for the employer to develop an ILM where it can contribute to profitability. It can thus be judged on criteria identical to those in the case of other markets, namely:

   (i) the speed of adjustment of labour supply to demand;
   (ii) the cost of having unfilled vacancies and of labour turnover;
   (iii) the transactions costs of hiring a worker from the ELM.[5]

Where pay is linked to seniority this may, of course, have the effect of reducing labour turnover. ILMs may also be beneficial to employees if their transactions costs of changing job are reduced and career prospects enhanced, but correspondingly their knowledge of alternative job opportunities may be reduced. Unions which place emphasis on seniority may support the emergence of an ILM. From the point of view of the economy the implied reduction in labour mobility could, on the other hand, have harmful consequences. Efficiency implies an absence of queues for particular jobs within the firm or of shortages of available labour to fill job openings.

There is some suggestion that ILMs predominate in high paying, large and well-organised firms, but Edwards *et al* (1975) argue that ILMs are a function not only of size of firm but also of bureaucratic control and the need for stability of the employment relationship. Size is important because the number of levels in a well-developed career hierarchy presupposes a certain minium size and as size increases the possibilities for satisfactory career development multiply. Size also tends to go hand in hand with high capital intensity and unionisation which increases the need both for bureaucratic control and habits of predictability and dependability on the part of the workforce. It is in this sort of enterprise also that specific skills are required and experience over the working lifetime is important. It has recently been suggested that females in particular tend to be found more than proportionately in small firms,[6] so that many of them will be excluded from the benefits of the ILM.

The relationship between relative pay in the ILM compared with the ELM is subject to a number of influences. Whilst the mean level of pay is likely to be lower for those excluded from the ILM because they are deprived of promotion opportunities the same need not be true for every skill level. Thus a worker low down the skill hierarchy of a particular ILM may be prepared to accept a lower current wage than he or she could obtain on the ELM because of the possibility of future advancement and higher earnings in the ILM. Taira (op. cit.) suggests, however, that the existence of ILMs will induce labour surpluses in the ELM from which selective recruitment is made such that:

> the higher the wages in ILMs, the larger the extent of the labour reserve that after a given fraction is employed by large firms, presses down the wages and working conditions in the ELM, accentuating internal-external wage differentials.[7]

Whether in aggregate wage dispersion widens as a consequence of labour market structuring is therefore uncertain and needs to be subjected to empirical investigation.

However, of crucial importance to the question of equal opportunity is the extent to which discrimination manifests itself as a consequence of the operation of the ILM. This involves two main aspects—the extent to which enterprises with well-developed ILMs fail to hire workers of equal ability as a consequence of screening devices or excessive use of credentials (which is basically a demand-side approach) and the extent to which women fail to advance up through the organisational hierarchy in the same proportion as men with equal abilities and qualifications which can be detected with the aid of a human capital (or supply-side) model.

Screening Devices and Entry Into the ILM

The existence of the ILM implies that the costs of defective hiring procedures are exacerbated since lifetime productivities rather than productivity in initial job grade are relevant and as prior assessment of potential productivity is difficult, if not impossible, this will intensify the tendency not only to use elaborate recruitment procedures but also to use sex (or education) as a screening device. An employer is said to be using a 'cheap screen' when he automatically distinguishes between individuals displaying a particular, readily ascertainable, characteristic (such as sex) with the implication that unfavourable treatment will be given on the basis of this characteristic, without consideration of other characteristics and attributes. Screening devices do not, therefore, sort perfectly but this must be assessed against the cost of fine sorting. An alternative way of evaluating prospective employees is to use a self-selection device. This is defined (Salop and Salop, 1976) as a pricing scheme which causes job applicants to reveal the true facts about themselves by their market behaviour. Thus wage structures favouring educational qualifications will exclude the less able from applying for jobs.[8] Whilst these forms of behaviour may be based on prejudice or misconception, there will also, however, be an economic rationale. Stiglitz (1973) has demonstrated that under certain plausible assumptions—differences in productivity between groups, individual productivity differences unascertainable prior to performance of the job, high fixed costs of replacement and equal pay—that discrimination in hiring practices based upon group attributes is an efficient means of allocating labour. Adopting a similar approach Spence (1974) has noted that whilst some individual characteristics observable to the employer prior to hiring are subject to manipulation by the individual, others are not. Thus, whilst education and training can be acquired, sex is unalterable; we may refer to alterable characteristics as 'signals' and unalterable ones as 'indices'.[9] Spence suggests that a situation in which employers draw inferences about productivity from indices because the latter are correlated with productive capacity within the population be referred to as 'statistical discrimination'. Discrimination may also be present in relation to signals since these are also frequently only proxies for underlying attributes and indeed this is covered by the indirect discrimination provisions of the Sex Discrimination Act. Thus if it is more difficult for women to enter certain educational courses than for men, a given level of education implies more talent in the former case and this casts doubt on the principle of equal treatment for people with the same test scores, signals or indices. Equal treatment in terms of social productivity may imply unequal treatment at the level of signals and justify 'reverse discrimination'.

To some extent education may also be used as a screen in the same way as sex when judging applicants and it is possible that employers may demand educational requirements which are higher and often unrelated to actual job performance—the problem of 'credentialism'.[10] To the extent that women have lower educational qualifications than men this will also work to their disadvantage. Thus one American study has found that in service and to some extent white-collar occupational categories 'dead end' jobs (as defined by employers) appeared to have higher entry requirements than those from which promotion was possible.[11] Whilst allowing for a desire by employers to 'cream the market' this would seem to point to requirements which for some reason or another were set too high.[12] One explanation which appears inadequate in itself is that higher educational requirements serve as an effective screening device for reducing applicant numbers to a manageable size for personnel decision-making. Whatever the explanation, the above constitutes a barrier for persons with less than the required level of education and these individuals are excluded from employment not because they cannot perform the work but simply because they fall outside the employer's hiring requirements.[13]

Other forms of job barrier are also apparent and may be equally linked to the ILM and aspects of discrimination. Thus employment tests, which lead to hiring and promotion only for those who achieve a pre-determined minimum score, are rarely validated in terms of job performance. Similar arguments apply to personnel interviews—the most widely used method of selecting employees. Likewise entry discrimination may be related to recruitment procedures. Some firms tend to establish rather narrow and stable channels of recruitment including referral of friends and relatives by present employees.[14] Reliance upon a narrow set of recruitment channels has advantages both to the employer and potential employee, producing applicant characteristics ressembling those of the incumbent workforce and possessing certain predictable traits, each of which is important in the context of the ILM. Relatives and friends can provide a clear picture of prospective employment for the applicant thereby reducing the costs of trial and error and job search. These benefits encourage the continuance of any set of recruitment channels once they are established and discriminatory recruitment practices may continue to yield employment patterns, excluding women from certain high level jobs, long after discriminatory intent has been removed.

Where behaviour is based on misconceptions, such as a mistaken belief that women are less productive than men, exclusion of women from employment means that there is no disconfirming experience. As Spence notes (op. cit.) once the pattern of exclusion is broken, employers' market experience changes and we might expect a fairly rapid 'tipping' phenomenon as employment moves to a new equilibrium. A minimum quota may be a useful policy device in this context. However, if the barrier is based upon prejudice such a change may not take place. Where failure to hire is based upon mis-conceptions or, more specifically, a failure to update stereotypes on the basis of labour market changes, such as the changed participation rates of married women,[15] legislation which has the effect of overriding employer hiring standards (e.g. quotas or affirmative action) need not distort the allocation of labour and might even improve it. Whilst detailed discussion of hiring in practice is postponed until the following section, it should be noted that we have little information on the extent to which employer hiring policies are sub-optimal or otherwise.

Finally, we should bear in mind the possibility that the relationship between the ILM and screening devices may operate in either direction in terms of cause and effect. An important *purpose* of the ILM is to provide a continuous screening function. Whilst credentials acquired elsewhere can be evaluated at the time of hire, individual performance in relation to specific skills must of necessity be assessed within the ILM.[16] As Wachter (op. cit.) notes, as long as the employer can rectify errors *ex-post* there is less necessity to establish entry barriers and form a well-developed ILM. Besides the possibility of dismissal of workers hired in error (increasingly difficult as a result of unionisation and protective legislation) workers may be held at a particular point on the promotion ladder. Statistical discrimination may still occur since employers will economise on costly information but this is more conveniently discussed in detail in the following section.

Human Capital Investment and Promotion Within the ILM
Though derived from a more theoretical approach there are obvious links between the study of human capital and the ILM concept.[17] At the post-hire level, the ILM is concerned with the numerous transactions that occur inside an organisation affecting employees in such matters as promotion, demotion, or transfer. Discrimination may occur with respect of each of these factors including the level at which an individual is hired, the rate of wage increase once hired or the rate at which he or she moves up through the organisational hierarchy. Discrimination may also be related to conscious and unconscious personnel policies related to personal characteristics of employees such as sex, marital status, education, and experience. Indeed, a major source of disadvantage among minority workers including women is the lack of human capital possessed by these groups.[18] Thus, it is not only the structure of the economic environment in which individuals and

minority groups work, but also the characteristics of individuals, on the supply side, which keep them in low income, low level jobs.

Whilst the screening hypothesis outlined above may be able to explain variations in starting salaries (though little testing of this has been undertaken) its ability to predict earnings of long-term employees within the ILM is limited by the fact that earnings are highly correlated with years of work experience as well as sex or educational level. As Blaug (op. cit.) notes, over time there is no reason why the employer should continue to rely on educational qualifications when independent evidence of job performance is available. Unlike the screening hypothesis, the human capital approach puts the emphasis on returns to investment in training in the context of individual utility maximisation. It is generally assumed that the individual is free (and sufficiently well-informed) to invest in the acquisition of skills where the rate of return is greatest. As Rosen (1976) has suggested, 'the theory of human capital is at heart a theory of "permanent" earnings'. The fact that attention is focused on lifetime rather than current earnings means that it is particularly appropriate for the analysis of ILMs. Further, where the costs of job change are high (e.g. where specific skills are crucial) the link between current earnings and skill will be weakened and the LMS approach discussed below may be more relevant than human capital theory in explaining *current* earnings.[19] Male/female earnings differences, in particular, will result from differences in lifetime participation in the labour market between the sexes (or varying quantities of specific capital) which in turn may give women a lower incentive to invest in skill acquisition. Here, it is necessary to examine the whole of lifetime earnings rather than a particular annual figure if the right inferences are to be drawn.

The basic human capital model developed by Jacob Mincer (1974) takes the form

$$\text{Log } E = a + bS + cX + dX^2 + U$$

where E = earnings
S = years of schooling
X = years of experience
U = error term.

Since earnings are the result of the interaction of supply and demand for labour, this is a reduced form equation. The amount of on-the-job training and other types of investment in human capital will tend to decrease with age or experience whilst depreciation and obsolescence reduce their value over time, and it is this fact which makes age/earnings profiles concave from below. It is generally assumed that the log of earnings is linearly related to years of schooling and quadratically related to years of work experience. Education and training and then, at the heart of the human capital approach, the former normally being undertaken prior to entry into the labour force and imparting general skills upon which a return is recouped over the whole working lifetime and the latter frequently being undertaken during the years of work, often imparting specific skills and sometimes involving learning on-the-job. Years of schooling are normally used to measure the extent of an individual's education but are in practice a crude proxy, hardly allowing adequately for qualitative differences and possibly biasing the results to indicate sex discrimination. To the extent that productivity is improved simply by doing a job, earnings will be related to experience.[20] Where there is a well-developed ILM, length of service within the enterprise will be more highly correlated with earnings than outside experience. Age is often used as a proxy for experience where data limitations prevent more appropriate measurement. Indeed, in macro-studies experience is often estimated indirectly as age minus years of education minus five years. In the case of females with breaks in length of service as a consequence of child-rearing this must give misleading results.

It is also important to bear in mind that marital status may influence the level of earnings in a number of ways. First, it is possible that employers may regard marital status as a proxy for commitment to work. If it is judged that family responsibilities make married men more stable employees than single men, then married men will predominate in the better paid jobs. On the other hand, the Malkiels (1973) and Gordon and Morton (1976) suggest that employers may prefer single to married females because they expect higher absence and turnover rates in the latter case, with the general assumption that a geographical job change by the husband will cause the married women to quit her job.[21] Ferber and Lowry (1976(a)) take the view that in the absence of labour market discrimination one would expect single women to earn more than single men on the grounds that 'strong independent career orientated' women will choose to remain single and 'less aggressive, perhaps unsuccessful' men fail to marry. This contrasts with the interpretation of Gwartney and Stroup (1973) who present evidence to suggest that the employment preferences of men and women are most similar for single employees and dissimilar for those married with spouse present. They do, however, acknowledge the difficulty of isolating supply side from demand side functions in a situation where neither employee preferences nor employer bias can be directly observed. A further difficulty, noted by Rosen (op. cit.) is the fact that 'never married' is an ex-post rationalisation. If females expect to become married at some uncertain future date this will affect the rate at which they invest in human capital and make it difficult to infer the precise part of the residual in adjusted male/female earnings equations which is the result of discrimination. At the minimum, however, it seems legitimate to expect, even in the absence of discrimination, that married women will fare worse than single women and either single or married men in terms of level of earnings and occupational advancement.

To summarise the above discussion of the concept of the ILM there are clearly a large number of ways in which earnings and occupational level may differ between various groups in the labour market, some of which may reflect efficiency criteria and some of which may reflect forms of discrimination. As Doeringer and Piore, (1971) note, since the ILM is at least in part the product of the employer's attempt to minimise the fixed costs of recruitment, hiring and training, it is not at all certain that the removal of discrimination will raise economic efficiency. Before examining empirical evidence on the extent and nature of ILMs, however, it is necessary to examine the related concept of labour market segmentation (LMS) and its stronger version—the dual labour market (DLM).

THE CONCEPT OF LABOUR MARKET SEGMENTATION

The distinction between the ILM and external labour market (ELM) implies some degree of segmentation in the labour market. Although certain authors treat LMS as though it were synonymous with the DLM,[22] it is perhaps more appropriate to regard the former as a more general approach to imperfections in the labour market and one, in fact, that has an established tradition in neoclassical theory. However, LMS is seen by the radical economists such as Edwards *et al* (op. cit.) to result from the attempt by employers to capture strategic control over product and factor markets through a policy of 'divide and rule'. For instance, the restructuring of the internal relationships of monopolistic corporations as part of the process of capitalistic development is held to have exacerbated LMS through the creation of ILMs and at the same time weakened the bargaining power of labour by heightening the difference of interests between various segments of the labour force. Whether LMS has resulted from conscious management decision designed to weaken the labour movement as the radical economists imply is, however, at the least debatable and differing interpretations can be placed on particular events in line with the mode of analysis being adopted.[23]

The essence of LMS theories is the all pervasive nature of barriers to mobility. Labour supply schedules may differ among otherwise similar groups because of differences in education and training, geographical location or work history, whilst labour demand schedules may differ because of differing industrial structures, discrimination by race and sex or trade union barriers to entry (Wachtel and Betsey 1972). As a result there is a whole series of possible wage and employment equilibria for particular groups of employee. Indeed, it is possible for individuals with low amounts of human capital to earn more than those with large amounts of human capital.[24] According to this view, then, public policy should concentrate not merely on the acquisition of human capital but on how this is utilised within the labour market. As Wachtel and Betsey (ibid.) note if an individual is sent on a training programme but on its completion simply returns to his original structural environment we should not be surprised at a lack of improvement in earnings capacity.

Dual Labour Markets

The concept of the DLM is not only an extreme form of LMS but also a logical progression from the analysis of the ILM since it broadens the coverage from the ILM (in the form of primary markets) to a consideration of the ELM and attempts to deal more specifically with mobility, or the lack of it, between the two sectors. An important feature of the hypothesis is the suggestion that the character of such markets is best explained by institutional and sociological factors rather than narrow economic variables in the neo-classical sense. Thus, according to Doeringer and Piore (1975), in contrast to the assumption of human capital theory, much on the job training is not so much the outcome of economic decisions as a process of socialisation (i.e. acceptance and conformity to group norms). In particular, social acceptability is a key factor in obtaining primary sector skills, which means that promotion may be influenced by factors such as shared social beliefs or sex.

The simple DLM theory states that the labour market can be divided into two quite distinct sectors. First, the primary labour market is characterised by high wages and fringe benefits, skilled jobs with opportunities for further training and promotion, employment stability and high levels of unionisation. By contrast the secondary labour market offers low wages and few fringe benefits, lack of skill and an absence of opportunities for promotion, employment instability and lack of unionisation. A high concentration of white adult males is to be found in the primary market, whilst there is a disproportionate number of females,[25] young workers, immigrants, coloured employees and other minorities in the secondary sector. As Andresani (1976) points out, this does not mean that all women, for instance, are confined to the secondary sector, that there is no upward mobility for such workers or that human capital has no value to them. Rather, it is held that

> What upward mobility occurs and what value there is from investments in the schooling and training of disadvantaged workers derives solely within the primary labour market sector, and that blacks and women are disproportionately relegated to the secondary sector at the very outset of their labour market career independently of their abilities and skills. Abilities and skills in other words are thought to be of no value within the secondary sector and of no value in escaping from secondary jobs.

The meaningfulness of the distinction is dependent upon the existence of mobility barriers between the two markets such that certain workers become trapped in the secondary market. 'Statistical discrimination' will occur where certain workers are trapped merely because their superficial characteristics resemble those of secondary workers.

The parallels to the concepts of ILMs and ELMs are clear. As Doeringer and Piore (1971) point out, the primary sector consists of a series of ILMs with employment queues at the ports of entry, whilst in the secondary sector there exist various kinds of employment situation of which they distinguish three; some workers are employed in casual labour markets which are too unstructured to qualify as an ILM; some are employed in establishments with formal internal structures but many ports of entry or other features of the secondary market (examples being foundry workers and hospital auxiliaries); others are to be found in non-promotable jobs in establishments where the remainder of jobs are primary (e.g. labourers). It is held that the distinction between the two sectors is not so much technologically as historically determined, since work in the primary sector can be moved to the secondary sector when, for example, pressure of demand is sufficiently great. The real difference between the DLM and other approaches is that segmentation *eliminates* opportunities for workers in the secondary sector as opposed to *limiting* them through either discrimination or market imperfections. It is also possible that the increasing importance of such factors as job training will tend to increase the separation between the two markets by making employment stability increasingly significant. In addition, the growth of non-wage elements in labour costs within the ILM implies the need to minimise numbers and maximise hours in order to spread those costs which are fixed in relation to the number of employees (Chiplin and Sloane (1976 (a)). In contrast Doeringer and Piore (1971) argue on the basis of the classification outlined above that:

> the distinction between primary and secondary markets need not imply the strict separation of the two embodied in the concept of a DLM. Whether a dichotomous or a continuous model of the labour market is appropriate is a matter of both emphasis and empirical judgement.[26]

This is very close to talking about segmentation along occupational lines and we are back to Cairnes' non-competing groups. If a continuous model does apply there seems little scope for an analysis of DLMs even if like Osterman (op. cit.) one believes that the concept of the ILM lacks sufficient generality for purposes of macro-economic analysis.

Later investigators have felt the need for a more precise definition of the primary and secondary sectors. As Osterman notes, 'simply segmenting the labour force into two parts . . . leaves a primary sector of enormous variety and poor definition'. Indeed it appears that the differences between groups within the primary sector are in some ways no less important than the distinction between the primary and secondary sector. Thus Piore (1970) suggests that at the minimum one should distinguish between an upper and lower tier of the primary sector, which are categorised by Edwards (op. cit.) as 'independent primary' and 'subordinate primary' segments. The former group consists largely of managerial and professional groups with a considerable degree of job discretion, general training and often substantial job mobility. The latter group comprises both white-collar and blue-collar employees engaged on routine tasks, with specific skills and consequently low mobility and it is this group upon which the emphasis is normally placed in DLM anlysis. It is likely that those women who gain entry to the primary sector are concentrated in the 'subordinate' segment.

Since particular jobs tend to draw workers from particular areas and employees tend to hold jobs in a certain sequence, Piore suggests that we should think in terms of mobility chains or seniority districts which have

stations at certain points along them, their division being determined by
the structure of technology. Thus:

> the critical distinction between primary and secondary sectors is that
> the mobility chains of the former constitute some kind of career
> ladder along which there is progress towards higher paying and
> higher status jobs. This is true on both the upper and lower tiers and
> constitutes the rationale for speaking of the two tiers together as the
> primary sectors. In the secondary sector by contrast, jobs do not fall
> into any regular progression of this kind; they are held in a more or
> less random fashion so that a worker coming into a job may take the
> place of another person moving to a job which the first person just
> left.[27]

Secondary markets may be expected where it is costly to create a well-
developed ILM, it is difficult to reduce turnover or the benefits of so
doing are relatively unimportant and unions are weak. Alternatively
certain groups of employees may not value job security very highly (e.g.
moonlighters or married women only temporarily in the labour
market). In the latter case it may be suggested that in some cases
workers in the secondary market may be relatively well-paid, such as
those engaged on civil engineering or construction contracts, though the
temporary nature of employment implies that differences in lifetime
earnings will be rather less and as a consequence of the nature of the
high-paying secondary jobs women may be excluded. The particular
case quoted also suggests that it is wrong to infer that secondary
markets are the sole preserve of small firms. Large firms may well
segment their operations in such a way that the effects of instability of
demand in the product market are felt by a clearly differentiated group
of their employees, since this is the only way in which the advantages of
an ILM can be obtained for part of the workforce.

It is suggested that the process of wage determination is quite
different in the two sectors. In the primary sector, wages, as in the ILM
analysis, are unresponsive to supply and demand because of sociological and institutional factors including equity considerations (Doeringer
and Piore, 1975). Further, incomes are determined by access to job
clusters and the speed with which the individual passes through the
structure of jobs, both of these being a function of the level of education.
Seniority provisions mean that wages generally increase with age. In the
secondary market variations in hours are more important than
variations in wage rates in determining income (Gordon op. cit.), those

with lower incomes and larger families working longer hours, *ceteris paribus*, and the employer's assumption of homogeneous labour and zero turnover costs strengthening the forces of supply and demand in the labour market. As noted above, it is held that quantities of human capital will not influence wages because employers, anticipating high turnover, do little screening and provide little subsequent on-the-job training,[28] so that age/earnings profiles will be flat as a consequence of lack of promotion opportunities. Two separate arguments are put forward to suggest that wage differentials between the two sectors will widen over time. First, high profits in the primary sector allow firms to pay for considerable on-the-job training, which in turn raises productivity allowing still higher wages (i.e. there is positive feedback). This presupposes that profits are indeed higher in the primary sector and neglects the possibility that some firms may operate in both markets. Secondly, Piore suggests that discrimination of any kind increases the labour force in the secondary sector, thus depressing the wage rate and giving the employers there, who in Becker's terms are presumably those with low discrimination coefficients or in Bergmann's terms members of the crowded sector, an interest in the perpetuation of discrimination. It is argued that higher wage costs for primary employers are offset by reduced costs in both screening and labour turnover. Klitgaard (1971), however, disputes the implication that discrimination can be in the interests of both primary and secondary employers because high voluntary turnover in the secondary sector should make that sector unattractive to employers. Otherwise it is difficult to explain why the primary sector should exist at all (unless unions are strong which in turn renders the conspiratorial theory redundant). Further, as Wachter notes we need to explain why, if secondary workers are basically sound employees, new firms do not enter the market to utilise their skills. Explanations could be found in lack of information, discrimination or feedback effects resulting in poor work habits.

The last of these suggests that the motivation of workers may be a key factor, and one with which human capital models find it difficult to cope.[29] The job satisfaction and performance of disadvantaged workers will be influenced by a number of factors in the social system including the organisation providing the job, community organisations, informal peer groups and family circumstances. Behavioural scientists generally agree that behaviour is a product of expectancies about behaviour-reward contingencies and the attractiveness of these rewards. Thus, high attendance (low rates of job turnover, absenteeism and tardiness) would occur when workers believe that remaining on the job leads to desired rewards, whereas leaving the job does not. It is not unreasonable to suggest that desired rewards will most frequently be forthcoming in the primary market and least often in the secondary market. Further, to be productive a worker must internalise a wide range of middle class values least likely to be found in the secondary market. Thus, it is held that performance is a function of three major types of skills—adaptive, functional and specific. Adaptive skills are those that enable an individual to meet the demands for conformity and change made by the physical, inter-personal and organisational arrangements and conditions of a job. These are generally acquired in the early years as a consequence of family and school background. Functional skills are those that enable individuals to function in relation to machines or equipment, data or people, and are normally acquired through training and reinforced through experience on the job. Specific skills are those that enable an individual to perform a particular job according to the standards demanded by employers and customers and require specific training, perhaps on-the-job. It is probably in relation to adaptive skills that differences between primary and secondary workers are most pronounced.

One consequence of such differences is that the process of self-selection alluded to earlier may operate to create marked occupational segregation, in so far as members of such groups do not apply for particular jobs or to particular firms (Chiplin and Sloane, 1976 (b)). A woman, for instance, may not apply for a particular job either because she has a high propensity to quit and the wage structure favours those with low quit rates or because she has a lower level of productivity than the minimum required for entrance to a particular job, or for advancement within it. Equally, however, a woman may have misconceptions about her own characteristics in respect of these variables. It is difficult to isolate this process of self-selection from demand-side job barriers reflected in employer hiring practices, since these practices influence self-selection and may result in self-confirming behaviour.

In general, the above discussion leads to the conclusion that the term duality is itself an over-simplification and that it may be more meaningful to talk in terms of multiple labour market segmentation, but discussion of this is postponed to the next section after the empirical evidence for the existence of DLMs has been examined.

EMPIRICAL EVIDENCE ON STRUCTURED LABOUR MARKETS

Examining first the extent of ILMs, the immediate question that arises is how far in practice it is possible to identify particular ILMs. Doeringer and Piore (1971) suggest that ILMs can be analysed according to three characteristics: their degree of openness to the external labour market in terms of the proportion of ports of entry and exit and criteria for entry; their scope in terms of size, geography and numbers of occupations; and the rules for internal job allocation. But in the case of 'manorial' markets at least this is extremely demanding in terms of data requirements and they limit themselves to estimates of the proportion of the labour force within the two types of ILM from data on employment by size and type of enterprise and by craft union membership. They conclude that about 80 per cent of the employed labour force in the USA works in ILMs, whilst the rest are engaged in agriculture or service occupations. The way in which an ILM is defined in this case seems, however, to be far from adequate for most purposes. For instance, they include under the heading of structured markets 27 per cent of workers employed in small enterprises, where administrative rules could well be relatively unimportant.

A more fruitful approach is perhaps that of Alexander (op. cit.), who classifies ILMs on the basis of labour mobility. Thus a manorial structure implies a low probability of turnover which as a rule of thumb he takes to be less than 10 per cent, whilst the unstructured market has a high probability of turnover which he takes to be greater than 20 per cent. The existence of a guild market implies that there will be a significant difference between the probability of leaving the firm and of leaving the industry (taken as 10 per cent). On this basis, using the Social Security 1 per cent work history file, he calculates the mobility of each individual from equations including both personal and establishment characteristics and averages them for each structural class. It appears that both manorial and guild structures influence mobility to a greater degree than would be anticipated on the basis of the characteristics of the labour force. That is, manorial industries reduce inter-firm mobility by almost seven percentage points and guild industries increase it by the same amount.

In comparison to the United States very little empirical work has been undertaken in Britain on the operation of the ILM. However, Bosanquet and Doeringer (1973) report that a brief survey undertaken by them of British hiring and promotion practices generally confirmed the significance of the distinction between open and structured markets. By contrast, Mackay *et al* (1971) found in their study of the British engineering industry that there was a major difference between American and British practice such that

None of the case study plants operated a procedure for internal promotion in which seniority was the only guiding principle, and there was no evidence that managements were under pressure from unions or workers to recognise the very informal procedures used to determine such promotion. This contrasts with much American experience, where promotion has become an important issue in labour-management relations, and the criteria used in selecting candidates for promotion have become a matter for collective bargaining.

Nonetheless the investigators conclude that plants did make use of their ILMs to meet those requirements for labour which could not be met satisfactorily by means of direct recruitment and other sectors of industry may well have ILMs which are rather more structured than in engineering. Thus, in an earlier study by S. W. Lerner *et al* (1969), which looked at four industries—engineering, chemicals, soap and baking— we are given some hints of the existence if ILMs with a stress on the concept of the internal wage structure—encompassing wage differentials, wage setting procedures and forms of wage payment at a particular plant. Further, there was some doubt if the local labour market even determined the rate for key jobs, for if it did the bottom rung of unskilled workers where there is an internal promotion system or the pay of fitters in engineering would not vary from works to works. Nonetheless, for reasons outlined below it is unlikely that ILMs are as significant in Britain as in the USA.

There is some evidence that American employers in general take more care in selecting employees than their British counterparts. In addition to having higher entry requirements than implied by the nature of the job, referred to earlier, far greater use appears to be made of entry tests than in the UK. Further, a comparison of the findings of Rees and Schultz (1970) and Mackay *et al* (op. cit.) suggests a tendency to rely on employee referral to a much greater degree and application at the gate to a much lesser extent in North America than Britain, which again might suggest greater care in hiring in North America. Further, Mackay *et al* note:

The outstanding impression of selection procedures is that they were extremely casual and informal. Judgments were made on the spot, often after a rather perfunctory interview, and no attempt was made to subject hiring standards to objective tests. Interviewers . . . seldom made any attempt to assess whether the recruit had potential for upgrading, possibly because the process of internal promotion was relatively little developed. Hiring was undertaken without particular thought to long-term considerations, and the requirements of the initial job had seldom been thought through systematically.

Further, there was little evidence that this informal procedure produced satisfactory results, but interestingly an exception to the general rule were those plants with American management which had more systematic methods of recruitment. A second factor to consider is the importance of seniority. Indeed this provides a simple method for identifying the existence or otherwise of ILMs for the stronger the relationship between inside experience (seniority) and pay and the less strong the relationship between pay and outside experience the more developed is the ILM. Thus in the Chiplin and Sloane study of a well-developed professional ILM (1976 (c)) inside experience was highly significant and outside experience negatively significant. In the USA Rees and Schultz (op. cit.) found that seniority was the most important determinant of pay for nearly all occupational categories. Unfortunately no comparable data exist for the UK.

This brings us on to the work that has been undertaken on the application of the human capital model to particular labour markets. Using his basic equation Mincer (1974) was able to explain a third of the variance in earnings for white non-farm men in 1959 based on the US Census and over a half on certain additional assumptions. Using the same model Psacharopoulos and Layard (1976) from a sample of 6873 adult males in the 1972 British General Household Survey were able to explain a third of the earnings inequality though the variance to be explained and the explained variance are lower than in the US. The conclusion that education and experience alone can account for as much as half of the observed variance in the distribution of earnings has been considered as 'somewhat surprising' (Blaug). Mincer and Polachek (1974), using data from the 1967 National Longitudinal Survey of Work Experience, also found that the earnings function was able to explain 25 to 30 per cent of the relative dispersion in wage rates of white married women and 40 per cent in the case of single women. Comparing the results with those for comparable males it seemed that differences in work experience accounted for roughly half the gap in male/female wage rates. However, for reasons outlined earlier, studies of individual establishments seem more appropriate for the analysis of discrimination. Even here, however, commitment to work may differ among groups according to sex or marital status, which makes any precise measurement of discrimination difficult if not impossible. The human capital establishment studies have analysed, in the main, white-collar employees where measurement of productivity is most difficult. Results have also been influenced by the number of independent variables that investigators were able to include in their equations, by whether semi-log, double-log or absolute scales were specified and by whether linear or quadratic forms were used for certain of the independent variables such as education, age and experience.[30]

Also some investigators (e.g. Cassell *et al* [1975]) include sex as a dummy variable in single equation models, but the fact that separate equations for men and women generally show significant differences in values of the coefficients of the independent variables—and this is true also where marital status is identified[31]—indicates that the procedure of Cassell *et al* is, at the minimum, dubious. For instance, in an analysis of three British ILMs Sloane and Siebert (1977) found that the education variable was in most cases highly significant, but this did not apply to married women in two cases.[32]

In general, studies at establishment or units of employment level by the Malkiels, Cassell *et al*, Gordon and Morton, Ferber and Lowry (1976b), Smith, Chiplin and Sloane (1976c) and Sloane and Siebert have been able to explain between approximately 50 and 90 per cent in the variance of earnings for the various sex and marital status employment groups. Education and experience are highly significant in most but not all equations, whilst age is sometimes significant. This is in line with other studies including Rees and Schultz's major analysis (op. cit.) of the Chicago labour market, where seniority was the most important determinant of individual earnings and age was in most cases not significant, though more strongly associated with earnings in high wage occupations. The explanatory power of the human capital model seems remarkably high in some equations, given the number of independent variables in the model. The Malkiels (op. cit.) were also able to use an expanded model using publications as a proxy for productivity (as well as including possession of PhD, critical area of study, absence rate and marital status). The additional productivity variables did increase the power to predict salary levels, with more than three-quarters of the variance in male and over 80 per cent in the case of female salaries being explained (as opposed to 71 and 68 per cent respectively). In some equations the Malkiels include organisational job level which causes the earnings gap to disappear, but women with the particular levels of training and experience are found to be in lower job levels than similar males. Likewise in the Chiplin and Sloane study (1976c) there was some evidence of discrimination in terms of access to the higher job level. It is important, therefore, to conduct analyses in terms of occupations as well as pay. Cassell *et al*, following Birnbaum (in Edwards *et al*, op. cit.), as outlined above, consider also the impact of initial grade upon current grade and wage and find that in the current wage regression's explanatory power is raised from 33–57 per cent to 50–62 per cent and in the current grade regressions from 29–63 per cent to 64 percent; 86 per cent when initial grade is included. Further, all race coefficients become insignificant which might indicate that discrimination occurs at the time of hire rather than in employment. Cassell *et al* also suggest that there may be a relationship between the method of payment and the amount of discrimination or, more precisely, that the 'objectivity' of payment-by-results may diminish discrimination. Finally, Smith (op. cit.) finds that sex is an important source of difference in government differentials over the private sector. That is, women appear to enjoy a premium in wages as a result of government employment and this premium increases with the level of government. The public sector may therefore be less discriminatory than the private sector.

In general, these results provide considerable support for the human capital theory since low earnings can at least partly be explained by low levels of human capital investment. Evidence of lower rates of return on the investment for women might have to be taken to suggest that discrimination is also a factor but we should allow for possible differences in the real costs of education between men and women.[33] Further, experience may reflect on-the-job training and the flatter experience/earnings profiles for women are suggestive of less on-the-job training and less rapid movement up the promotion ladder.[34]

The most complete test of the LMS theory is that of Wachtel and Betsey (op. cit.) who adopt a two stage regression procedure. This involves running regressions with wages specified as a function of personal characteristics (education, years in present job, race, age, sex and marital status), then calculating an adjusted wage variable with the characteristics variable removed. The process is then reversed to test for the effects of personal characteristics upon wage after eliminating the effects of structural variables (occupation/industry, region, city size and union status). All the independent variables proved to be significant, though only about one third of the variance was explained.

An important aspect of the LMS theory is the question of self-confirming behaviour. Thus as workers become categorised as members of a particular group they may well adopt behaviour patterns predominant in that sector, which implies that career origin may be a major if not the major determinant of career ending. Adopting this approach Birnbaum finds that the inclusion of career origin (i.e. job grade at which entry is made into a particular labour market) as well as conventional variables such as education and race raises the explained variance of earnings from 39 to 41 per cent and the additional independent variable is statistically significant. However, the interpretation of this result as support for the LMS view depends on the assumption that career origin measures the job rather than some attribute of the individual concerned. Segmentation theories seem particularly appropriate in the context of female employment for, as referred to earlier, there is some suggestion that women are not only segregated by occupation but within any occupation where substantial numbers of male workers are to be found they may be segregated by firm. Thus Blau (in Edwards *et al*; op. cit.) found from a sample of clerical employees in three large cities a strong and consistent pattern of intra-occupational segregation of this kind. The policy implication is clear. Increasing the supply of female employees within particular occupations may not improve integration of the sexes unless demand side forces creating segregation can be overcome.

Some investigators have attempted to detect the existence of DLMs using a single measure. Thus Bosanquet and Doeringer suggest that an appropriate test for the evidence of a DLM is differential rates of increase with age of age-earnings profiles of particular groups of employee, though one problem that emerges is the fact that labour statistics do not divide workers into a classification which accords precisely with that of the DLM theory. However, age-earnings profiles would hardly seem by themselves to be an adequate test of DLM theory since such results are capable of a number of interpretations. An alternative approach is to examine job tenure and turnover. Thus, Edwards finds that there are significant differences in the job tenure rates of those groups said to be heavily represented in the primary sector (i.e. white males) and those in the secondary market (i.e. blacks, youths and all females over twenty-five). Here again, however, demographically defined groups are used as proxies for market determined categories, and the results can be interpreted in a number of ways. The same criticism would apply to a third possible measure: unemployment rates for different segments of the labour force. To some extent Gordon's (1971) factor analysis of multiple occupational and industrial characteristics[35] overcomes the problem of a single measuring rod. He examines weeks worked per year, whether or not the worker was looking for work during the year, and personal characteristics such as marital status, whether or not head of household and years in the labour force. Both primary white and black males exhibit larger average job tenure in their first and present job than secondary white and black males, but the average duration of tenure seems remarkably stable even in the secondary sector—8.90 years for secondary whites and 5.95 years for secondary blacks in their present job.[36]

In the case of Great Britain, Barron and Norris (1974) examined evidence for sexual differences between the primary and secondary sectors. Firstly, in examining job security they note that redundancy procedures based on last in/first out (LIFO) will work to the disadvantage of women and whilst higher quit rates for women should make it possible for firms to adjust employment without the necessity for redundancy, rates of redundancy are higher for women (see Mackay *et al.*). Secondly, they examine occupational mobility and opportunities for promotion in terms of movement to higher skill levels within the manual sector and movement from the manual sector and non-manual class III and IV sectors to the professional and managerial sectors. Reworking labour mobility data of Amelia Harris covering the period 1953–63, they find greater upward mobility for men than for women (though it should be pointed out that upward mobility is by no means negligable for women, e.g. 13 per cent as opposed to 27 per cent in the case of men in relation to movement from unskilled to skilled manual work). From this they conclude that the British labour market is characterised by a fairly well-defined line between primary and secondary jobs. However, they admit that they were not able to use conventional statistical techniques such as cluster analysis to test the DLM hypothesis and one might suggest that the fragmentary evidence that they present is more consistent with LMS than rigid dualism.

Two rather more rigorous examinations of the DLM hypothesis than the studies referred to above have, however, been undertaken. Osterman (op. cit.), using data from the 1967 US Survey of Economic Opportunity, assigns each male worker to one of the three segments in the Piore model, which provides 4130 observations in the lower primary tier and only 242 in the upper primary tier and 234 in the secondary tier.[37] Semi-log regressions were run to establish whether there were fundamental differences in the earnings functions among the three segments of the labour force and if so whether these were in line with the predictions of the DLM theory.[38] Substantial differences in the earnings function were found among the three segments and this was taken to support the theory.[39] One problem with this particular study, acknowledged by the author, is the fact that workers were assigned to each segment on the basis of subjective judgments and this increases the importance of further research currently underway to develop more refined classification procedures. In a rather different type of analysis Andresani (op. cit.) set out to explain three empirical issues—the incidence of mobility between the two sectors, the importance of skills in obtaining access to the primary sector and differences in the importance of skills within each sector—using a cohort of males aged 14 to 20 in 1966 from the National Longitudinal Survey and examining them over a period of three years. He found that although 43 per cent of whites and 64 per cent of black youths started their careers in the secondary labour market only 17 per cent and 38 per cent (respectively) remained there at the end of the period.[40] Secondly, among both blacks and whites investments in human capital increase the likelihood that the individual will be in a primary rather than a secondary job. Thirdly, the returns to investment in human capital appear to be just as high in the secondary as in the primary sector for both groups. Thus the secondary sector hardly appears to be 'a prison from which there is no escape'. All in all the empirical evidence in favour of the DLM is hardly conclusive, rather what firm evidence there is tends to cast doubt on the dichotomous model. However, the two major examinations of the DLM hypothesis outlined above were confined to male employees and further analyses are required to ascertain how far female employment conforms to the dualist model. In particular we need to explain how sex segregation occurs *within* both the primary and secondary sectors.[41]

CONCLUSIONS AND POLICY IMPLICATIONS

Sex is an obvious means of differentiating between workers, which is likely to be practised where employers (or employees) are resistant to the idea of hiring women in particular occupations or where they judge that differences between the sexes are important in terms of their value as employees. Predominantly female occupations will tend to be characterised by lower educational requirements, little training, fewer promotion possibilities and more numerous ports of entry than is the case for many 'male' jobs.

ILMs are likely to be more significant for non-manual rather than manual occupations and here it should be borne in mind that approximately two thirds of females in the British labour force are employed in non-manual occupations. Since it is suggested that ILMs are a function of size of firm and also that women are concentrated more than proportionately in small firms, it follows that many women will be excluded from the high earnings possibilities that characterise the ILM. On the other hand, it should be noted that ILMs are possibly less significant in Britain than in the US as reflected in less sophisticated methods of recruitment in the former and greater emphasis on seniority in the latter. That is not to say that seniority is unimportant in the British context—or that examples of well-developed ILMs are lacking. Indeed pay does appear to be linked to seniority in many cases and the few British human capital studies that have been undertaken confirm the American results, with a high proportion of the variance in earnings being explained in terms of a simple human capital framework. Female earnings are influenced to a considerable degree by intermittant participation in the labour force and by a relative lack of educational qualifications and experience. Further, married women fare significantly worse in terms of pay and occupational level than do single women. Associated with these differences is the use of sex as a screening device such that certain women, who might have made satisfactory employees, are excluded merely because they are assessed on the basis of the characteristics of the group to which they belong. Discrimination of various types may be manifested in relation both to entry into particular labour markets, through the use of sex as a cheap screening device, and in relation to advancement within such a market, characterised by lower rates of return on investments in human capital. It should also be borne in mind, however, that screening devices, whether based on sex or education, and ILMs themselves may be, under certain circumstances, economically efficient labour market mechanisms.

A second major approach is to concentrate on labour market segmentation and barriers to mobility such as education, training, geographical location and work history on the supply side and industrial or occupational distribution, discrimination and perhaps trade union restrictions on the demand side. One particular formulation is the DLM approach which sees women as being confined to the secondary sector and excluded from the advantages of primary markets even when they possess the necessary skills to be productive there. It is also assumed that the secondary sector is characterised by low pay, though difficulties of isolating the secondary sector empirically mean that this proposition has yet to be fully demonstrated. Further, some investigators have distinguished an upper and lower tier within the primary sector and the relative concentration of women in non-manual employment suggests that many of them may well be found in the lower tier, so that their problem may be lack of access to the upper tier rather than exclusion from the primary sector *per se*. To the extent that women are confined to the secondary sector, a problem of motivation may arise as women develop adverse characteristics which are predominant there and continue to self select themselves for jobs within that sector. However, the evidence for such a dichotomy in the labour market, as opposed to more complex segmentation, is far from convincing given the evidence of a significant amount of mobility between the 'two sectors' in both US and Britain. Most American studies have been concerned with racial rather than sexual divisions and there is perhaps a need for further empirical work, particularly in Britain, in order to detect whether a simple dichotomy is an appropriate means of analysing the relative position of women in the labour force.

The above suggests that there are three broad types of manpower policy which might be utilised to assist female workers. Firstly, taking labour supply and demand as given, one might attempt to make the labour market operate more efficiently by means of placement activities, worker counselling and labour mobility or related measures to broaden the job horizon of female employees which would be appropriate regardless of the structure of labour markets.

Secondly, one might attempt, consistent with the human capital approach, to upgrade the labour supply of women by means of greater investment in education and training, though a note of caution may be required since it is possible that labour market efficiency requires equilibrium of supply and demand in all sectors including the unskilled, and it is possible to have supra-optimal as well as sub-optimal investment even in this area. Thirdly, the labour market segmentationists, broadly defined, would see the solution as lying on the demand rather than the supply side with a requirement for government employment and expenditure policy to favour those in the secondary sector. This would include equal opportunity and affirmative action programmes.

Following the third of these broad approaches, Doeringer and Piore argue that it is possible with determination to create more primary jobs or to stabilise most secondary jobs and provide levels of wages and career hierarchies characteristics of the primary sector. Such a policy might include increasing the coverage and extent of minimum wage laws, encouraging unionisation and expanding social legislation in general. This, hower, ignores the contribution that the secondary labour force makes to the adjustment of labour supply to fluctuations in product demand and the fact that some workers may prefer not to form long-term relationships with a particular employer. It is also held by the dualists that full employment has a primary role in encouraging the structural transformation required to expand the primary labour market and facilitate the absorption of minority employees into it.

As far as the ILM is concerned the crucial role of hiring practices in perpetuating discriminatory behaviour is emphasised, and as Doeringer and Piore note in this respect,

> to achieve any degree of control over discrimination occurring through screening procedures will require the formalisation, precise definition, and validation of screening procedures.

Such evidence that is available suggests that in the UK, in particular, hiring practices are informal, imprecise and rarely validated, and to the extent that this is not amenable to change, the alternative for anti-discrimination policy would appear to lie either with quotas or subsidies. The analysis also suggests, however, that both 'cheap' screening and the operation of the ILM itself can increase efficiency, and public policy both in the USA and UK has been slow to recognise the fact that the elimination of discriminatory practices involves the balancing of competing interests, not least of which is the protection of the job security of other groups in the labour force. If, as Doeringer and Piore suggest, the costs of changing hiring and promotion standards vary with the conditions surrounding each ILM, general rules should perhaps be subordinated to *ad hoc* judgment.

Given the multiplicity of factors operating in the ILM including the supply of and demand for human capital, technology, capital intensity, unionisation and the bureaucracy of large organisations (Alexander, op. cit.) it is most unlikely that anti-discrimination legislation is a sufficient as opposed to a necessary condition for the elimination of inequality between men and women in the labour force, though its long run effects in eliminating that part of the differential in job and wage opportunity which reflects discriminatory behaviour remains to be determined.

APPENDIX

1 EXPLAINING EARNINGS DIFFERENCES AT ESTABLISHMENT LEVEL

Preliminary results of an attempt to apply a Mincer-type human capital model at individual establishment level, which parallels earlier work by

Chiplin and Sloane, are contained in Table 4A.1 below. In each case a sample of individual personnel record cards was taken and data collected on earnings, occupation, sex, marital status, age, education and experience. In the case of the Financial Institution, however, education was not available and in order to correct for this, results are presented for a sub-sample of employees who had joined the organisation at the age of sixteen and thus would be approximately of the same educational level. It follows from this that outside service, (age minus service with the company, minus years of education, minus five) is not relevant in this case. Results are presented only for the preferred equations and exclude age, for instance, which is highly correlated with service. Separate results are provided for each sex/marital status group for reasons outlined above.

In each case it was possible to explain over 50 per cent of the variance of earnings for married men and in two cases out of three rather more in the case of married women. In every case more of the variance is explained in the case of single employees and support is provided for the importance of marital status. Thus in the Financial Institution married men appear to be the exceptional group; running a regression for all groups other than married men revealed that the intercept was considerably lower than for married men and the relationship to length of service and professional qualifications much closer. In the Light Engineering company, in contrast, married women are the exception with a depreciation of salary for each year outside the plant and a much lower coefficient on education.

In the two cases where educational data were available, it proved to be highly significant (with the one exception referred to above) and in general the rate of return on education (given by the value of the coefficient) is not lower for women than for men, unlike many of the other studies to which reference has been made. It is the lower length of service of women that really depresses their earnings. It is noticeable in the case of the Light Engineering establishment that the coefficient in outside service is in fact higher than for inside service which is not suggestive of a pronounced ILM. The Local Government Service length of service data are more difficult to interpret since outside service includes experience within the local government sector and, therefore, relevant to the broader ILM in the sector as a whole. Since service with the company is a very good predictor of pay (other than for married men) in the case of the Financial Institution one would suggest that there is a strong ILM in that case. In general these factors do explain why married men earn more than single men who in turn earn more than

TABLE 4A.1 Earnings functions by sex and marital status for three Scottish establishments 1975/6

	Constant	Service	Service²	Outside Service	Outside Service²	Education	Diploma or Qualification	R²	Sample Size
1. *Local Government Service—White-Collar Employees*									
(a) Married Men	7.28	.0166 (3.83)	−.0008 (0.80)	.0366 (5.92)	−.0010 (5.70)	.0709 (8.45)	.1801 (2.82)	.69	78
(b) Married Women	6.35	.0474 (3.44)	−.0012 (2.44)	.0104 (1.56)	−.0001 (1.04)	.1174 (8.70)	−.0942 (0.34)	.62	64
(c) Single Men	6.48	.1124 (5.00)	−.0030 (3.24)	.0728 (3.21)	−.0006 (0.20)	.0832 (4.43)	.1787 (1.04)	.86	35
(d) Single Women	6.60	.0665 (8.53)	−.0012 (4.88)	.0624 (6.20)	−.0028 (6.02)	.0773 (7.46)	.4260 (2.95)	.88	68
2. *Financial Institution —White-Collar Employees*									
(a) Married Men	7.40	.0472 (2.10)	−.0005 (1.09)				.104 (1.21)	.52	52
(b) Married Women	7.24	.0619 (5.29)	−.0013 (2.73)					.76	33
(c) Single Men	7.01	.1117 (5.46)	−.0019 (4.42)				−.039 (0.40)	.97	13
(d) Single Women	7.03	.0889 (19.62)	−.0019 (12.72)				.139 (3.70)	.91	103

TABLE 4A.1 (contd.)

	Constant	Service	Service²	Outside Service	Outside Service²	Education	Diploma or Qualification	R²	Sample Size
3. Light Engineering—All Employees (on Common Salary Structure)									
(a) Married Men	6.66	.0526 (3.40)	-.0012 (1.80)	.0234 (2.03)	-.0009 (2.26)	.1037 (7.39)		.53	77
(b) Married Women	7.51	.0269 (1.54)	-.0002 (0.25)	-.0093 (0.89)	.0002 (0.71)	.0242 (0.96)		.30	50
(c) Single Men	6.88	.0379 (1.21)	-.0006 (0.49)	.0410 (1.33)	-.0020 (1.50)	.0799 (3.34)		.72	19
(d) Single Women	6.39	.0716 (6.97)	-.0018 (4.57)	.0137 (1.53)	-.0009 (2.09)	.1062 (9.99)		.75	54

( ) = t statistic

SOURCE
P. J. Sloane and W. S. Siebert (1977).

single women, with married women earning least of all (though married women do fare rather better in the Financial Institution). The fact, however, that not all the differences can be explained in such terms, implies that discrimination or variations in commitment to work are also relevant.

NOTES

1. For a full discussion of this in relation to female employment, see Chiplin and Sloane (1976(b)).
2. Thus Laws (in Blaxall & Reagan (eds) 1976) notes that 'after thirty years of research the question of the formation of occupational aspiration remains virtually pristine'.
3. Thus equity theory suggests that workers will adjust quantity or quality of output (according to the method of payment), where they feel under- or over-paid, in order to achieve an 'equitable' reward for their endeavours.
4. Blau and Justinius (in Blaxall & Reagan, 1976, op. cit.).
5. This interpretation of the ILM contrasts with that of the DLM theorists who claim, according to Wachter (1974), that:

> although efficiency factors are relevant to managerial decision-making in the ILM, they are not dominant. More specifically they claim that productivity at a high wage adheres to the job rather than the worker; that the wage structure is dominated not by efficiency considerations but rather by custom and habit; and that good jobs go to people who are already with the firm by methods of promotion that largely reflect institutional arrangements. Consequently the distribution of jobs and income in the primary sector is not dictated by ability and human capital.

6. See Chiplin and Sloane (1976(a)), the same authors (1976(b)) and Blau (in Edwards *et al.* (eds) 1975).
7. It is appropriate to assume, in general, that workers in the ELM are subject to unionisation to a smaller degree than workers in the ILM, if at all.
8. Salop and Salop suggest that a major problem for employers is to identify slow quitters and this can be achieved by a wage structure favouring length of service. This will make the income distribution more disparate, favouring men relative to women.
9. Spence notes that 'it is possible (and may be desirable) to make observable, unalterable characteristics like sex and race unobservable. To do so would probably involve an institutional or social decision. Colleges, for example, are forbidden in many states to seek to acquire information about an applicant's race, colour, religion, or national origin. There are obvious difficulties in designing effective disguises. But suppressing the observability of a characteristic does not make it adjustable.'
10. This is not to say that education does not provide any useful information, since in that event we would expect it to be discarded as a screen.

11. Standing (1976) has argued in contrast that screening may not favour educated women since such women may be prepared to undertake routine tasks to meet particular needs such as part-time employment or a job near to home, but be excluded on the grounds that they would not stay long in such a job.

12. G. S. Hamilton and J. D. Roessner (1972).

13. See H. C. Jain, 'Is Education Related to Job Performance?' in the same author (ed., 1974).

14. For the UK see *Department of Employment Gazette* (1975).

15. Steinberg (1975) found that over a five year period attachment to a particular ILM was *higher* among women than among men, among older workers than younger, and among middle as opposed to lower income recipients. However, despite their higher attachment to given ILMs, women did not exhibit as much upward mobility as men. But, these results may have been affected by the fact that workers employed at the beginning but not at the end of the period covered were excluded from the sample and individual employers are equated with ILMs.

16. Williamson *et al.* (1976) suggest that the principal impediment to effective inter-firm experience-rating is one of communication.

17. Thus as Williamson *et al.* (op. cit.) point out, both make the distinction between specific and general training whilst the human capital approach suggests that 'incumbent employees who have received specific training become valuable resources to the firm. Turnover is costly, since a similarly qualified but inexperienced employee would have to acquire the requisite task-specific skills before he would reach a level of productivity equivalent to that of an incumbent. A premium is accordingly offered to specifically trained employees to discourage turnover, although in principle a long-term contract would suffice.'

18. As Blaug (1976) and Mincer (in Atkinson, 1976) point out, a large number of phenomena including health, education, job search, information retrieval, migration and in-service training may be regarded as investments rather than consumption and are consequently aspects of human capital formation in which individuals may share unequally. Blaug also sees the 'screening hypothesis' or 'credentialism' as a rival to the human capital approach linking up to DLM or LMS theory.

19. Cf. Flanagan (1973):

> This is particularly relevant to the discussion of LMS, since the occupational wage structure should be weakly related to human capital investments if for a given level of investment there are barriers to moving freely among occupations.

20. Though as Blaug (op. cit.) notes, this model does not take into account 'the role of costless learning by doing as a simple function of time, not to mention the organisational imperatives of the ILM'.

21. They also point out, particularly in relation to marriage, that a bias may emerge because certain independent variables measure different things in men and women. Thus, using the equation for men together with the means of the women's characteristics variables in order to measure discrimination

is tantamount to saying that in the absence of discrimination married women would earn more than single ones. This suggests that it is necessary to run separate regressions not only according to sex but also according to marital status or, as in the case of Smith (1976) to introduce interaction terms between marital status and experience.

22. Thus the title of Osterman's Paper (1975) which is intended as a test of the DLM hypothesis is 'An Empirical Study of Labour Market Segmentation'.
23. See, for instance, Cain (1975).
24. Though the empirical results summarised below suggest that this is not common in practice.
25. Thus, Gordon (1972) notes:

> women are much less able than previously 'dis-advantaged' workers to identify with 'advantaged' workers and to follow their model in the transition to stable work. Further the social definition of family and sex roles continues to undercut employment stability among women. And, as the percentage of women in the labour force continues to increase, some employers seem more and more likely to move many jobs into the secondary market in response to the (expected) behavioural characteristics of secondary women employees.

26. Op. cit., p. 157.
27. Some doubt might, however, be cast on Piore's view that jobs neatly divided into 'good' and 'bad' categories. Thus dockers with unstable work and car workers with monotonous working conditions are but two examples of high wage jobs with poor job characteristics. Perhaps also some secondary jobs are 'exploratory' jobs for young people. See the discussion in Wachter (op. cit.).
28. The fact that the secondary sector contains the bulk of those with a low level of education and possibly a majority of the less able will lower the observed rate of return on education, thereby biasing downwards human capital coefficients.
29. Though they still explain a substantial part of the variance in earnings.
30. This problem is particularly well illustrated in the analysis of Ferber and Lowry (op. cit.). In order to investigate the extent to which sex segregation of jobs influences female earnings they set up regression models as below

$$(1) \quad Ym_i = b_0 + b_1 \ Em_i + b_2 \ Mi$$
$$(2) \quad Y_{fi} = b_0 + b_1 Ef_i + b_2 \ Mi$$

where Yi = median earnings in occupation i separately for men and women
Ei = median years of schooling
Mi = proportion of male employees in occupation i.

The results reveal that schooling is a better investment for men than for women, that earnings rise with the proportion of male employees, whilst the addition of an interaction term raises the explained variance from 76 to 84 per cent in the case of males and from 50 to 84 per cent in the case of females. They conclude that

> the lower earnings in occupations with a higher proportion of women cannot be ascribed solely to the lower productivity of women, unless, of course, one is prepared to believe that women's productivity is somehow adversely affected by the mere presence of men and that men become less productive when they work with women.

Given, however, that their model excludes experience this result is hardly surprising. If mean male experience exceeds that of females and is a significant determinant of earnings, then one would expect a positive relationship between the proportion of males in the labour force and earnings. But the implications to be drawn are quite different from those stated by the authors.

31. Thus, Gordon and Morton (op. cit.) found that unmarried males earned 2.7 per cent ($t = -2.25$) less than married males, whereas there was no such effect for women.

32. Details of these results are provided in Appendix 1.

33. Thus Becker in *Human Capital*, University of Chicago (1964) points out that:

> Many women drop out of college after marriage, and college women are more likely to marry educated and wealthy men. These well known facts suggest that women go to college partly to increase the probability of marrying a more desirable man. If the marriage factor were important, the gains to women from additional schooling should be determined by family earnings classified by the wife's education rather than by personal earnings so classified, and the full money gains to women may be much higher than previous estimates have indicated.

34. Flanagan notes that when employers are uncertain of the employment stability of job applicants, it may be possible to protect themselves against capital loss by shifting a larger proportion of the training costs (and returns) on to the trainee. However, anti-discrimination legislation prohibits the implied lower wage for a given amount of training. For what may be required is a lower wage for women, say, during training and a higher wage than men thereafter. It is doubtful, however, if employers would be allowed by male workers or their representatives to pay higher wages to female workers in this way on completion of training.

35. 'Class Productivity and the Ghetto: A Study of Labour Market Stratification' unpublished Ph.D. thesis, Harvard, Mass. (1971) reported in Edwards (1975).

36. Wachter (op. cit.) notes that neither the distribution of industries nor the distribution of workers by earnings shows any evidence of bipolarity. Whilst it is preferable to consider several rather than one variable, even here the results are mixed and the null hypothesis is that there is a continuum of jobs. Barron and Norris (op. cit.) do find, however, using British NES data bipolarity in relation to male and female earnings.

37. The danger of this procedure is that by segmenting workers into three separate groups one is denying the possibility of movement between groups. Yet upward mobility is precisely the way in which most of the gains to education are secured.

38. The independent variables in the model are age, years of schooling, race, weeks unemployed in the previous year, hours worked in the previous week and dummy variables for the industry in which the individual worked.

39. Osterman claims that the results show that policies designed to increase the human capital of secondary workers are not likely to improve their earnings. This claim is surprising in view of the fact that when separate equations were run for whites and blacks the education variables was significant for blacks in the secondary sector.

40. Leigh (1976) also found that inter-firm and inter-industry mobility was similar for blacks and whites in similar age groups and in general his findings 'cast doubt on the literal interpretation of the dual hypothesis as a guide for explaining labour market processes—at least during periods of full employment'.

41. See Blau and Justinius in Blaxall & Reagan (eds), 1976.

REFERENCES.

Alexander, Arthur J., 'Income, Experience and Internal Labour Markets', *Quarterly Journal of Economics* (February 1974).

Andresani, P. J., 'Discrimination, Segmentation and Upward Mobility: A Longitudinal Approach to the Dual Labour Market Theory', mimeographed, Temple University, Philadelphia (1976).

Atkinson, A. B. (ed.), *The Personal Distribution of Incomes* (London: Allen and Unwin, 1976).

Barron, R. D. & Norris, G. M., 'Sexual Divisions in the Labour Market', paper presented to the Conference on Sexual Divisions in Society, British Sociological Association (1974).

Blaug, M., 'The Empirical Status of Human Capital Theory: A Slightly Jaundiced Survey', *Journal of Economic Literature* (September 1976).

Blaxall, M. & Reagan, B. (eds), *Women and the Workplace: The Implications of Occupational Segregation* (Chicago: University of Chicago Press, 1976).

Bosanquet, N. & Doeringer, P. 'Is there a Dual Labour Market in Great Britain?' *Economic Journal* (June 1973).

Cain, G. G., 'The Challenge of Dual and Radical Theories of the Labour Market to Orthodox Theory', *American Economic Review*, Papers and Proceedings (May 1975).

Cassell, F. H., Director, S. M. and Doctors, S. I., 'Discrimination within Internal Labour Markets', *Industrial Relations* (October 1975).

Chiplin, B. & Sloane, P. J., 'Male/Female Earnings Differences: A Further Analysis', *British Journal of Industrial Relations*, (March 1976(a)).

——, *Sex Discrimination in the Labour Market* (London: Macmillan, 1976(b)).

——, 'Personal Characteristics and Sex Differentials in Professional Employment', *Economic Journal* (December 1976c).

Doeringer, P. B. & Piore, M. J., *Internal Labour Markets and Manpower Analysis*, D. C. Heath and Co. (Lexington, Mass., 1971).

——, 'Unemployment and the Dual Labour Market', *Public Interest* (Winter 1975).

Edwards, R. C., Reich, M. & Gordon, D. M. (eds), *Labour Market Segmentation*, D. C. Heath and Co. (Lexington, Mass., 1975).

Department of Employment 'Employers, Recruitment and the Employment Service', *Department of Employment Gazette* (December 1975).

Ferber, M. A. & Lowry, H. M., 'The Sex Differential in Earnings: A Reappraisal', *Industrial and Labour Relations Review*, vol. 29, no. 3 (1976a).

——, 'Sex and Race Differences in Non Academic Wages in A University', *The Journal of Human Resources*, vol. XI, no. 3 (1976b).

Flanagan, R. J., 'Segmented Market Theories and Racial Discrimination', *Industrial Relations* (October 1973).

Gordon, D. M., *Theories of Poverty and Under-employment: Orthodox, Radical and Dual Wage Perspectives* (Lexington, Mass., 1972).

Gordon, Nancy M. & Morton, T. E., 'The Staff Salary Structure of a Large Urban University', *The Journal of Human Resources*, vol. XI, no. 3 (1976).

Gwartney, J. & Stroup, R., 'Measurement of Employment Discrimination According to Sex', *Southern Economic Journal* (April 1973).

Hamilton, G. S. & Roessner, J. D., 'How Employers Screen Disadvantaged Job Applicants', *Monthly Labour Review* (September 1972).

Jain, H. C. (ed.), *Contemporary Issues in Canadian Personnel Administration* (Scarborough, Ontario: Prentice Hall, 1974).

Kerr, C., 'The Balkanisation of Labour Markets', in E. Wight Bakke *et al.*, *Labour Mobility and Economic Opportunity*, (Cambridge: Technology Press, 1954).

Klitgaard, R. A., 'The Dual Labour Market and Manpower Policy', *Monthly Labour Review* (November 1971).

Leigh, D. E., 'Occupational Advancement in the Late 1960s: An Indirect Test of the Dual Labour Market Hypothesis', *The Journal of Human Resources*, vol. XI, no. 2 (Spring 1976).

Lerner, S. W., Cable, J. R. & Gupta, S. (eds), *Workshop Wage Determination* (Pergamon, 1969).

Mackay, D. I. *et al.*, *Labour Markets under Different Employment Conditions* (Allen & Unwin, 1971).

Malkiel, G. B. and J. A. 'Male and Female Pay Differentials in Professional Employment', *American Economic Review* (September 1973).

Mincer, J., *Schooling, Experience and Earnings*, NBER (New York: Columbia University Press, 1974).

Mincer, J. & Polachek, S., 'Earnings of Women', *Journal of Political Economy*, part II (March/April 1974).

Osterman, Paul, 'An Empirical Study of Labour Market Segmentation', *Industrial and Labour Relations Review* (July 1975).

Piore, M. J., 'Jobs and Training', in *The State and the Poor*, S. H. Beer and R. E. Berringer (eds) (Winthrop, 1970).

Psacharopoulos, G. & Layard, R., 'Human Capital and Earnings: British Evidence and A Critique', unpublished manuscript, LSE (1976).

Rees, A. & Schultz, G. P., *Workers and Wages in an Urban Labour Market* (University of Chicago Press, 1970).

Rosen, Sherwin, 'Human Capital: A Survey of Empirical Research', *Department of Economics, University of Rochester, Discussion Paper* 76–2 (January 1976).

Salop, J. & S., 'Self-selection and Turnover in the Labour Market', *Quarterly Journal of Economics* (November 1976).

Slichter, S. H. *et al.*, *The Impact of Collective Bargaining on Management* (Washington: Brookings Institution, 1960).

Sloane, P. J. & Siebert, W. S., 'Hiring Practices and the Employment of Women', Paisley College of Technology, mimeographed (1977).

Smith, Sharon P., 'Government Wage Differentials by Sex', *The Journal of Human Resources* (Spring 1976).

Spence, A. M., *Market Signalling: Informational Transfer in Hiring and Related Screening Processes* (Cambridge, Mass: Harvard University Press, 1974).

Standing, G., 'Education and Female Participation in the Labour Force', *International Labour Review*, vol. 114, no. 3 (November/December 1976).

Steinberg, E., 'Upward Mobility in the Internal Labour Market', *Industrial Relations*, Berkeley, vol. 14, part 2 (May 1975).

Stiglitz, J. E., 'Approaches to the Economics of Discrimination', *American Economic Review, Papers and Proceedings* (May 1973).

Taira, K., 'Internal Labour Markets, Human Resource Utilisation and Economic Growth', *International Institute for Labour Studies*, Research Conference on Urban Labour Markets, Geneva (9–13 September 1976).

Wachtel, H. M. & Betsey, C., 'Employment at Low Wages', *Review of Economics and Statistics* (May 1972).

Wachter, M. L., 'Primary and Secondary Labour Markets: A Critique of the Dual Approach', *Brookings Papers on Economic Activity*, 3 (1974).

Williamson, O. E., Wachter, M. L. & Harris, J. E., 'Understanding the Employment Relation: The Analysis of Idiosyncratic Exchange', *The Bell Journal of Economics*, vol. 6, no. 1 (Spring 1976).

5 Low Pay and Female Employment in Canada with Selected References to the USA*

M. GUNDERSON and H. C. JAIN

INTRODUCTION

The pay position of females is becoming an increasingly important issue in the analyses of poverty and income distribution. Although the relationship between the wages of an individual and the long-run wealth of a family unit is extremely complex, the wages of females have important implications for the income position of various groups including the poor, those families who are out of poverty simply because both husband and wife work, the working poor, female-headed households, as well as single unattached females.

The purpose of this chapter is to discuss the low-pay position of females with particular emphasis on the relationship between their wages and the issue of poverty and income distribution. Although the focus of the analyses and the data sources are Canadian, the conclusions also pertain to the US; whenever major differences arise they are discussed in the text.

The second section provides a picture of the relationship between female employment and poverty by discussing the incidence and distribution of poverty by sex, the relationship between labour force

* Some of the Canadian data published in this report was collected for an earlier study, Gunderson (1976), which was financially supported by Statistics Canada and the Howe Research Institute.

participation and poverty, and the extent to which the low-pay jobs are dominated by females. The third section provides empirical evidence on male/female pay differentials and on their time patterns. The fourth discusses the factors associated with the low earnings of women, including their occupational-industrial distribution, hours and weeks worked, age, experience, education and unionisation. The paper concludes with a discussion of various policy options that are available to alter the low-pay position of women.

POVERTY AND FEMALE EMPLOYMENT

The relationship between poverty[1] and female employment is extremely complex. Economic poverty is related to long-run family wealth, of which the wages and employment of females is only one part. However, especially in recent years, the pay position of females has become increasingly important, not only for poverty families but also for all families and for unattached individuals, and not only for male-headed families but also for female-headed families.

INCIDENCE AND DISTRIBUTION OF POVERTY BY SEX

The incidence of poverty refers to the propensity of a particular group to be poor (i.e., the percentage of persons in each group who are poor). The distribution of poverty refers to the extent to which a particular group constitutes a large portion of the poor (i.e., the percentage of the poor who are in a particular group). The two can differ because of the size of the group under question.

As Table 5.1 indicates, female-headed families (and individuals) have a much higher incidence of poverty than male-headed families (or individuals); however, because there are fewer female-headed families than male-headed families, a larger proportion (distribution) of the poor are male-headed families. Over the 1969 to 1974 period the incidence of poverty fell markedly for male-headed families whereas it remained extremely high for female-headed families. In part of this reason, and in part because of the growth of female-headed families, by 1974 female-headed families constituted 30 per cent of poor families, compared to only 18 per cent in 1969.[2] In addition, almost half the unattached females were poor in 1969 and 1974, according to standards that considered the fact that they had no dependents.

The picture that emerges then is rather bleak. Almost half the

TABLE 5.1   Characteristics of poor[a] families and unattached individuals, Canada 1969 and 1974

Characteristic	Families Incidence[b] 1969	1974	Families Distribution[c] 1969	1974	Unattached individuals Incidence[b] 1969	1974	Unattached individuals Distribution[c] 1969	1974
Total	17	11	100	100	36	38	100	100
Sex[d]								
male	15	9	82	70	26	29	36	35
female	41	41	18	30	45	45	65	65
Age[d]								
under 25 years	16	16	5	8	24	38	25	23
25 to 65[e] years	14	10	65	70	23	24	25	31
over 65[e] years	38	19	30	22	57	58	50	46
Education[d]								
elementary[e]	36	18	40	50	65	62	32	45
some secondary	17	12	48	30	39	41	41	25
complete secondary[e]	7	6	10	18	25	25	23	26
complete university	4	3	2	2	12	16	4	4
Workers								
none	n.a.	51	n.a.	42	n.a.	74	n.a.	69
one	n.a.	13	n.a.	43	n.a.	18	n.a.	31
two plus	n.a.	3	n.a.	15	n.a.	0	n.a.	0
Major Income								
earnings	8	4	34	29	15	} 16	25	} 82
self employed	31	16	17	12	30		3	
transfers	79	56	43	52	85	84	58	6
other	25	15	6	7	29	23	14	12
Labour Force Status[d]								
in	n.a.	7	55	48	n.a.	19	35	31
out	48	34	45	52	68	67	65	69
Worked[d]								
full time	8	4	27	25	10	6	11	6
part time	21	16	30	26	32	39	26	28
didn't	53	38	43	49	71	72	63	66

SOURCE
Adopted from Statistics Canada, *Income Distribution in Canada*, no. 13–307, Tables 64 and 65 for 1974 figures and Statistics on Low Income in Canada, no. 13–554, 1969 Table 1 and for 1969 figures

NOTES
[a] Those below the poverty line, based on Statistics Canada revised and updated low-income cut-offs.
[b] Percent of families (unattached individuals) in each group who are poor.
[c] Percentage of poor who are in each group.
[d] Refers to head in the case of families.
[e] Figures are approximations since groups were often aggregated because of a similar incidence of poverty within groups.

unattached females and families headed by females are poor and they have remained so over a period when the incidence of poverty dropped rather markedly, even according to revised and updated poverty standards. In addition, females constitute a much larger and growing proportion of the poor:[3] almost one third of poor families are headed by a female and two thirds of poor unattached individuals are female.

Unfortunately, the data do not enable one to compare the labour market behaviour of female versus male headed families. However, unpublished data from the 1971 Canadian census indicate that 44 per cent of the 370,825 female-headed, one-parent families participated in the labour force, a figure that is higher than their overall participation rate of approximately 40 per cent for all females. Clearly labour market activity will be an important source of income for many female-headed families. The problems of the working poor (and hence the importance of the labour market) are highlighted by the figures for the distribution of poverty for families in 1974. The work status variable indicates that one half of the heads of poor families worked, and almost half of these in turn worked full time. The number of workers variable indicates that 15 per cent of poor families even had two or more persons working. The major income variable indicates that 29 per cent of poor families relied on employee earnings and 12 per cent on self-employed earnings for their major source of income; the proportions are much higher for unattached individuals. Clearly the labour market is an important source of income for most poor people and yet it does not provide sufficient income to raise many out of poverty.

The age variable indicates that the vast majority of poor families are headed by persons in the working ages of 25 to 65, although if the head is under 25 or over 65 then the family is more likely to be poor. For unattached individuals both the distribution and incidence of poverty is higher for the young and old. Increased education is associated with a lower incidence and distribution of poverty.

Table 5.2 also indicates the income problems of female-headed families, whether the head works or is not in the labour force. Much larger proportions of female rather than male-headed families are in low income groups, and this pattern prevails whether the head is employed or is not in the labour force. Since income comes from all sources (e.g., earnings, alimony, inheritances, transfers) then the low income position of employed female-heads is particularly striking: even with income from a variety of possible sources they are more likely to fall into low income groups than are male-headed families. One obvious reason for

TABLE 5.2   Percentage distribution of families by income group, labour force status and sex of head, Canada 1974 and 1967.[a]

Income Group	Employed		Not in Labour Force	
	Male	*Female*	*Male*	*Female*
		1974		
Under 4,000	1.6	9.3	16.3	39.2
4,000– 6,999	4.6	25.6	36.0	27.1
7.000– 9,999	11.6	22.5	17.4	13.2
10,000–14,999	31.0	27.3	16.5	11.4
Over 15,000	51.2	15.3	13.8	9.1
Total	100.0	100.0	100.0	100.0
Average Income	16,491	9,770	9,073	6,930
		1967		
Under 4,000	8.7	30.0	59.6	60.7
4,000– 6,999	32.5	39.5	24.9	26.8
7,000– 9,999	32.1	18.5	8.2	12.9
10,000–14,999	20.5	9.1	4.9	6.9
Over 15,000	6.2	2.9	2.4	2.6
Total	100.0	100.0	100.0	100.0
Average Income	8,430	6,063	4,539	4,905
Number (in '000)	3,026	112	519	213

SOURCE
Statistics Canada, *Income Distribution by Size in Canada*, no. 13–207, p. 36 of 1974 report for 1974 figures and p. 23 of 1967 report for 1967 figures.
NOTE
[a] The same money income groups are used for the two years even though inflation averaged about 5 per cent per year over that period.

this is that many male-headed families may have a working spouse, a possibility that is obviously precluded for female-headed families.

LABOUR FORCE PARTICIPATION AND POVERTY

The rapid growth in the labour force participation rate of women highlights the point that increasingly the family income depends heavily on the earnings of both the husband and wife. Regarding women's earnings as secondary or supplementary is becoming increasingly archaic under today's circumstances of large numbers of female-headed families and families whose income depends crucially on the earnings of both the husband and wife or on the earnings of the wife if the husband is unemployed.

The primacy of the economic motives for working are all illustrated in the large number of studies analysing the labour force participation decisions of married women. The Canadian studies are reviewed, for example in Spencer (1974) and Gunderson (1977(a)). Other things equal, married women are more likely to participate when they can earn a high wage in the labour market, when family obligations for the care of the children are not present, and when economic necessity compels them to engage in labour market activities.[4] Married women in families with low income are much more likely to participate in the labour force so as to raise their family income. Gunderson (1977(a)), for example, finds that married women in families with an income of less than 3000 dollars (excluding their own income) are almost 30 per cent more likely to participate in labour force activity than married women in families whose income exceeds 15,000 dollars. The higher participation rate of married women in low-income families suggests that many families may have income above the poverty line simply because both husband and wife work. Alternatively stated, labour force participation by many married women may be a prerequisite to raise families from poverty. If this is the case, then earnings in the labour market become an important focus for the study of poverty.

LOW PAY JOBS AND FEMALE EMPLOYMENT

The previous analysis highlighted the importance of the pay position of women in the overall picture of poverty and income distribution. Female-headed families are likely to be poor and they constitute a large and growing percentage of the poverty population. In addition, labour market earnings are an important source of income for the working poor who constitute a large portion of the poor and for the large and increasing number of families where both husband and wife work. Obviously the pay position of women must be given serious consideration in any analysis of poverty and income distribution.

Table 5.3 lists the current low-pay jobs (earnings below the average) in Canada and ranks them, for low to high, in terms of their earnings. Clearly, relative to their overall representation of 29 per cent in all jobs, females are much more heavily represented in the low-pay jobs. They constitute a disproportionately large share of the low-wage service, trade and nondurable manufacturing jobs. This pattern is also evident in the data of Appendix 11 and in other tabulations to follow, especially on the occupational and industrial distribution of females.

TABLE 5.3   Low pay jobs[a] and female employment, Canada, 1976

Industry[b]	Earnings	Percentage female
Total industrial composite	234.81	29
Motion picture: service	99.56	16
Hotels, restaurants: service	113.01	51
Variety stores: trade	116.31	67
Apparel stores: trade	126.09	62
Service to buildings: service	126.61	42
Laundries: service	140.82	63
Department stores: trade	142.32	63
Children's clothing: manufacturing	144.53	78
Fish products: manufacturing	151.49	37
Women's clothing: manufacturing	151.62	80
Shoe: manufacturing	151.92	62
Men's clothing: manufacturing	153.30	72
Luggage: manufacturing	156.44	57
Hosiery: manufacturing	157.76	69
Food stores: trade	161.38	42
Toy: manufacturing	172.96	49
Rubber footware: manufacturing	178.48	52
Furniture stores: trade	182.85	32
Woollen: manufacturing	184.40	38
Fruit canners: manufacturing	186.15	36
Cotton: manufacturing	186.16	36
Forestry services: forestry	186.98	2
Household furniture: manufacturing	189.26	24
Confectionery: manufacturing	199.82	49
Plastic: manufacturing	199.86	31
Alcohol stores: trade	201.12	12
Drug preparation: trade	204.01	39
Bakeries: manufacturing	206.87	26
Biscuits: manufacturing	208.31	47
Wholesalers: trade	210.18	37
Lumber: trade	210.86	18
Misc. electric prod.: manufacturing	211.61	47
Door and flooring: manufacturing	215.29	15
Miscellaneous textiles: manufacturing	216.11	57
Radio, television: manufacturing	216.30	44
Synthetic textiles: manufacturing	216.81	28
Furniture: manufacturing	217.14	21
Insurance carriers	219.19	54
Clay products: manufacturing	220.40	17
Electric appliances: manufacturing	221.08	16
Bus transport: transportation, communications and utilities	221.36	20

Table 5.3   *(contd.)*

Industry[b]	Earnings	Percentage female
Food: trade	224.30	29
Motor vehicles: trade	225.63	17
Advertising: service	228.41	63
Heating equipment: manufacturing	229.82	15
Other paper: manufacturing	229.77	33
Soft drinks: manufacturing	232.31	11
Miscellaneous food: manufacturing	232.91	32
Paint: manufacturing	234.04	19
Hardware: manufacturing	234.62	29

SOURCE
Statistics Canada, *Employment Earnings and Hours*, no. 72–002 (Nov. 1976) Table 2. The data are based on the monthly survey of employment and payrolls in companies of 20 or more employees only. Consequently, the small firms which pay disproportionately lower wages are not covered.

NOTES
[a] Jobs with weekly earnings below the average industrial composite of 235 dollars per week. The jobs are ranked from low to high in terms of the average weekly earnings of all employees.
[b] The title following the colon refers to the major industry group.

EVIDENCE OF MALE/FEMALE PAY DIFFERENTIALS

Although few in number, existing Canadian studies tend to confirm the existence of substantial differences in pay between men and women. These studies are reviewed in Gunderson (1975(b)) and Agarwal & Jain (1978). As expected, as one controls or standardises for productivity-related factors the gap diminishes. Care must be exercised in following this procedure, however, since many of the productivity-related factors themselves may be subject to discrimination: to 'remove' the effect of productivity-related factors, then, is not to remove the effect of discrimination. Even after controlling for productivity factors, however a sizeable gap still remains.

UNADJUSTED AND ADJUSTED EARNINGS RATIO

Ostry (1968), for example, computes the ratio of female to male annual earnings for all workers to be .54 based on 1961 Canadian census data. Adjustments for part-time and part-year employment, occupational distribution, age and education raised the ratio to .81. Based on 1967 data from the Survey of Consumer Finances, Holmes (1976) estimates the potential lifetime earnings of females to average only 41 per cent of male potential earnings. Adjusting for productivity-related factors raises the ratio to .56 for males and females with similar productivity-related characteristics. In rough rank order of importance these characteristics were weeks worked, occupation and marital status, with class of worker, residence region and immigration status having a distinctly minor impact.

WAGE DIFFERENTIALS IN THE SAME JOB

The use of aggregate data, as in the Ostry and Holmes study, necessitates controlling for productivity-related factors so as to compare wage differentials for similar (productivity-adjusted) workers. Data limitations usually preclude anything more than crude adjustments for these productivity factors. Consequently it is instructive to examine wage differentials within narrowly-defined occupations with identical job descriptions and within the same industry. Thus inter-industry and interoccupational wage differentials do not get compounded with the sex differential in earnings; in effect, it becomes possible to focus on wage discrimination rather than occupational and industrial segregation.

Table 5.4 gives such a tabulation. Clearly the ratio of female to male wages is higher when we focus on wage differentials only, yet a considerable wage gap remains, even within the same occupation and industry. There appears to be considerable variation in the wage gap, and yet no obvious pattern emerges. Within the same industry, different occupations have considerably different earnings ratios, and for the same occupation, the ratios vary considerably by industry. In addition there does not appear to be any systematic relationship between the magnitude of the earnings gap and the female wage in the job.

This latter statement is confirmed in a more systematic study by Gunderson (1978) based on both US and Canadian data. The study concludes:

The earnings ratio was nonlinearly related to the average income of the occupations, with females doing best relative to males in upper-middle income jobs and females doing poorest relative to males in lower-income jobs and in the very high income jobs. Although the nonlinear relationship between the earnings ratio and the income of

TABLE 5.4   Female wages and ratio of female/male wage in same narrowly defined occupations, Canada 1966–72

Industry: Occupation[a]	1966 W_f	1966 W_f/W_m	1967 W_f	1967 W_f/W_m	1968 W_f	1968 W_f/W_m	1969 W_f	1969 W_f/W_m	1970 W_f	1970 W_f/W_m	1971 W_f	1971 W_f/W_m	1972 W_f	1972 W_f/W_m
Fish: packer	.89	.80	.99	.83	1.10	.89	1.15	.92	1.25	.90	1.41	.88	1.60	.93
Biscuits: helper	1.61	.89	1.81	.90	1.93	.91	2.18	.88	2.24	.86	2.51	.90	2.85	.94
Bakeries: helper	1.39	.79	1.57	.81	1.76	.84	1.89	.80	2.12	.85	2.10	.81	2.22	.78
machine operator	1.59	.79	1.71	.80	1.88	.78	1.92	.72	2.10	.75	2.56	.88	2.85	.92
Tobacco: machine op.	2.65	.94	2.76	.94	3.17	.96	3.36	.93	3.70	.94	4.02	.95	4.11	.87
labourer	2.23	.92	2.38	.92	2.64	.96	2.73	.90	3.16	.91	3.44	.90	3.62	.91
Rubber products: inspector	1.42	.65	1.62	.72	1.76	.77	1.74	.71	1.78	.67	1.94	.70	2.17	.68
Tanneries: finisher	1.55	.83	1.73	.88	1.92	.94	2.02	.90	2.29	.99	2.44	.90	2.79	.98
Cloth: twister	1.28	.84	1.36	.85	1.59	.86	1.71	.86	1.88	.89	1.95	.89	2.14	.96
operator	1.39	.87	1.45	.85	1.61	.88	1.86	.94	n.a.	n.a.	2.06	.91	2.28	.92
Textiles: grader	1.64	1.01	1.79	1.01	1.91	1.01	2.14	1.12	2.25	1.06	2.50	1.16	2.74	1.17
spinner	1.46	.67	1.69	.74	1.85	.76	1.90	.71	2.22	.72	2.22	.69	2.45	.72
thrower	1.39	.67	1.59	.75	1.70	.75	1.82	.72	1.95	.74	2.11	.73	2.69	.87
Knitted goods: knitter circular	1.18	.69	1.25	.70	1.41	.76	1.44	.73	1.55	.75	1.74	.79	2.06	.86
knitter	1.29	.73	1.34	.71	1.48	.76	1.60	.76	1.77	.81	1.87	.80	2.01	.81
cutter	1.26	.66	1.37	.69	1.42	.66	1.53	.69	1.75	.74	1.84	.71	2.07	.75
hand operator	1.19	.85	1.22	.79	1.29	.76	1.41	.79	1.48	.73	1.67	.80	1.84	.80
Clothing: fitter	1.31	.66	1.37	.69	1.44	.66	1.56	.71	1.60	.72	1.69	.71	1.90	.77
joiner	1.27	.68	1.41	.71	1.41	.71	1.58	.72	1.82	.78	1.85	.77	1.99	.81
lining sewer	1.33	.77	1.42	.77	1.57	.88	1.66	.86	1.74	.83	1.91	.88	2.09	.80
pocket maker	1.34	.66	1.41	.68	1.53	.71	1.63	.71	1.77	.74	1.91	.74	2.05	.73
finish presser	1.44	.65	1.59	.65	1.76	.70	1.86	.66	2.13	.71	2.52	.79	2.81	.77
sewing operator	1.25	.79	1.37	.59	1.49	.61	1.50	.58	1.70	.55	1.90	.61	2.11	.68

TABLE 5.4 (contd.)

Industry: Occupation[a]	1966 W_f	1966 W_{fl}/W_m	1967 W_f	1967 W_{fl}/W_m	1968 W_f	1968 W_{fl}/W_m	1969 W_f	1969 W_{fl}/W_m	1970 W_f	1970 W_{fl}/W_m	1971 W_f	1971 W_{fl}/W_m	1972 W_f	1972 W_{fl}/W_m
Fur goods: fur op.	2.14	.72	2.30	.76	2.63	.79	2.97	.89	3.05	.83	3.24	.83	3.41	.85
Plywood mills: grader	1.73	.90	1.94	.90	2.25	1.04	2.00	.78	2.19	.77	2.28	.77	2.31	.70
patcher	2.26	.94	2.36	.87	2.57	.90	2.86	.94	3.08	.97	3.60	.97	3.78	.94
Paper boxes: bundler	1.39	.72	1.65	.89	1.62	.72	1.86	.77	1.99	.77	2.37	.85	2.60	.88
stitcher operator	1.78	.82	2.00	.87	2.14	.86	2.18	.87	2.32	.80	2.74	.92	2.89	.87
Wire: assembler	n.a.	n.a.	1.81	.66	2.05	.72	1.94	.66	2.01	.82	2.06	.76	2.22	.70
Motor parts: machine op.	1.64	.66	1.51	.57	1.68	.60	1.89	.61	2.25	.67	2.24	.66	2.42	.68
Appliances: assembler	1.37	.71	1.47	.68	1.53	.69	1.74	.74	1.88	.78	2.03	.89	2.21	.85
press operator	1.40	.84	1.48	.80	1.60	.79	1.84	.89	2.01	.93	2.20	.94	2.49	1.02
Radio: aligner	n.a.	n.a.	n.a.	n.a.	2.02	.80	2.16	.82	2.48	.89	2.76	.92	2.88	.90
assembler	1.53	.86	1.56	.83	1.83	.92	1.90	.87	2.15	.90	2.34	.90	2.41	.93
inspector	1.68	.82	1.77	.77	2.22	.88	2.00	.78	2.40	.75	2.89	.90	3.18	.99
Communications: assembler	1.50	.87	1.62	.92	1.70	.86	1.88	.87	2.01	.80	2.10	.76	2.23	.76
fitter	1.87	.80	1.99	.78	2.07	.76	2.13	.75	2.44	.78	2.42	.76	2.89	.83
wirer	1.84	.84	1.87	.72	2.11	.84	2.31	.87	2.13	.76	2.27	.77	2.37	.76
inspector, electrical	1.64	.68	1.78	.66	1.94	.71	1.99	.64	1.94	.59	2.39	.71	2.38	.67
inspector, receive	1.66	.65	2.11	.79	2.22	.79	2.30	.77	2.40	.75	2.61	.82	2.60	.71
Electric eqpt.: assembler	1.67	.70	1.76	.75	1.88	.74	1.95	.73	1.90	.70	2.13	.72	2.29	.77
winder	1.91	.89	1.94	.85	2.07	.83	2.19	.80	n.a.	n.a.	2.47	.77	2.84	.86
Pharmacy: packager	1.46	.81	1.59	.85	1.66	.84	1.86	.90	2.07	.89	2.25	.94	2.39	.86
Paint: labeller	1.77	.83	1.79	.76	1.93	.74	2.17	.77	2.44	.79	2.52	.76	2.82	.82

Table 5.4 (contd.)

Industry: Occupation^a	1966		1967		1968		1969		1970		1971		1972	
	W_f	W_{fl}/W_m	W_f	W_{fl}/W_m	W_f	W_{fl}/W_m	W_f	W_{fl}/W_m	W_f	W_{fl}/W_m	W_f	W_{fl}/W_m	W_f	W_{fl}/W_m
Laundry: presser	1.32	.73	1.39	.75	1.46	.77	1.56	.75	1.64	.79	1.84	.83	1.83	.73
Hotel (large): dishwasher	2.39	1.06	2.47	1.02	2.63	1.02	1.61	1.06	1.59	.96	1.83	.99	2.06	1.05
Hotel (small): dishwasher	2.00	.94	2.13	.99	2.32	.97	1.35	.99	1.50	1.02	1.62	1.01	1.79	1.02

SOURCE:
Computed from data in *Wage Rates, Salaries and Hours of Labour*, Ottawa; Canada Dept. of Labour, annual.

NOTES:
a The industry preceeds the colon: the occupation follows. Additional occupations are indented. The occupations were selected if they had male-female wage data for the years 1966–72. Changes in the survey since 1972 precluded getting more recent estimates.

the occupation was statistically significant it was quantitatively not very large. Similarly, although the relationship between the female to male earnings ratio and the ratio of female to male employment was positive and statistically significant, it was quantitatively unimportant. The conclusion that emerges is that there is little systematic relationship between the male-female earnings gap and the average income or sex composition of the occupation.

It is also instructive to examine male-female wage differentials for the same narrowly-defined occupations within the same *establishment*, in part, because equal pay legislation is applied at the level of the establishment, and in part because *intra*establishment differentials also control for compensating differentials associated with location (region, urban/rural) or the establishment itself (size, profitability). In Gunderson (1975(a)) only those occupations with identical detailed job descriptions were compared (consequently the important issue of job segregation was not considered). Although the use of identical job descriptions does not necessitate that males and females do exactly the same work, the following observations suggest that the work is very similar. First, the occupations are extremely narrowly defined and where they are not sufficiently narrow, they were broken into subgroupings. Second, where obvious discrepancies exist between the work of males and females, then females are put into different groupings.

The study found that the ratio of female to male wages within the same narrowly-defined occupations within the same establishment averaged 0.82. Even in such identical jobs the productivity of males and females may not be the same. In jobs with an incentive pay system the female to male pay ratio was 0.88. To the extent that wages are paid according to productivity under an incentive pay system then the earnings ratio of 0.88 could be taken to reflect the true productivity of females relative to males in those jobs. If this were the case then wage discrimination (unequal pay for equal work) would account for one third of the wage gap and productivity differences the remaining two thirds. That is, in narrowly-defined occupations, if female productivity is 0.88 of male productivity, but they are paid only 0.82 of male wages, then this wage discrimination of 0.06 (i.e., $0.88 - 0.82$) is one third (.06/.18) of the wage gap of 0.18, and productivity differences of 0.12 (i.e., $1.00 - 0.88$) are two thirds (0.12/0.18) of the wage gap of 0.18.

As the author points out, however, not only does this measure not consider the important issue of job segregation, but also it is probably a conservative measure of wage discrimination because it does not account for possible discrimination in the incentive system itself. Such discrimination could occur if women received a lower guaranteed wage than men, or if they were given job assignments that make it more difficult to earn production bonuses or if the evaluation system itself is based somewhat on the subjective judgement of individuals.

In spite of these problems, the measure probably provides a more accurate picture of the amount of *wage* discrimination than the gross and productivity-adjusted ratios discussed earlier. It is simply hard to believe that profit maximising (or even cost conscious) firms would pass up the opportunity to employ females who are as productive as males but who would accept a wage only 50, or 60 or even 80 per cent of the male wage. It seems much more believable that female labour market productivity in narrowly-defined occupations is 0.88 of male productivity (for reasons outlined later) but that they tend to be paid only 0.82 of male wages so that wage discrimination accounts for about one third of the wage gap and productivity differences the remaining two thirds.[5]

HOUSEHOLD VERSUS WAGE DISCRIMINATION

The extent to which the productivity differences themselves arise because of discrimination is really an unanswered question. The rubric 'productivity differences' tends to be a catch-all to reflect differences in such factors as absenteeism, turnover, experience and on-the-job training. Sex differences in these characteristics in turn arise in large part because of discrimination outside the labour market, in particular within the household (see Gunderson, 1976(a), and Agarwal and Jain, 1978). High female absenteeism can be associated with their segregation into tedious dead-end jobs as well as their bearing the primary responsibility for household tasks including the care of children (and husbands!) when they are ill and absent from school or work. Because of their primary responsibility for household tasks, women also have shorter and more intermittent stays in the labour force, thus preventing them from acquiring continuous work experience and on-the-job training. The vicious circle is obvious: women have a comparative advantage in household tasks because of their low wages in the labour market; they have low wages in the labour market in part because of their prime responsibility for household tasks. Hence the possibility that equal pay is not possible without a more equitable division of labour in the household.

The preceding discussion suggested that about one third of the male/female wage gap in identical jobs could be attributed to wage discrimination in the labour market and the remaining two thirds to productivity differences, with an undetermined part of the productivity differences attributable to non-labour-market discrimination, particularly to discrimination within the household.[6] Since it is difficult to imagine innate (be there such a thing) productivity differences that matter for the occupations analysed, it seems reasonable to assume that most, if not all, of the two thirds of the wage gap attributable to productivity differences arises because of non-labour-market discrimination.

Assigning more of the wage gap to non-labour-market discrimination rather than wage discrimination in the labour market seems reasonable since non-labour-market institutions (including the household) are not as subject to the profit-maximising, cost-minimising constraints of employers in the labour market. In the long run, firms may go out of business (or in the public sector come under taxpayer criticism) if they do not hire the cheapest labour. However, educational institutions that channel females into 'female-type' courses, or households that require females to do their full complement of household tasks while maintaining a job in the labour market, need not adjust as quickly to labour market realities. In essence, non-labour-market institutions, including the household, are more tradition and custom bound and are under less external pressure to adjust, than are employers in the labour market. Consequently, the quest for equal pay must go beyond the attack on wage discrimination in the labour market.

CHANGES IN MALE/FEMALE EARNINGS OVER TIME

Economic theory does not yield unambiguous predictions concerning the impact of the passage of time (both trend and cycle) on the male/female earning gap. There are, of course, a variety of powerful forces at work over time that should serve to reduce the earnings gap. Competition should ensure that profit maximising firms would hire lower wage females who are as productive as males and this should serve to raise the wages of females relative to males. Increased education and knowledge would reduce discrimination arising out of erroneous information and may even alter tastes and preferences away from discrimination. The large growth of the female labour force, especially since the 1950s, may serve to break down sex stereotypes. Increased urbanisation and improved transportation and communication may break down monopsonistic discrimination that can arise because females do not have the effect threat of mobility (they are often tied to the household and to their husband's place of employment) necessary to command a competitive wage. Recent adoption of equal pay and fair employment laws should also narrow the gap over time.

On the other hand, there are a variety of forces at work to widen the male/female earnings gap over time. As income grows over time, individuals may be able to satisfy more or all of their wants, perhaps including their tastes for discrimination. Also, the rapid increase in female labour force participation may depress female wages both directly because of the supply influx, and indirectly because their greater numbers may increase discrimination because they are regarded as more of a threat. Equal pay and equal employment laws may even have a perverse effect, widening the earnings gap, by reducing training options for women who would accept low present wages to acquire training for higher future wages. In addition, equal pay laws may create unemployment amongst females and crowd them further into low productivity jobs.

Unfortunately, there is little systematic empirical evidence on the trend of female earnings relative to male earnings. The Canadian and US studies are reviewed in Gunderson (1976(b), pp. 57 and 58) and the conclusion reached that, although the evidence is scant and often contradictory, it certainly does not point to an unambiguous narrowing of the gap over time; if anything, the gap appears to be widening over the long run.

In that same study which was designed specifically to ascertain the time pattern of male/female wage differentials, it was found that the gap actually widened over time, especially during the 1960s, and that there was no narrowing of the gap during periods of prosperity and tight labour markets; in fact, it may even widen in such times. In addition, there was no clear narrowing of the differential over time in response to stricter enforcement of equal pay legislation. This later conclusion is confirmed in a separate cross-sectional analysis in Gunderson (1975(a)).

FACTORS ASSOCIATED WITH LOW EARNINGS OF WOMEN

Labour-market earnings have both a price and quantity dimension in that they are a combination of wages times hours employed. Low earnings, therefore, can result from being employed for a small number of hours and/or having low hourly earnings. Each of these components—hours and wages—in turn has a variety of dimensions.

Reduced hours of work may be associated with part-time, part-year work. Low hourly wages may be associated with being in a low wage industry or occupation, having small endowments of human capital (experience, education), as well as receiving unequal pay for equal work. In the following sections, we discuss various factors associated with the earnings of women and attempt to relate these factors to their low pay position and to male/female earnings differences.

OCCUPATIONAL PATTERN

Table 5.5 gives the occupational pattern of the female labour force in Canada as of 1971 for the approximately 20 broad intermediate occupations. As the last column indicates, over half the female labour force is distributed in the low-wage clerical, service and sales occupations—31.7, 15.0, and 8.4 per cent respectively. The male labour force, in contrast, is distributed much more evenly across the various occupations. As the second column indicates, whereas females constitute approximately 34 per cent of the labour force, they constitute a much smaller proportion of the managerial and administrative jobs and a much larger portion of the jobs in the clerical and service sectors.[7]

Broad occupational groupings can mask considerable occupational segregation that goes on within occupations. To illustrate this point, Table 5.6 gives the occupational pattern of the female labour force for select occupations that were broken down to highlight the occupational segregation that can occur within the broader categories. For example, the high proportion of the female labour force in medicine and health (8.2 per cent from earlier Table 5.5) occurs because of the large numbers of females in nursing (6.9 per cent of the female labour force according to Table 5.6) rather than in the higher paying physician/surgeon categories. This pattern of being in the lower wage jobs within the broad occupation aggregates is repeated in various cases. Their large numbers in the teaching profession (7.1 per cent from Table 5.5) occur because 6.9 per cent of the female labour force is in elementary and secondary school teaching, rather than in the higher paid colleges and universities.[8] Their large numbers in the service sector are concentrated in the general service categories rather than the higher paid protective service jobs.

Column 2 of Table 5.6 also highlights some interesting points concerning this intraoccupational segregation. For example, within the processing sector where they are under-represented (17.8 per cent according to Table 5.5), they are more important in the food and textile

TABLE 5.5 Occupational pattern of female labour force in Canada, intermediate occupational groups, 1971 census

| Occupation | Female labour force | Proportion female[a] | Distribution of labour force[b] | |
			Male	Female
Managerial & administrative	58,305	15.7	5.5	1.9
Science, engineering, math.	17,110	7.3	3.8	0.5
Social sciences	29,525	37.3	0.9	1.0
Religion	3,710	15.7	0.3	0.1
Teaching	211,125	60.4	2.4	7.1
Medicine & health	242,690	74.3	1.5	8.2
Arts & recreation	21,895	27.2	1.0	0.7
Clerical	940,180	68.4	7.6	31.7
Sales	247,760	30.4	10.2	8.4
Service	447,985	46.2	9.2	15.0
Farm	106,845	20.7	7.2	3.6
Fishing, hunting, trapping	520	1.9	0.5	0.1
Forestry, logging	1,410	2.1	1.2	0.1
Mining	380	0.6	1.0	0.1
Processing	59,565	17.8	4.9	2.0
Machining	13,680	5.7	4.0	0.5
Product fabricating	150,210	23.7	8.5	5.1
Construction	5,125	0.9	9.9	0.2
Transport operating	8,190	2.4	5.8	0.3
Material handling	40,450	19.7	2.9	1.4
Other crafts & equip. op.	13,545	12.4	1.7	0.5
Not elsewhere classified	21,730	12.7	2.6	0.7
Not stated	319,275	43.3	7.4	10.8
Total	2,961,210	34.3	100	100

SOURCE
Computed from *Occupations by Sex*, 1971 Census. Statistics Canada no. 94–
717, vol. III, part 2, Bulletin 3.2–3 (September 1974).

NOTES
[a] Proportion of the labour force in each occupation that is female. The male
proportion is simply 100 minus the female proportion.
[b] Proportion of the labour force for each sex that is in each occupation. When
the occupation had less than 0.1 per cent of the labour force, it was rounded
upwards to 0.1.

processing as opposed to metal, chemical or wood processing. Similarly,
within fabricating they are over-represented in textile fabricating and
under-represented in non-textile fabricating. Their activities in the
labour force appear to be a carry-over from many of their household
tasks.

TABLE 5.6 Occupational pattern of female labour force in Canada, select occupations,[a] 1971 census

Occupation	Female Labour Force	Proportion Female[b]	Distribution of labour force[c]	
			Male	Female
Managerial & admin.	58,305	15.7	5.5	1.9
Professional	141,040	24.0	7.9	4.8
School teaching	180,515	66.2	1.6	6.1
Nursing	204,500	87.7	0.5	6.9
Clerical	940,180	68.5	7.6	31.6
Sales	247,760	30.4	10.0	8.4
Protective service	7,930	3.9	3.5	0.3
Service	440,055	57.4	5.6	14.8
Primary	109,155	16.4	9.9	3.7
Metal & chemical proc.	11,260	10.5	1.7	0.4
Food processing	31,910	25.9	1.6	1.1
Wood processing	2,165	3.1	1.2	0.1
Textile processing	14,220	38.8	0.4	0.5
Machinery	13,680	5.7	4.0	0.5
Non-textile fabricating	50,605	10.3	7.9	1.7
Textile fabricating	99,605	70.0	0.8	3.4
Construction	5,125	0.9	9.9	0.2
Transport operator	8,190	2.4	5.8	0.3
Materials handling	40,450	19.7	2.9	1.4
Craftworker	13,545	12.4	1.7	0.5
Not elsewhere classified	21,730	13.0	2.6	0.7
Not stated	319,275	43.3	7.4	10.7
Total	2,961,210	34.3	100	100

SOURCE
Computed from *Occupations by Sex*, 1971 Census. Statistics Canada no. 94–714, vol. III, part Bulletin 3.2–3 (September 1974).

NOTES
[a] The occupations were broken down so as to highlight certain female dominated occupations, e.g. textile fabricating versus non-textile fabricating.
[b] Proportion of the labour force in each occupation that is female. The male proportion is simply 100 minus the female proportion.
[c] Proportion of the labour force for each sex that is in each occupation.

This later point highlights the importance of tradition and historically determined roles in the job allocation of labour. It is hard to imagine there being much real carry-over of skills from household production of food and clothing to factory production as it occurs today. Surely most of the skills applicable to food and textile processing and fabricating are also applicable to metal and wood processing and non-textile fabricating. And yet females dominate the former, and males the latter, to an extent that hardly seems explicable on grounds other than tradition and historical determinancy.

This suggests that we should not uncritically accept the argument that females dominate certain occupations because they have a comparative advantage in performing these jobs, perhaps because of their strength, dexterity or because of the limited time they can commit to such jobs. While this may explain some occupational choice, it does not seem capable of explaining their predominance, for example, in the food and clothing sectors within the processing and fabricating industries.

Appendix 11 provides an even more detailed picture of the representation of females in more narrowly-defined occupations, specifically the four digit CCDO level. The more detailed occupation groups provide further confirmation that within the broad occupational categories women predominate in the lower ranks and in many of the jobs that are a carry-over from household activities. They are, for example, over-represented as administrators in medicine and health but under-represented in other managerial capacities; they predominate in teaching at the elementary and kindergarten levels, but their relative importance declines at higher levels.

The recent time pattern of the occupational distribution of the female labour force is given in Table 5.7. Clearly dramatic changes have not occured in recent years in spite of the fact that equal employment opportunity legislation (fair employment laws) became prominent in that period.

In an earlier study, Gunderson (1976(a), p. 116) also indicated that during the 1960s when equal opportunity laws generally came into force, the decline in occupational segregation was only normal; not large as one may expect if the laws had a wide impact. However, over the longer period from 1901 to 1971 the distribution of females across the broad occupational categories consistently became more even; that is, there was a modest decline in occupational segregation (at least between broad occupational aggregates) over the extreme long run. It appears that legislation has not had an impact over and above the impact of basic forces that have been at work over time.

INDUSTRIAL PATTERN

The industrial pattern of female employment also exhibits considerable segregation into the low wage sector and into those industries that are

TABLE 5.7 Occupational distribution[a] of employed women, Canada 1966–1973

Occupation[b]	1966	1967	1968	1969	1970	1971[c]	1972	1973
Clerical	30.6	30.7	31.6	32.1	32.2	32.7	32.9	34.1
Service, recreation	22.2	22.6	22.5	22.3	22.6	22.3	21.4	20.6
Professional, technical	17.5	17.2	17.4	17.4	17.5	17.5	17.3	17.5
Crafts, production	12.0	11.8	11.0	11.2	10.5	10.2	10.9	11.1
Sales	8.3	8.4	8.4	8.2	8.3	8.3	8.1	8.3
Managerial	3.6	3.7	3.8	3.6	3.9	3.9	4.2	4.2
Farm	3.0	3.0	2.8	2.8	2.5	2.5	2.5	2.2
Communications	1.6	1.6	1.5	1.3	1.3	1.3	1.3	1.2
Labourers	1.0	0.9	0.8	0.8	0.9	1.0	1.1	0.7

SOURCE
Canada Manpower and Immigration Review, vol. 8, no. 1 (First Quarter 1975) p. 20.

NOTES
[a] Female employment in each occupation as a percentage of the total female employment in all occupations. Columns may not sum to 100 due to rounding.
[b] The occupations are ranked in descending order according to their percentage distribution.
[c] Figures for 1971 may not correspond to those given in earlier tables because the earlier tables referred to the labour force (not just employed women) and because they were based on the 1971 census whereas the above estimates are from the Labour Force Survey.

closely related to household tasks. As the last column of Table 5.8 indicates, relative to their typical representation of 34 per cent in all industries, women are over-represented in the leather-textile-knitting-clothing manufacturing, retail trade, finance-insurance-reality, and in the service sector.[9]

The 'all industries' ratio (last entry but one) gives the considerable growth of the female labour force in Canada, constituting 17 per cent of the total labour force in 1961 and 34 per cent by 1971. As the consistently declining coefficient of variation (last entry) indicates, the female labour force also became more evenly dispersed across the various industries over time. As with the occupational distribution, it appears that some desegregration has occurred in the industrial distribution of females, yet considerable occupational and industrial segmentation still persists.

Table 5.9 gives an alternative picture of the industrial pattern of

TABLE 5.8 Proportion of labour force, in each industry, that is female, census years 1931–71

Industry	1931	1941	1951	1961	1971
Agriculture	.02	.02	.04	.12	.23
Forestry	.01	.01	.08	.02	.05
Fishing & trapping	.01	.01	.01	.01	.04
Mines, quarries, oil	.01	.01	.02	.04	.07
Manufacturing	.17	.19	.20	.21	.24
Durable manufacturing	.05	.07	.09	.10	.14
Wood products	.02	.03	.05	.06	.07
Furniture & fixtures	.07	.08	.10	.12	.19
Metals[a]	.07	.10	.13	.13	.17
Transport equipment	.02	.04	.05	.06	.11
Non-metallic	.05	.09	.11	.10	.13
Non-Durable manufacturing	.29	.32	.31	.31	.32
Food & beverages	.16	.18	.22	.24	.27
Tobacco products	.49	.57	.55	.49	.41
Rubber	.23	.25	.24	.22	.19
Leather	.20	.26	.32	.38	.50
Textile	.40	.38	.35	.33	.38
Knitting	.60	.60	.60	.63	.64
Clothing	.60	.62	.62	.66	.71
Paper	.11	.14	.13	.12	.13
Printing	.20	.21	.25	.26	.30
Petrol & coal	n.a.	n.a.	.09	.10	.14
Chemical products	.18	.19	.22	.24	.24
Miscellaneous mfg.	.18	.28	.33	.31	.35
Construction	.01	.01	.02	.02	.05
Transport & communications	.08	.07	.12	.14	.17
Trade	.22	.24	.30	.32	.37
Wholesale	.14	.16	.19	.18	.23
Retail	.23	.27	.34	.38	.42
Finance, insurance, realty	.27	.32	.44	.46	.51
Services[b]	.54	.58	.50	.50	.50
Unspecified	.02	.11	.19	.26	.44
All industries	.17	.20	.22	.28	.34
Coefficient of variation[c]	.91	.89	.77	.75	.65

SOURCE
1931–61 figures based on tables D1–D3 in N. Meltz, *Manpower in Canada 1931–1961*. Ottawa: Dept. of Manpower and Immigration (1969). Figures for 1971 are from *Industry by Sex*, 1971 Census, Statistics Canada No. 94–740, vol. III, part 2, Bulletin 3.4–3 (December 1974).

NOTES
[a] For 1931–61 metals consists of iron and steel products, non-ferrous metal products, and electrical apparatus and supplies. For 1971 metals consists of primary metals, metal fabricating, machinery and electrical products.
[b] Includes public administration and defence.
[c] Standard deviation of the series divided by its mean.

Table 5.9 Distribution of female labour force across each industry, census years 1931–71

Industry	1931	1941	1951	1961	1971
Agriculture	3.64	2.30	3.02	4.47	3.77
Forestry	.11	.06	.20	.12	.11
Fishing & trapping	.11	.04	.04	.03	.03
Mines; quarries, oil	.05	.07	.20	.27	.42
Manufacturing	18.46	21.77	23.61	17.42	13.42
Durable manufacturing	2.51	4.59	5.60	4.17	3.87
Wood products	.19	.29	.50	.35	.24
Furniture & fixtures	.19	.19	.26	.24	.29
Metals[1]	1.55	3.07	3.66	2.68	2.51
Transport equipment	.36	.74	.84	.64	.60
Non-metallic	.21	.30	.33	.26	.24
Non-durable manufacturing	15.95	17.17	18.02	13.26	9.55
Food & beverages	1.99	1.83	2.96	2.70	2.17
Tobacco products	.55	.54	.40	.25	.12
Rubber	.48	.48	.44	.23	.16
Leather	1.00	1.19	1.05	.80	.49
Textile	2.72	3.02	2.37	1.15	.88
Knitting	.88	1.02	1.19	.71	.39
Clothing	5.67	5.92	5.25	3.59	2.28
Paper	.69	.81	.98	.72	.54
Printing	1.16	.93	1.38	1.23	1.04
Petrol & coal	n.a.	n.a.	.11	.10	.09
Chemical products	.44	.86	.99	.96	.63
Miscellaneous mfg.	.36	.58	.91	.82	.74
Construction	.24	.18	.52	.65	.89
Transport & communications	3.40	2.37	4.19	3.59	3.85
Trade	12.80	13.54	18.19	17.13	15.71
wholesale	1.32	1.90	3.13	2.99	2.69
retail	11.47	11.64	15.06	14.14	13.06
Finance, Insurance, Realty	3.75	3.41	5.50	5.93	6.22
Services[2]	56.72	55.43	42.97	47.52	45.23
Unspecified	.56	.59	1.12	2.38	10.17

SOURCE
1931–61 Figures based on tables D1–D3 in N. Meltz, *Manpower in Canada 1931–1961*. Ottawa: Dept. of Manpower and Immigration, 1969. Figures for 1971 are from *Industry by Sex*, 1971 Census, Statistics Canada no. 94–740, vol. III, part 2, Bulletin 3.4–3 (December 1974).

NOTES
[1] For 1931–61 metals consists of iron and steel products, non-ferrous metal products, and electrical apparatus and supplies. For 1971 metals consists of primary metals, metal fabricating, machinery and electrical products.
[2] Includes public administration and defence.

female employment by indicating the proportion of the total female work force that is in each industry. In 1971, nearly half the female work force were still in the service sector and almost 60 per cent were in services or retail trade.[10] Obviously many of the problems of low wages for women are problems of being in the low wage service and retail trade sector. Unfortunately, policies to alter their position will be difficult because these sectors are traditionally ones that are hard to unionise or to enforce legislation upon.

The recent time pattern of the industrial distribution of the female workforce is given in Table 5.10. As with the occupational distribution no dramatic changes in the broad industrial distribution have occurred in recent years. Fair employment laws notwithstanding, the recent changes are simply a part of the long-run evolution as documented earlier.

TABLE 5.10   Industrial distribution[a] of employed women, Canada 1966–73

Industry[b]	1966	1967	1968	1969	1970	1971[c]	1972	1973
Services	45.1	45.6	46.0	45.6	47.1	46.7	46.0	45.1
Trade	17.8	17.7	18.1	17.8	17.8	17.5	18.3	18.7
Manufacturing	17.7	17.2	16.1	16.3	15.3	15.4	15.6	15.6
Finance[d]	6.6	6.4	6.7	6.9	7.0	7.4	7.2	7.5
Public admin.	4.4	4.6	4.6	4.8	4.7	5.1	5.0	5.3
Trans/com/ut.[e]	4.1	4.2	4.4	4.4	4.2	4.0	4.0	4.3
Agriculture	3.1	3.1	2.9	2.9	2.7	2.6	2.7	2.3
Construction	0.8	0.8	0.8	0.9	0.8	0.9	0.9	0.9

SOURCE
Canada Manpower and Immigration Review, vol. 8, no. 1, (First Quarter 1975) p. 19.
NOTES
[a] Female employment in each industry as a percentage of the total female employment in all industries. Columns may not sum to 100 due to rounding.
[b] The industries are ranked in descending order according to their percentage distribution.
[c] Figures for 1971 may not correspond to those given in earlier tables, which referred to the labour force (not just employed women) and because they were based on the 1971 census whereas the above estimates are from the Labour Force Survey.
[d] Includes insurance and real estate.
[e] Transportation, communications and utilities.

HOURS AND WEEKS WORKED

For a variety of reasons, including their responsibility for household tasks, women tend to work fewer weeks per year and fewer hours per week than do men. Table 5.11 indicates the rapid growth in part-time employment (less than 30 hours per week) for the labour force as a whole, and the last column indicates that women constitute a large and increasing share of this growing total part-time employment. However, as the last three columns indicate, although married women still have a higher probability of working part-time, in recent years the importance

TABLE 5.11   Part time employment,[a] Canada 1953–1973

Year	Proportion employment that is part-time	Proportion part-time that is female	Proportion of employed women working part-time		
			Single	Married	Other[b]
1953	3.8	63.5	n.a.	n.a.	n.a.
1954	4.0	64.4	n.a.	n.a.	n.a.
1955	4.2	64.4	n.a.	n.a.	n.a.
1956	4.4	67.5	n.a.	n.a.	n.a.
1957	5.0	66.1	n.a.	n.a.	n.a.
1958	6.1	65.3	n.a.	n.a.	n.a.
1959	6.3	65.9	n.a.	n.a.	n.a.
1960	6.7	66.5	n.a.	n.a.	n.a.
1961	7.9	66.4	n.a.	n.a.	n.a.
1962	8.0	65.8	n.a.	n.a.	n.a.
1963	8.3	66.9	n.a.	n.a.	n.a.
1964	9.0	67.0	n.a.	n.a.	n.a.
1965	9.6	67.9	n.a.	n.a.	n.a.
1966	9.5	68.7	12.4	28.6	18.1
1967	10.1	67.8	13.7	28.3	18.2
1968	11.0	67.8	16.4	29.0	17.9
1969	11.6	67.4	17.7	29.1	19.2
1970	12.3	65.8	19.5	28.9	19.1
1971	12.5	65.9	20.7	28.0	19.5
1972	12.5	67.0	21.4	27.7	19.0
1973	12.4	67.9	21.8	27.2	18.2

SOURCE
Canada Manpower and Immigration Review, vol. 8, no. 1, (First Quarter 1975) p. 17.
NOTE
[a] Usually worked less than 30 hours per week.
[b] Separated, widowed or divorced.

of part-time employment has grown most for single women.[11] This suggests that family responsibilities are not the only reason for the high rate of part-time employment amongst women.

Table 5.12 gives a more detailed breakdown of the hours worked per week by men and women. Clearly, women tend to work fewer hours per week than do men, and between 1964 and 1974 they increased their representation in the lower categories of hours worked per week.

TABLE 5.12   Cumulative percentage distribution of employed labour force by hours worked per week, Canada 1964 and 1974

	1964			1974		
Hours per week	Men	Women	Percentage female[a]	Men	Women	Percentage female[a]
0	4.4	4.3	28.5	6.9	6.5	33.4
1–14	6.9	12.9	60.6	9.6	15.4	63.0
15–24	9.6	21.8	56.9	13.2	26.5	61.8
24–34	17.3	34.4	39.1	18.3	36.2	50.2
35–44	65.2	86.9	30.7	73.3	92.2	35.1
45–54	84.0	95.7	15.9	88.3	97.2	15.0
55 +	100.0	100.0	9.8	100.0	100.0	11.1
Total	n.a.	n.a.	28.8	n.a.	n.a.	34.6

SOURCE
Women in the Labour Force: Facts and Figures, Women's Bureau, Canada Department of Labour, Ottawa: Information Canada (1975) p. 25.
NOTE
[a] Women as percentage of the total labour force in each category of hours worked per week.

Not only do women tend to work fewer hours per week than men, but also they tend to work fewer weeks per year. Table 5.13 indicates that with the exception of the youngest age groups, larger proportions of women than men tend to work only part of the year. For the age groups of prime working age (25 to 54), for example, the proportions of women working only 1–13 weeks tend to be four or five times as high as the proportion of men working only 1–13 weeks, and the proportion of women working 14–26 weeks tends to be twice as high as the proportion of men working only 14–26 weeks. Conversely whereas almost three-quarters of males aged 25 to 54 work 49–52 weeks, only about half the females aged 25 to 54 work 49–52 weeks. The pattern is similar for full-time workers also.

Obviously the earnings of women and their earnings relative to male

TABLE 5.13 Proportion of workers in each category of weeks worked, by age and sex, Canada 1970

Age (years)	1–13 Weeks		14–26 Weeks		27–39 Weeks		40–48 Weeks		49–52 Weeks	
	M	F	M	F	M	F	M	F	M	F
					All workers					
15–19	.43	.41	.22	.22	.11	.12	.08	.09	.16	.16
20–24	.13	.14	.17	.17	.15	.13	.15	.13	.41	.43
25–34	.03	.14	.06	.14	.09	.12	.14	.14	.68	.48
35–44	.02	.12	.04	.11	.07	.11	.13	.15	.73	.50
45–54	.03	.10	.05	.09	.07	.10	.14	.15	.72	.56
55–64	.04	.09	.06	.09	.08	.10	.14	.15	.67	.57
65 +	.12	.12	.13	.12	.12	.12	.14	.16	.49	.47
					Full-time workers only					
15–19	.42	.36	.20	.22	.11	.12	.09	.10	.17	.20
20–24	.10	.11	.15	.15	.14	.12	.15	.14	.46	.49
25–34	.02	.08	.05	.11	.08	.11	.14	.14	.71	.56
35–44	.02	.07	.04	.08	.06	.09	.13	.15	.75	.62
45–54	.02	.05	.04	.06	.06	.07	.14	.15	.75	.67
55–64	.03	.05	.05	.06	.07	.07	.14	.15	.71	.67
65 +	.08	.08	.10	.09	.10	.09	.15	.16	.57	.58

SOURCE
Computed from data given in 1971 Census of Canada, *Labour Force Activity–Work Experience*, Catalogue 94–779, pp. 21–2.

earnings will reflect their greater propensity to work part-time and part-year. It is especially important in comparing annual earnings, for example, to control for differences in hours and weeks worked. Based on 1961 Canadian census data, Ostry (1968, p. 41) estimated the ratio of female to male annual earnings to be 0.54 for all wage earners and 0.59 for first-year, full-time workers only. Based on 1971 data, Gunderson (1976, p. 121) estimates the ratios to be 0.50 for all wage earners and 0.59 or full-year, full-time workers.

These ratios highlight a number of important points. The overall earnings gap between the sexes has actually widened over the 1960s for all workers, although the constancy of the gap for full-time, full-year workers suggests that much of this widening occurred because of increases in part-time, part-year employment of females. Also, although the adjustment for hours and weeks worked did close the earnings gap somewhat, the magnitude of the reduction was not large; even for men and women who work full-time all of the year, the earnings gap is extremely large. When the ratios were computed for separate occupations in 1971, the hours and weeks work adjustment raised the earnings ratio most for the predominantly female sales and service occupations, suggesting that the extremely low unadjusted earnings ratio for these occupations is due in large part to the lower hours and weeks worked by females in these occupations.

For various separate categories of weeks worked, Table 5.14 gives the ratio of female to male earnings. Tabulating by the separate categories of weeks worked indicates that even when they work approximately the same number of weeks as men (that is, within each category), females earn only a fraction of what males earn. Although the pattern is not definite, especially in 1972, it appears that the earnings ratio rises as the number of weeks worked falls. Thus women who are part-year workers tend to earn closer to what male part-year workers earn, although the gap is still large.[12]

TABLE 5.14   Ratio of female/male annual earnings, by weeks worked, Canada 1967 and 1972

Weeks worked	1967	1972
50–52	.54	.55
40–49	.55	.58
30–39	.53	.54
20–29	.59	.59
10–19	.66	.61
0–9	.71	.54

SOURCE
Computed for data given in *Women in the Labour Force: Facts and Figures*, Women's Bureau, Labour Canada (1975) p. 67.

AGE-EXPERIENCE

Because they tend to leave the labour force for household responsibilities—especially the bearing and rearing of children—females tend to have shorter and more intermittent stays in the labour force than males. Consequently they do not accumulate as much continuous labour market experience, on-the-job training, and leaning-by-doing. In addition, both females and employers are reluctant to invest heavily in their human capital, for fear of not being able to reap the full benefits. In part, for these reasons, female earnings may fall below male earnings, and females may enter jobs where continuous work histories are not so important.

Empirical evidence on experience differences between males and females is extremely hard to come by, in part because of the dearth of longitudinal, work-history data. Consequently age (or age minus education minus six) is often used as an imperfect proxy for accumulated work experience, realising that it may over-estimate the experience of females with interrupted labour market careers.

Table 5.15 gives the percentage distribution of the labour force by age group for men and women in 1964 and 1974. Clearly a larger proportion of the female labour force is in the younger age groups. However, this pattern is much more noticeable in 1964 than in 1974: over time the age distribution of the female work force is becoming more like that of the male work force. Appendix 13 also indicates that proportionately more of the female labour force is in the younger age groups and that females have less cumulated and continuous labour market experience than do men.

TABLE 5.15 Percentage distribution of the male and female labour force, Canada 1964 and 1974

	Women		Men	
Age group	1964	1974	1964	1974
14–19	15.3	14.6	8.0	10.2
20–24	16.8	19.2	11.0	14.3
25–34	18.3	23.0	22.7	24.8
35–44	20.6	17.7	23.6	19.5
45–54	17.8	16.0	19.0	17.8
55–64	8.9	8.3	12.1	11.3
65 and over	2.3	1.2	3.6	2.2
All ages	100.0	100.0	100.0	100.0

SOURCE
Women in the Labour Force: Facts and Figures, Women's Bureau, Labour Canada, Ottawa: Information Canada (1974).

Based on 1971 Canadian census data on full-time, full-year workers, Gunderson (1976(a), p. 138) finds that proportionately more females are in the younger age groups and that, more important, the dollar earnings increments associated with additional age are smaller for females than males: in essence their age-earnings profiles are lower and flatter, reflecting their lack of rewards for cumulated work experience. This is also reflected in the fact that (ibid., p. 125) female/male earnings ratios decline with age. The ratio is 0.89 for 15 to 19 year olds, 0.77 for 20 to 24 year olds, 0.66 for 25 to 34 year olds, and thereafter it declines to approximately 0.60. Obviously younger males and females are more similar in their (lack of) accumulated work experience and this is reflected in the much smaller earnings differential for younger workers.

US data also indicate that female earnings rise less rapidly with age than do male earnings. Oaxaca (1971, p. 67) finds that 'the estimated experience-net wage profiles tend to be flatter and peak earlier for females'. He also finds (ibid., p. 77) that single, never-married females have experience-wage profiles vary similar to those of men. In other words, women who accumulate similar labour market experience as men will have their wages rise over their lifetime in a similar fashion as male wages.

Blinder also finds that working males and females differ only by a small amount with respect to their average age, but that the percentage wage increments associated with additional age are much larger for males than females. He concludes (1973, p. 448):

> women exhibit an almost flat age-wage profile—that is, their wages do not show any tendency to rise over the life cycle, whereas wages for white men certainly do. Thus, the failure of women in the same education-occupation category to rise on the economic ladder over their working lives is seen to be the single largest cause of the male/ female different·al amongst   ·ites.

Clearly, one of the important explanations for the low wages of females is their lack of cumulated work experience. From a policy point of view it is not possible to give people such work experience. However, it is possible to alter factors that prevent women from accumulating continuous work history. Since most of the discontinuities in work history occur because women tend to have primary responsibilities for household tasks—usually associated with the bearing and raising of children—then policies to ease those responsibilities will have an obvious impact on their work history. Day care, maternity leave, and flexitime are obvious policies. More difficult to change—but perhaps more important in their impact—would be attitudes within the household itself concerning the shared responsibility of household tasks when both husband and wife work in the labour market.

EDUCATION

The relationship between the education of females and their low pay position is a complicated process and depends on a variety of factors, including the extent of their education, their type of education, the effect of education on their earnings and the determinants of their education decision. Especially important in the latter regard is the effect of family income, since if education is a means of breaking the poverty cycle, and if high family income is a prerequisite to acquiring education, then the vicious circle of low income and low education is obvious.

In Canada, the average years of education of the female labour force is slightly higher than that of the male labour force, although the difference is small. For full-year, full-time wage earners, for example, females have an average of 11 years education versus 10.8 years for males. Robb and Spencer (1976, p. 76) also indicate similar enrolment rates for males and females between the ages of 16 and 21. Although their average educational attainment tends to be similar for males and females, the dispersion is larger for males since they are more likely to drop out earlier but also they are more likely to acquire more advanced education.

Although their level of education tends to be similar, the *type* of education acquired by males and females tends to be dissimilar. As Robb and Spencer point out, females remain concentrated in their traditional fields of study such as arts, education and nursing.[13] In addition, the rapid expansion of education in job-oriented community colleges has been male dominated and females remain insignificant in numbers in the government-supported, job-oriented apprenticeship system. On the other hand, females have made notable inroads into some traditionally male fields of study, notably law, medicine and commerce.[14] Also their representation in government-sponsored institutional and industrial training programmes tends to be increasing slightly and is roughly equal to their representation in the labour force. On net then it appears that women tend to acquire education and training that is less job-market oriented than males and that most of the inroads into male-dominated fields of study have occurred at higher professional level jobs. Consequently, one cannot expect that changes in the education or training of females will have a dramatic impact on their position as low wage employees.

The effect of education and training on the earnings of females and on male/female earnings differentials is still a matter of considerable debate. Appendix 2 indicates that increased education improves the earnings of both males and females but that the impact is larger for females as evidenced by the increased ratio of female to male earnings at higher levels of education. Holmes (1976, p. 114) finds that 'with higher levels of education, females are better able to compete with males for higher paying jobs and are less likely to be forced into overcrowded occupations where their productivity and rate of pay is low'. Gunderson (1977(b)) also finds that for full-time, full-year wage earners, the percentage increase in annual earnings associated with an additional year of education is greater for women than for men. For example, for men and women with eight years of education, the percentage increase associated with an additional year of education is 5.5 per cent for women and 3.7 per cent for men. This suggests that working women with low levels of education could improve their earnings position relative to similar men by acquiring additional education. In this sense, education seems to be a viable policy to improve the wages of the less educated working women.

This conclusion should be regarded as highly tentative not only because of the preliminary analysis on which it is based, but also because it is not one that has been substantiated by various empirical studies. In the US, for example, Blinder (1973, p. 448) finds that although males and females have similar levels of education, 'men earn much larger wage increments for advancing to higher educational levels'. A careful examination of his regression coefficients, however, indicates that *at lower levels of education* (up to 11 years) women get larger percentage wage increases than men when they advance their education levels. Consequently, our conclusion regarding the viability of education in increasing the earnings of low wage women may still hold. Oaxaca's (op. cit., p. 133) empirical evidence, on the other hand, indicates that even for low levels of education, the return to an additional year of education is greater for males than females. Specifically, evaluating his regression coefficients (ibid., p. 133) indicates that for men and women of eight years of schooling, the percentage increase in hourly wages resulting from an additional year of education is 3.5 per cent for males and only 1.9 per cent for females. Obviously these differences would have to be reconciled before it is possible to derive conclusive statements on the viability of increased education as a mechanism to improve the wages of low wage women and, for that matter, men.

If it were found that increased education improved the earnings of low wage women, then the next step would be to examine the possibility of altering their education decision. Based on their analysis of the 1971 Canadian census data, Robb and Spencer (op. cit., p. 82) conclude that 'enrolment rates for both sexes rise with education of the father, with the education of the mother, and, although with less consistency, with family income. Less support is found for independent systematic effects of province of residence, language of the home, and family size.' This suggests the pesimistic conclusion that women from low income, uneducated families will themselves be unlikely to acquire much education to improve their low earnings position. It also suggests, however, that once the cycle is broken, it is likely to remain broken.

The Robb and Spencer analyses for Canada also indicate that these background factors did not account for much of the variation in enrolment rates. The large unexplained variance led them to speculate that less quantifiable factors such as social pressures, the media, the school system itself and career opportunities may be important factors, and that (p. 87) 'fundamental changes in the way that people view the roles of men and women in society would be required to reduce the differentials'.

UNIONISATION

The total effect of unionisation on the average earnings of women relative to men depends both on the impact of unions on the wages of males and females and on the extent of unionisation of males and females. In the study by Gunderson (1975(a), pp. 467–8) unions were shown to have a substantial impact on raising the wages of females relative to males. Specifically, within narrowly-defined occupations within the same establishment unions raised the ratio of female to male wages from 0.82 to 0.90, thereby closing almost half the gap. The higher earnings associated with unionisation is also illustrated in the more aggregate data of Appendix 12 where the female/male earnings ratio is 0.42 for non-union workers and 0.60 for union workers. Based on US data, the percentage increase in wages associated with unionism was 0.28 for females and 0.23 for males according to Blinder (op. cit., p. 453) and 0.15 for females and 0.11 for males according to Oaxaca (op. cit., p. 133).

Although unionism appears to have a larger impact on the wages of females relative to males, a much smaller percentage of women are unionised, and consequently only a few get the wage benefits of unionisation. The total impact of unionisation—which is the product of the union impact on wages and the proportion of the labour force unionised—actually favours male wages because their larger proportion organised dominates their smaller union impact. Alternatively stated, males have a larger 'endowment' of unionisation, and this tends to swamp the fact that their returns from unionisation are smaller. Thus,

Oaxaca's estimates (op. cit., p. 141) indicate that the total impact of unionisation is to raise wages by 0.021 for males (union impact of 0.11 times extent organised of 0.28) and to raise wages by only 0.018 for females (larger union impact of 0.15 times smaller extent organised of 0.12), and that consequently the presence of unionism lowers the ratio of female to male wages.

The policy implications that follow from this analysis are important. Unions can be an effective device for raising the wages of both males and females and for narrowing the male/female wage differential. Consequently the encouragement of the unionisation of the female work force can be an important device to raise the wages of low-wage females and to reduce the earnings gap between the sexes. This would be especially effective in raising the wages of low-wage females because by bargaining for (roughly) equal absolute wage increases for different skill levels, unions have a larger percentage wage impact on the wages of the low paid.

The encouragement of the unionisation of low-wage females may be expecially important to counteract the spillover effect that may occur as the excess supplies of labour from the more heavily unionised male workforce exerts downward pressure on wages in the less unionised female workforce. In essence, the unionisation of the male workforce fosters the labour market segmentation and overcrowding into the non-unionised female jobs. Extending the benefits of unionisation into the female workforce, especially into the low-wage sectors, may be a way of breaking up the labour market segmentation and improving the wages of low-wage women.

There is considerable scope for increased unionisation of the female work force in Canada. As Table 5.16 indicates, by 1972 only 22 per cent of the female workforce was organised, compared to 38 per cent for men. In addition, industries with lowest degree of unionisation—trade, finance and services—are predominantly female.[15]

Increased unionisation of females will not be without its difficulties, since there are powerful forces that have restricted the growth of unionism amongst females. The predominantly female industries are difficult to organise for various reasons including the small firm size and the lack of militancy and worker consciousness amongst white-collar workers. The organising difficulties in these sectors is confirmed by the fact that male unionisation is also low in trade, finance and services. Also, because of their shorter and more intermittent stays in the labour force and because their income is often regarded as a supplement to family income, females may place a lower value on the benefits of

TABLE 5.16   Union membership as a proportion of paid workers, by industry and sex, Canada 1967–1972[a]

	1967		1968		1969		1971		1972	
Industry	Males	Females	Males	Females	Males	Females	Males	Females	Males	Females
Manufac-turing	47.7	32.1	46.5	34.3	45.9	36.5	46.9	35.0	45.5	34.5
Transpor-tation	54.3	38.3	60.3	39.8	56.0	41.8	53.9	50.9	52.2	51.1
Trade	8.7	9.4	11.7	9.7	10.5	6.1	9.8	6.7	8.4	6.9
Finance	5.4	2.1	4.0	1.3	2.8	2.0	0.8	0.8	1.7	0.9
Services	18.4	14.4	22.5	16.5	22.0	17.2	24.0	20.9	23.0	20.9
Public admin.	72.5	61.3	64.6	52.3	74.8	53.5	69.9	61.6	61.4	59.7
Total[b]	39.9	19.3	39.7	20.1	39.5	20.4	39.8	22.6	38.1	22.3

SOURCE
Women in the Labour Force: Facts and Figures. Workmen's Bureau, Labour Canada, Ottawa: Information Canada, unions issues.

NOTE
[a] Figures for 1970 are not available.
[b] Total includes all industries, including construction, agriculture, forestry and fishing.

unionism. Since many of these inhibiting factors are diminishing over time, we would expect some increase in the unionisation of women over time. This is confirmed by the data of Table 5.16 which indicates that even between 1967 and 1972 the proportion of the female workforce that is unionised increased from 19 to 22 per cent, compared to a slight decline from 40 to 38 per cent for males.[16]

If unionisation of female workers is to expand and if that unionisation is to be effective in representing women, then women must take a more active role in the management of the union. During the early 1970s, for example, women constituted only about 10 per cent of the executive board members of unions, even though they constituted about 25 per cent of all union membership.[17] Obviously any growth in female union membership would have to be accompanied by an increased role in running the unions, otherwise it is unlikely that they would share in the benefits of unionisation.

SUMMARY AND POLICY IMPLICATIONS

SUMMARY

The pay position of females is becoming an increasingly important issue in the analysis of poverty and income distribution. Females are a large and growing component of the labour force. Their contribution to the earnings of the family is increasingly being regarded as essential rather than secondary; in fact for some families, female earnings are necessary to raise the family out of poverty. Female-headed families are growing, they are likely to be poor, and they constitute a large and growing percentage of the poverty population. In addition, labour market earnings are an important source of income for the numerous working poor and for the large and increasing number of families where both husband and wife work. Obviously the pay position of women has important implications for the income of the poor, the non-poor, the working poor, and for both male and female-headed households as well as single unattached individuals.

Empirical evidence tends to confirm the existence of a substantial pay gap between the sexes. Typically, the earnings of females tend to be about 0.50 of the earnings of males, and for full-time, full-year workers the ratio is more in the neighbourhood of 0.60. Even within the same narrowly-defined occupation within the same industry the ratio is in the neighbourhood of 0.75 (with considerable variation) and within the same establishment the ratio is about 0.80. Wage discrimination probably accounts for about a third of the remaining gap with productivity differences accounting for two thirds: most of the productivity differences probably arise because of discrimination outside of the labour market, especially in the household.

Limited empirical evidence also suggests that the earnings gap between the sexes is not obviously narrowing over time (it may even be widening), it does not narrow during the tight labour markets at the peak of a business cycle and most important, there is no obvious narrowing in response to stricter enforcement of equal pay for equal work legislation. Occupational and industrial segregation appear to have been reduced somewhat; however, the process has been extremely slow and does not appear to have been accelerated by recent equal employment opportunity (fair employment) laws.

A variety of factors are associated with the low earnings of women. They tend to work in the low-wage clerical, service, sales and nondurable manufacturing jobs and even when they are in higher earnings jobs, they are at the lower rungs of the pay scale. Many of their jobs are ones that are traditionally hard to unionise or to enforce legislation upon. To a large extent their occupational-industrial distribution tends to reflect many of their household tasks, suggesting the importance of historically determined roles in the allocation of labour.

Women constitute a large and increasing share of the growing part-time employment and they tend to work fewer weeks per year than men. Adjusting for these factors, however, only raises the ratio of female to male earnings by a small amount, at most from 0.50 to 0.60.

Women also have shorter and more intermittent stays in the labour force, and hence do not accumulate as much continuous labour market experience as do men. The importance of this factor is highlighted by the fact that when accumulated work experience is similar, as it is for young males and females or with males and single, never-married females, then female earnings are much closer to male earnings.

Increased education is associated with higher earnings for both males and females; however, its impact on the earnings differential is still a matter of debate. Although males and females tend to have similar amounts of education, female education is not as job-oriented as male education. Making their education more labour-market oriented, however, will require fundamental changes in the attitudes concerning the roles of men and women in society.

Unionisation tends to be associated with higher earnings for both males and females; however, the effect appears to be larger for females as evidenced by the smaller earnings gap in unionised sectors. Since a much smaller percentage of women are unionised, however, only a few get the benefits of unionisation. Consequently the total impact of unionisation—which is the product of the union impact on wages and the proportion of the labour force unionised—actually favours male earnings because their larger proportion organised dominates their smaller wage impact.

POLICY IMPLICATIONS

Subject to the various reservations and qualifications outlined in the text, a variety of policy implications arise from the analysis.

1. Although the feasibility and desirability of altering the wage structure so as to alter the income distribution is beyond the scope of this chapter, the analysis of poverty and income distribution clearly requires an analysis of the pay position of women.
2. The passage of time will not remove the problem of unequal pay, although it may *slowly* erode occupational and industrial segregation.
3. Equal pay for equal work and equal employment opportunity legislation, at least as they have been enforced in Canada, have not

had significant impact on narrowing male/female wage differentials or occupational segregation. Perhaps in time their impact will be felt; however, the results are not yet apparent.

4. Increased unionisation of the female workforce has the potential for a large impact on closing the earnings differential both because unionisation appears to raise the relative wages of females more than males and because the small proportion of females presently unionised provides the opportunity for increased unionisation of the female workforce. There is also ample room for increased participation of women in the managing of unions.

5. Policies such as daycare, maternity leave and flexitime, could have a large potential impact on the earnings of women by enabling them to maintain more continuous work experience in the labour market. Their total effect on income distribution as well as allocative efficiency, however, merits detailed examination.

6. Perhaps the largest potential impact on the earnings of women can come about from something that may be extremely difficult to change—the attitudes of society and the household towards the role of women and men in both labour market and household work. Such attitudes not only affect those who may discriminate in the labour market (employers, co-workers, customers) and the educational institutions which are responsible for much of the job streaming, but also these attitudes affect the perception of women themselves concerning their own potential. That such attitudes can change is evidenced by the differing roles of women in various societies: that such attitudes are difficult to change is evidenced by the restortion of traditional roles even after major changes such as wars. To the extent that attitudes change as a result of other changes—such as unionisation or equal pay or fair employment laws—then the policy impact of these other factors is obviously broadened.

APPENDIXES

1
TABLE 5A.1.1   Low income Cut-Off, 1969

Family size	Low income cut-off $
1	1894.00
2	3157.00
3	3788.00
4	4420.00
5 or more	5051.00

SOURCE

Statistics of Low Income in Canada, 1969,
Statistics Canada (January 1974) p. 13.

2
TABLE 5A.2.1   Low income Cut-Off, 1974

Family size	Low income cut-off $
1	2518.00
2	4196.00
3	5034.00
4	5872.00
5 or more	6713.00

SOURCE

*Income Distributions by Size in Canada,
1974.* Statistics Canada (July 1976) p. 18.

3

Table 5A.3.1   Average and median income of families in constant (1971) and current dollars for selected years

| | Constant dollars (1971) | | | | | | |
	1965	1967	1969	1971	1972	1973	1974
Average income	8,127	8,788	9,490	10,368	10,780	11,780	11,866
Median income	7,320	7,906	8,465	9,347	9,847	10,217	10,827
			Current dollars				
Average income	6,536	7,602	8,927	10,368	11,300	12,716	14,833
Median income	5,909	6,839	8,008	9,347	10,367	11,533	13,516

SOURCE
Income Distributions by Size in Canada, 1974, Statistics Canada (July 1976) Table 1, p. 23.

4

Table 5A.4.1   Average and median income of individuals by income groups in constant and current dollars for selected years

| | Constant dollars (1971) | | | | | | |
	1965	1967	1969	1971	1972	1973	1974
Average income	4,446	4,882	5,006	5,371	5,560	5,691	5,933
Median income	3,724	4,106	3,981	4,186	4,334	4,447	4,644
			Current dollars				
Average income	3,579	4,222	4,710	5,371	5,828	6,416	7,416
Median income	3,029	3,553	3,769	4,186	4,576	5,046	5,833

SOURCE
Income Distributions by Size in Canada, 1974, Statistics Canada (July 1976) Table 57, p. 57.

5

TABLE 5A.5.1 Average and median income of individuals by sex, 1971 to 1974

| | *Males* | | | |
	1971	*1972*	*1973*	*1974*
Average income	$7,984	8,634	9,563	11,059
Median income	7,319	7,970	8,752	10,016
	Females			
Average income	$4,010	4,275	4,737	5,545
Median income	3,731	3,882	4,412	5,157
Ratio: females/males	.51	.49	.50	.51

SOURCE
Income Distribution by Size in Canada, 1971, 1972, 1973, 1974, Statistics Canada.
NOTE
The above mentioned figures represent income for all the workers in the labour force (irrespective of the length of time they were in the labour force).

6

TABLE 5A.6.1   Changes between 1959 and 1974 in the consumer price index and the average low-income threshold for a non-farm family of four in the USA

Year	Consumer Price Index (1963 = 100)	Average threshold for a non-farm family of four persons
1974	161.1	$5,038
1973	145.1	4,540
1972	136.6	4,275
1971	132.3	4,137
1970	126.8	3,968
1969	119.7	3,743
1968	113.6	3,553
1967	109.1	3,410
1966	106.0	3,317
1965	103.1	3,223
1964	101.3	3,169
1963	100.0	3,128
1962	98.8	3,089
1961	97.7	3,054
1960	96.7	3,022
1959	95.2	2,973

SOURCE
Consumer Income, Characteristics of the Population below the poverty level, 1974, Current Population Reports, US Department of Commerce, Bureau of the Census, P–60, no. 102 (January 1976,) Table A–1, p. 143.

7
TABLE 5A.7.1 Median earnings of year-round full-time civilian workers 14 years old and over with earnings by sex: 1960 to 1974

| Year | Median Earnings (in current dollars) | | Ratio Women/Men |
	Women	Men	
1974	$6,772	$11,835	0.57
1973	6,335	11,185	0.57
1972	5,903	10,202	0.58
1971	5,593	9,399	0.60
1970	5,323	8,966	0.59
1969	4,977	8,455	0.59
1968	4,457	7,664	0.58
1967	4,134	7,174	0.58
1966	3,946	6,856	0.58
1965	3,828	6,388	0.60
1964	3,669	6,203	0.59
1963	3,525	5,980	0.59
1962	3,412	5,754	0.59
1961	3,315	5,596	0.59
1960	3,257	5,368	0.61

SOURCE
US Department of Commerce, Bureau of the Census, *Current Population Reports*, Series p. 60, nos. 99, 93, 90, 85, 80, 75, 66, 60, 53, 51, 47, 43, 41, 39, and 37.

As reproduced in *A Statistical Portrait of Women in the US*, Current Population Reports, Special Studies Series p. 23, no. 58 (April 1976) Table 10–3, p. 48.

8

TABLE 5A.8.1 Median income of year-round full-time civilian workers 14 years old and over with income by age and sex: 1960, 1970, and 1974

Age (at March of following year) and sex	1974		1970		1960	
	Number ('000s)	Median income ($)	Number	Median income	Number[1]	Median income
Women						
Total with income	18,017	$6,957	15,518	$5,440	10,337	$3,296
14–19 years	467	3,875	335	3,783	311	2,450
20–24 years	2,704	5,849	2,224	4,928	1,223	3,155
25–34 years	4,411	7,604	2,899	5,923	1,795	3,549
35–44 years	3,410	7,418	3,081	5,531	2,553	3,404
45–54 years	3,943	7,359	3,865	5,588	2,581	3,296
55–64 years	2,716	7,044	2,690	5,468	1,541	3,275
65 years and over	365	6,085	423	4,884	283	2,838
Men						
Total with income	38,915	$12,152	36,146	$9,184	32,165	$5,435
14–19 years	696	4,492	419	3,950	321	1,974
20–24 years	3,567	7,709	2,700	6,655	1,973	3,916
25–34 years	10,492	12,037	8,763	9,126	7,790	5,450
35–44 years	8,617	13,586	8,649	10,258	8,868	5,907
45–54 years	8,758	13,641	8,756	9,931	7,452	5,678
55–64 years	5,776	12,454	5,757	9,071	4,730	5,079
65 years and over	1,009	8,670	1,102	6,754	1,156	4,115
Ratio: women/men						
Total with income	0.46	0.57	0.43	0.59	0.32	0.61
14–19 years	0.67	0.86	0.80	0.96	0.97	1.24
20–24 years	0.76	0.76	0.82	0.74	0.62	0.81

TABLE 5A.8.1   (contd.)

Age (at March of following year) and sex	1974 Number ('000s)	1974 Median income ($)	1970 Number	1970 Median income	1960 Number[1]	1960 Median income
25–34 years	0.42	0.63	0.33	0.65	0.23	0.65
35–44 years	0.40	0.55	0.36	0.54	0.29	0.58
45–54 years	0.45	0.54	0.44	0.56	0.35	0.58
55–64 years	0.47	0.57	0.47	0.60	0.33	0.64
65 years and over	0.36	0.70	0.38	0.72	0.24	0.69

SOURCE
US Department of Commerce, Bureau of the Census, *Current Population Reports*, Series P-60, nos. 99, 80 and 37, as reproduced in *A Statistical Portrait of Women in the US*, op. cit., p. 47.

NOTE
1. Numbers were derived by multiplying total number of persons with income by the percentage of year-round full-time workers with income; figures, therefore, are less exact than comparable ones for 1974 and 1970.

9

TABLE 5A.9.1 Number of households, median income, mean income, and aggregate household income in 1975 and 1974 (revised)

(*Households as of March of the following year*)

Item	1975	1974 In current dollars	1974 In 1975 dollars	Percentage Change In current dollars	Percentage Change In 1975 dollars
Number of households (thousands.)	72,867	71,163	71,163	2.4*	2.4*
Median income	$11,800	$11,197	$12,220	5.4*	−3.4*
Mean income	13,779	13,094	14,291	5.2*	−3.6*
Aggregate income (billions.)	1,004.0	931.8	1,017.0	7.7*	−1.3*

NOTE

An asterisk (*) preceding percentage change indicates statistically significant change at the 95 per cent confidence level.

10

TABLE 5A.10.1   Percentage share of aggregate income, lower limit of each fifth and top 5 per cent of households ranked by size of household money income in 1967 to 1975, by race of head

Race of Head and Year	Mean Income		Percent Distribution of Aggregate Income						Lower Income Limit (Dollars)				
	Value (Dollars)	Standard Error (Dollars)	Lowest Fifth	Second Fifth	Third Fifth	Fourth Fifth	Highest Fifth	Top 5 Percent	Second Fifth	Third Fifth	Fourth Fifth	Highest Fifth	Top 5 Percent
All races													
1975	13,779	43	4.3	10.4	17.1	24.7	43.4	16.3	5,018	9,439	14,181	20,487	32,295
1974*	13,094	41	4.4	10.6	17.0	24.5	43.5	16.6	4,881	9,106	13,359	19,362	30,796
1974	12,893	38	4.3	10.7	17.2	24.4	43.4	16.5	4,774	8,969	13,170	13,447	30,309
1973	12,157	37	4.3	10.6	17.2	24.4	43.5	16.9	4,452	8,435	12,510	17,459	28,735
1972	11,286	35	4.1	10.5	17.2	24.5	43.7	17.0	4,093	7,804	11,566	16,364	26,742
1971	10,383	33	4.1	10.7	17.3	24.5	43.4	16.9	3,825	7,312	10,702	15,257	24,197
1970	10,001	32	4.1	10.8	17.4	24.5	43.3	16.8	3,699	7,126	10,342	14,687	23,199
1969	9,544	30	4.1	11.0	17.5	24.5	42.8	16.5	3,614	6,914	9,949	13,890	21,782
1968	8,760	28	4.2	11.1	17.6	24.6	42.5	16.2	3,353	6,382	9,132	12,733	19,812
1967	7,989	26	4.0	11.1	17.6	24.6	42.7	16.3	3,025	5,876	8,380	11,775	18,432

SOURCE
Both Appendix 9 and Appendix 10 above are extracted from *Household Money Income in 1975 and Selected Social and Economics Characteristics of Households*, Series P-60, no. 104 (March 1977) US Dept of Commerce, Bureau of Census, pages 1 & 23 respectively.

* Revised series

11
TABLE 5A.11.1 Proportion of women in various occupations[a] for full-time,[b] full-year workers,[c] and earnings ratio for similar[d] workers age 45–54 and education 9–13 years, Canada 1971

Occupation	Female earnings $	Female/male earnings	Production female in %
General managers and senior officials	14,569	.55	2.5
Management occupations: social sciences	11,221	1.24	27.0
Administrators in medicine and health	7,801	.68	45.2
Financial management occupations	7,933	.42	6.0
Personnel, industrial relations management	6,655	.51	8.6
Sales and advertising management	8,314	.45	2.5
Purchasing management	6,814	.60	7.5
Services management	9,505	.67	5.4
Production management occupations	6,246	.41	2.1
Accountants, auditors, financial officers	6,744	.57	13.0
Personnel and related officers	7,364	.59	19.0
Purchasing officers and buyers	7,046	.70	7.8
Electrical engineers	9,158	.81	1.0
Draughtsmen	6,861	.71	5.6
Systems analysts, computer programmers	7,751	.68	12.3
Economists	6,626	.57	9.0
Psychologists	6,020	.82	43.1
Social workers	6,898	.80	49.9
Welfare and community services	5,910	.71	36.5
Lawyers and notaries	7,955	.40	4.1
Librarians and archivists	5,962	.80	75.6
Educational and vocational counsellors	7,480	.77	26.2
Ministers of religion	2,968	.81	3.4
Elementary and kindergarten teachers	7,204	.82	80.1
Secondary school teachers	7,890	.75	39.8
Community college, vocational teachers	6,632	.88	21.5
Fine arts school teachers	5,268	.59	38.0
Supervisors: nursing occupations	8,032	1.01	91.1
Nurses, graduate, except supervisors	6,764	.94	93.7
Nursing assistants	5,071	.79	89.3
Nursing aides and orderlies	4,513	.73	67.4
Physiotherapists, therapists	6,244	.76	77.0

TABLE 5A.11.1   *(contd.)*

Occupation	Female earnings $	Female/male earnings	Proportion female in %
Pharmacists	6,193	.54	14.8
Dispensing opticians	7,076	.81	12.6
Medical lab technologists, technicians	5,923	.70	72.8
Dental hygienists, assistants, technicians	4,436	.55	68.1
Painters, sculptors and related artists	7,703	1.32	13.5
Product and interior designers	4,756	.48	24.0
Advertising and illustrating artists	6,815	.71	14.7
Photographers and cameramen	5,337	.65	6.4
Musicians	3,416	.30	12.9
Writers and editors	6,805	.65	24.2
Translators and interpreters	6,830	.54	46.8
Supervisors: stenographic and typing	6,514	.66	81.7
Secretaries and stenographers	5,550	.59	97.0
Typists and clerk-typists	4,917	.73	94.5
Supervisors: bookkeeping, account-recording	6,368	.63	44.6
Bookkeepers and accounting clerks	5,226	.66	62.0
Tellers and cashiers	4,409	.64	88.2
Insurance, bank and other financial clerks	5,166	.68	78.8
Statistical clerks	5,604	.71	59.8
Supervisors: office machine, data processing	6,730	.57	31.0
Office machine operators	5,060	.67	76.1
Telephone operators	4,734	.71	95.3
Adjusters: claim	5,246	.62	47.7
Hotel clerks	4,236	.91	40.9
Sales clerks, commodities	3,610	.47	49.3
Insurance salesmen and agents	6,217	.59	11.3
Real estate salesmen	6,238	.70	14.8
Salesmen and traders: securities	5,585	.54	6.5
Advertising salesmen	5,635	.49	9.1
Buyers: wholesale and retail trade	6,220	.59	20.3
Chefs and cooks	3,788	.59	42.7
Waiters, hostesses: food and beverage	3,285	.64	71.3
Managers: hotel, motel	4,249	.49	44.5
Barbers, hairdressers	4,567	.80	51.4
Laundering and dry cleaning occupation	3,716	.68	62.2
Pressing Occupations	3,573	.67	63.0

Table 5A.11.1 (*contd.*)

Occupation	Female earnings $	Female/male earnings	Proportion female in %
Janitors, charworkers and cleaners	3,577	.57	19.0
Elevator operating occupations	4,002	.76	21.8
Farmers	2,530	.59	2.6
Farm management occupations	4,364	.74	2.4
Farm workers	3,022	.62	24.0
Nursery and related workers	5,700	.85	2.7
Foremen: material processing	5,657	.54	3.8
Foremen: food processing	4,572	.47	5.3
Baking, confectionery-making	4,142	.59	24.3
Fish canning, curing and packing	4,586	.83	24.9
Fruit, vegetable canning	3,978	.50	40.3
Milk processing	3,998	.59	5.7
Foremen: textile processing	5,447	.61	11.1
Textile spinning and twisting	3,637	.59	48.6
Textile winding and reeling	3,882	.54	67.3
Knitting	2,146	.39	46.1
Textile finishing and calendering	3,748	.56	30.2
Inspecting, testing, grading, sampling	4,087	.59	59.7
Tobacco processing	6,229	.81	57.3
Machinist and tool setting up	5,641	.68	2.8
Machine tool operating	4,378	.54	4.1
Cutting and shaping clay, glass	3,662	.44	5.9
Motor vehicle fabricating and assembling	4,610	.59	10.7
Aircraft fabricating and assembling	6,145	.79	3.9
Business machines assembling	5,426	.60	38.1
Precision instrument assembling	5,228	.69	27.7
Electrical equipment assembling	5,024	.65	41.5
Electrical equipment installing	5,143	.59	1.8
Electronic equipment assembling	4,642	.60	66.8
Cabinet and wood furniture makers	3,882	.61	4.7
Tailors and dressmakers	3,678	.59	61.0
Furriers	4,113	.77	40.7
Shoemaking and repairing	4,106	.68	40.6
Upholsterers	5,157	.75	11.5
Sewing machine operators: textile	3,850	.61	87.3
Bonding: rubber, plastics	6,250	.76	4.4
Moulding: rubber, plastics	4,268	.55	24.5
Cutting and finishing: rubber, plastics	3,560	.47	20.6
Watch and clock repairs	5,823	.81	1.9
Jewellery and silverware assembling	3,620	.50	20.6

TABLE 5A.11.1 (*contd.*)

Occupation	Female earnings $	Female/male earnings	Proportion female in %
Painting and decorating	4,305	.57	7.0
Bus drivers	4,275	.56	1.4
Taxi drivers and chauffeurs	3,921	.70	2.5
Truck drivers	5,039	.67	0.7
Typesetters and compositors	5,125	.60	9.3
Printing press occupations	5,029	.56	5.7
Printing engravers	4,737	.46	5.0
Photo-engravers	6,218	.59	6.8
Bookbinders	4,461	.57	63.4
Telegraph operators	5,480	.67	8.8

SOURCE
Computed from unpublished tabulations from Statistics Canada and reported in *Women in the Labour Force: Facts and Figures* (1975) Tables 1–148, pp. 87–263.

NOTES

[a] The occupations used in the above report were 'selected from approximately 500 occupational categories on a subjective basis for their general interest'.

[b] Persons who reported that they worked mainly full-time.

[c] Worked 49–52 weeks.

[d] The earnings ratio is for full-time, full-year workers age 45–54 and education 9–13 years, whereas the proportion of women in various occupations is for all full-time, full-year workers regardless of age or education.

12

TABLE 5A.12.1   Average earnings of males and females by select characteristics Canada, 1972

| Characteristics | Earnings ($) | | |
	Males	Females	Female/ male
Age: <25 years	4,481	3,061	.68
25 to 34 years	8,492	4,354	.51
35 to 44 years	10,290	4,254	.41
45 + years	8,698	4,339	.50
Experience[1] <4 years	4,500	2,957	.66
5 to 9 years	7,654	3,938	.51
10 to 19 years	9,351	4,542	.49
20 + years	9,111	5,194	.57
Experience: discontinuous	6,744	3,258	.48
continuous	8,404	4,281	.51
Education: less high school	7,179	3,129	.44
completed high school	8,647	3,935	.46
some advanced	9,385	4,509	.48
completed nonuniversity	9,287	4,951	.53
completed university	13,712	7,208	.53
Training: none	7,870	3,788	.48
completed	9,394	4,497	.48
Union: nonmember	8,137	3,456	.42
member	8,531	5,103	.60
Marital Status: single	4,673	4,134	.88
married	9,148	3,830	.42
other	n.a.	4,599	n.a.
Total	8,302	3,969	.48

SOURCE
Computed from data given in Statistics Canada, *Earnings and Work Histories of the 1972 Canadian Labour Force*, No. 13–557 (Ottawa: Information Canada, 1976).

NOTE
1. Actual length of work experience gained since entering the labour force on a regular basis. The experience may or may not be related to the Job.

13
Table 5A.13.1 Percentage distribution of workers by select
characteristics Canada, 1972

Characteristic	Males	Females
Age <25 years	.16	.28
25–34 years	.26	.27
35–44 years	.22	.18
45+ years	.36	.27
Experience[1] <4 years	.14	.33
5–9 years	.14	.26
10–19 years	.23	.24
20+ years	.49	.17
Experience: discontinuous	.06	.30
continuous	.94	.70
Education: less high school	.61	.47
completed high school	.19	.27
some advanced	.06	.06
completed non-university	.05	.13
completed university	.09	.07
Training: none	.72	.74
completed	.28	.26
Union: nonmember	.42	.31
member	.58	.69
Marital Status: single	.18	.26
married	.80	.66
other	.02	.08

SOURCE and NOTES
As in Appendix 12.

14

TABLE 5A.14.1   Median earnings of civilians 14 years old and over with earnings by work experience and sex, 1974

(Numbers in thousands. Medians in current dollars)

Weeks worked and sex	Worked at full-time job		Worked at part-time job	
	Number	Median earnings	Number	Median earnings
WOMEN				
Total with earnings	28,705	$5,311	13,945	$1,097
Worked 50 to 52 weeks	17,977	6,772	4,645	2,243
Worked 40 to 49 weeks	2,669	4,680	1,485	2,149
Worked 27 to 39 weeks	2,638	3,513	1,864	1,467
Worked 14 to 26 weeks	2,699	2,041	2,659	817
Worked 13 weeks or less	2,722	647	3,292	330
MEN				
Total with earnings	51,392	$10,288	8,361	$1,222
Worked 50 to 52 weeks	38,898	11,835	2,942	2,203
Worked 40 to 49 weeks	4,440	8,214	832	2,240
Worked 27 to 39 weeks	2,932	5,747	1,004	1,832
Worked 14 to 26 weeks	2,671	3,133	1,572	979
Worked 13 weeks or less	2,450	899	2,010	346
RATIO: WOMEN/MEN				
Total with earnings	0.56	0.52	1.67	0.90
Worked 50 to 52 weeks	0.46	0.57	1.58	1.02
Worked 40 to 49 weeks	0.60	0.57	1.78	0.96
Worked 27 to 39 weeks	0.90	0.61	1.86	0.80
Worked 14 to 26 weeks	1.01	0.65	1.69	0.83
Worked 13 weeks or less	1.11	0.72	1.64	0.95

SOURCE

US Department of Commerce, Bureau of the Census, *Current Population Reports*, series P-60, no. 101. Reproduced from *A Statistical Portrait of Women in the US*, US Dept. of Commerce, Bureau of the Census, Special Studies Series P-23, no. 58 (USGPO, Washington, DC: USGPO, April 1976) p. 50.

1. Figures for the poverty line, and in relation to average and/or median earnings and household/family income for both Canada and the US are provided in Appendixes 1 to 10. For definitions, explanations and methodology, see sources cited in the tables.

2. In the US over time the relative importance of families with female heads has increased as well (as in Canada). For instance, between March 1962 and March 1972 female heads of families increased by 46 per cent compared with a 17 per cent increase among male headed families. Families headed by women were 13 per cent of all families in 1975.

   There has also been an increase in the number and proportion of low-income female-headed families. In 1960, there were about 31 female-headed families for every 100 male-headed families below the poverty level, while in 1974 there were 85 female-headed families for every 100 male-headed families (1976, *A Statistical Portrait of Women in the US*).

3. In the US, three-fifths of the adult population in poverty were women (1974, US Department of Labour).

4. These and other factors are also applicable to the labour force participation rates of married women in the US (Kahne, 1975).

5. Studies of individual establishments, using a human capital model, indicate that men and women are rewarded differently, with females earning a lower rate of return on their investment in human capital (e.g. education, training etc.); secondly, the level of earnings is influenced by marital status with marriage enhancing the prospects of males and depressing that of females; thirdly, these studies find that women with particular levels of training and experience are employed at lower job levels than males with similar characteristics; fourthly, internal labour markets reward experience within the enterprise as opposed to general labour market experience; and finally, there may be a relationship between the method of payment and the amount of discrimination (Jain & Sloane, 1979).

6. Sawhill (1973) has reviewed the relevant empirical studies in the US in this (wage discrimination) area.

7. In the US, in both the census years 1960 and 1970, over half of the employed women were working in clerical, operative or service occupations. In fact, a higher proportion of employed women were clerical or service workers in 1970 than in 1960 (48 per cent to 43 per cent). Just as in Canada, the male labour force, on the other hand, was distributed more evenly among the various occupations. In the US females constituted approximately 38 per cent of the labour force. However, only 20 per cent of the managerial and administrative jobs were held by women. It is therefore apparent that the general trends are similar in both Canada and the US. See *A Statistical Portrait of Women in the US* (1976) Table 8.1, p. 35.

8. Similar trends were also apparent in the US. In 1970 men were in the more prestigious, better paying professional-technical occupational groups relative to women. The vast majority of women professionals were employed in normally lower-paying occupations—health workers, except practitioners (mostly registered nurses), and elementary and secondary school teachers.

For instance, in the education industry, about 70 per cent of the teachers in colleges and universities were men; about 70 per cent of teachers in elementary and high schools were women. Doctors, lawyers, engineers and many other professional-technical occupations also remained male-intensive. These (e.g. medicine, law and engineering) were among the ten top-paying occupations for men and not for women (in 1970). In that year (1970) about 30 per cent of the men professional and technical workers were employed in these (e.g. medicine, law and engineering) fields; only about 2 per cent of women professionals were in these occupations (Waldman and McEaddy (1974); Sommers (1974); *A Statistical Portrait of Women* (1976).

9. In the US, as in Canada, women are over-represented (relative to their typical representation of 38 per cent in all industries), in most of the same industrial sectors such as in textile products, retail trade, finance, insurance, real estate, and in the service sector (Table 8.3, p. 37, *A Statistical Portrait of Women in the US* [1976]).

10. In the US in 1970, just as in the three previous census years—1940, 1950 and 1960—the service industry ranked first in the employment of women. Over this 30 year span, about 60 per cent of all employees in the service industry were women; some 60 per cent of the workers in the educational services; around 75 per cent in the medical-health industry; and about 75 per cent in personal services, including those in hotels and private homes. Within other major industrial categories, such as manufacturing and trade, certain sub-groups remain as female-intensive today as they were yesterday. Examples are the manufacture of clothing and general merchandise, where at least 50 per cent of all employees are women (Waldman & McEaddy [1974]; Jain & Pettman, [1976]).

11. In the US as well (as in Canada) part-time employment (less than 35 hours a week) has grown from almost seven million workers in the 1950 Census of population to more than 16 million in the 1970 Census. As well, there were more women than men working part-time (8.9 million v. 7.2 million in 1970)—in 1960 and 1970 relative to 1950 when slightly more males worked part-time, (Table 7.6, p. 31, *A Statistical Portrait of Women in the US* [1976]). For voluntary part-time workers by age and sex from 1963 to 1973 and part-time for economic reasons, see Tables A.24, A.25, *Manpower Report to the President (1974)*.

12. Overall, a similar pattern is discernable for the US in Appendix 14.

13. In 1974 women constituted a very small proportion of students enrolled in some of the traditional 'male' majors in the US as well. For example, the percentage of women who majored in engineering, agriculture/forestry were 7 per cent and 14 per cent respectively (in 1974). Female college students remained a large proportion of traditional female majors, such as education (73 per cent), English or Journalism (59 per cent), and health or medical professions (64 per cent) (*A Statistical Portrait of Women in the US* [1976]).

14. In the US, women's enrolment in the professions accelerated after 1960 and is continuing to rise in law, medicine and engineering through 1974 (Parrish, 1975).

15. In the US, women's proportion of total union membership was 21.7 per cent in 1972 even though they made up almost 40 per cent of the civilian labour

force at that time. The type of industry in which women are most frequently employed partially explains the small proportion of women in unions. For instance, unions had organised less than 25 per cent of the workers in five of the nine industries in which women constituted more than 40 per cent of total employment: textiles, finance, service, and state and local governments (Bergquist, 1974).

16. Contrary to the growth in union membership for all workers, and females in particular in Canada, the proportion of working women who were members of labour unions in the US declined between 1966 to 1970. The proportion of working men who were union members also declined during this period, but the decline was greater among women. These opposite trends have continued in the two countries as of 1976 (Wood & Kumar, [1978]; Raphael [1974]).

17. Similarly, in the US women have remained rare at the governing and high appointive levels of almost all of the 177 unions in the country; they held leadership roles more frequently at local rather than national levels (Bergquist, 1974).

REFERENCES

A Statistical Portrait of Women in the US, Current Population Reports, special studies series P. 23, no. 58, US Dept. of Commerce, Washington, DC: USGPO (April 1976).

Agarwal, Naresh and Jain, Harish, 'Pay Discrimination Against Females in Canada: Issues and Policies', *International Labour Review* 117 (March–April 1978) pp. 169–77.

Bergquist, Virgina A., 'Women's Participation in Labor Organizations', 97, *Monthly Labour Review*, (October 1974) p. 3–9.

Blinder, Alan, 'Wage Discrimation: Reduced Form and Structural Estimates', *Journal of Human Resources*, 8 (Fall 1973) pp. 436–55.

Gunderson, Morley (1975(a)), 'Male-Female Wage Differentials and the Impact of Equal Pay Legislation'. *Review of Economics and Statistics*, 57 (November 1975) pp. 462–9.

—— (1975(b)) 'Equal Pay in Canada: History, Progress, Problems', in *Equal Pay for Women: Progress and Problems in Seven Countries*, (ed.) B. Pettman (Bradford, England: MCB Books, 1975).

—— (1976(a)) Work patterns in *Opportunity for Choice: A Goal for Women in Canada*. (ed.) G. Cook (Ottawa: Information Canada, 1976).

—— (1976(b)) 'Time Patterns of Male-Female Wage Differentials: Ontario 1946–71', *Relations Industrielles/Industrial Relations*. 31 (no. 1, 1976) pp. 57–71.

—— 'The Influence of the Status and Sex Composition of Occupations on the Male-Female Earnings Gap'. *Industrial and Labour Relations Review*, 31 (January 1978) pp. 217–26.

—— (1977(a)) 'Logit Estimates of Labour Force Participation Based on Census Cross Tabulations', *Canadian Journal of Economics*, 10 (August 1977) pp. 453–62.

—— (1977(b)) Statements based on this source are from published tabulations and separate wage equations for males and females based on Public Use Sample Data derived from the 1971 Canadian Census of Population supplied by Statistics Canada. The responsibility for the use and interpretations of these data is entirely that of the authors. Since the tabulations and wage equations, at this stage, are preliminary, and the analysis has not been completed or written up, the statements based on this data should be used with caution.

Holmes, R., 'Male-Female Earnings Differentials in Canada', *Journal of Human Resources*, 11 (Winter 1976) pp. 109–12.

Jain, Harish C. and Pettman, Barrie O., 'The Impact of Anti-Discrimination Legislation on the Utilization of Minority Groups: The American Experience', *International Journal of Social Economics*, 3 (1976) pp. 109–34.

Jain, Harish C. and Sloane, Peter J., 'The Structure of Labour Markets, Minority Workers and Equal Employment Opportunity Legislation' (forthcoming, 1979).

Kahne, Hilda, 'Economic Perspectives on the Roles of Women in the American Economy', *Journal of Economic Literature*, 13 (December 1975) pp. 1249–92.

Oaxaca, R., 'Sex discrimination in wages'. In *Discrimination in Labour Markets.* (eds) O. Ashenfelter and A. Rees (Princeton University Press, 1974).

Ostry, S., *The Female Worker in Canada,* 1961 Census Monograph (Ottawa: Dominion Bureau of Statistics, 1968).

Parrish, John B., 'Women in Professional Training—An Update', *Monthly Labour Review*, 98, (November 1975) pp. 49–51.

Robb, A. and Spencer, B., 'Education: Enrollment and Attainment' in *Opportunity for Choice: A Goal for Women in Canada*, (ed.) G. Cook (Ottawa: Information Canada, 1976).

Sawhill, I. W., 'The Economics of Discrimination Against Women: Some New Findings', *Journal of Human Resources*, 8 (Summer 1973) pp. 383–94.

Sommers, Dixie, 'Occupational Ranking for Men and Women by Earnings', 97, *Monthly Labour Review*, (August 1974) pp. 34–51.

Spencer, Byron G., 'The Increase in Female Labour Force Participation in Canada: A Survey of Some Causes and Consequences', in Harish C. Jain (ed.), *Contemporary Issues in Canadian Personnel Administration* (Scarborough, Ontario: Prentice-Hall, 1974).

Waldman, Elizabeth and McEaddy, Beverly, 'Where Women Work—an Analysis by Industry and Occupation', *Monthly Labour Review*, 97 (May 1974) pp. 3–13.

Wood, W. D. and Kumar, P., *The Current Industrial Relations Scene in Canada 1978*, Kingston, Ontario: Industrial Relations Centre, Queen's University (1978).

US Department of Labour (1974). Bureau of Labour Statistics, *Release* (10 June 1974).

6 Shortcomings and Problems in Analyses of Women and Low Pay

W. S. SIEBERT and P. J. SLOANE

INTRODUCTION

Women on average are less well paid than men, and in this Chapter we consider the chief explanations of why this should be the case, with a view to highlighting areas where better statistical material and/or further theoretical developments are needed. The indications are that lack of data is indeed a constraint on further British research in this area, and consequently informed public policy-making on issues concerning women's employment. However, the costs of data retrieval and tabulation must be considered. It is therefore necessary to form a judgment on those areas in which our main surveys (the Population Census, the New Earnings Survey and the General Household Survey) might usefully be supplemented in the context of women's pay relative to men.

In considering why women have lower average earnings than men it is useful to adopt the following classification. Average earnings differ because:

(a) women have less access than do men to productivity augmenting opportunities such as schooling and training;

(b) they have less favourable jobs than men, given qualifications such as education and experience. In this case, if tastes for jobs do not differ, and differences in qualifications have been properly allowed for, we have 'employment discrimination';

(c) women receive lower pay given the job. This reflects 'wage discrimination' if similar jobs are in fact being compared.

Discrimination is, in fact, most simply defined as the receipt of lower pay on average for given productivity. It is, however, often worth separating out its wage and employment components so as to cater for those circumstances where women are receiving the same pay as men given the job, yet have inferior job opportunities (unions, for example, might promote the former, yet cause the latter).

These categories are useful for analysing policy with respect to low pay. Thus the lower education of women, which comes under the first head, tends to be mainly a result of conditions facing them *before* entering the labour market. There are different patterns of upbringing or 'role discrimination', as it has been described,[1] different school syllabuses, and anticipation of lower labour force commitment. Measures to change the cultural milieu and the education system would be most important here, rather than measures to counter discrimination in the market.[2] The second two categories, on the other hand, point to labour market factors, and relate to the need for measures opening up job opportunities for women, or enforcing equal pay, or both.

On the question of market discrimination, in a competitive market and under certain conditions it is sufficient for some groups in society to have a 'taste' for discrimination in order for discrimination to occur. Such a theory has been developed by Becker,[3] as noted in Chapter 4, but it does beg the question of what determines these tastes, and ignores non-competitive contexts, that is, where there is exertion of power by employers and trade unions. Thus alternative theories have developed in which certain types of discrimination occur because the discriminators find such practices profitable. For example, trade union members may collude to raise their pay by barring entry to women. It is also profit maximising for a monopsonistic employer to pay lower rates given the job to workers in less elastic supply, who tend to be women. In the same vein, but on a less orthodox level, there are the 'dual labour market' theories, positing permanent barriers to movement. These have been assessed in Chapter 4. Recently, however, a further important theoretical strand has been developed which suggests that even where collusion is absent, it can be income maximising to discriminate for *informational* reasons. If employers cannot easily assess job applicants' qualifications, they might use sex as a substitute test. Accordingly, to the extent that some members of the group do not possess the characteristics of the *stereotype*, individuals will be subject to discrimination. This source of discrimination becomes more important if the stereotype is in fact incorrect. This is likely under present circumstances, when motivations and labour force participation of groups such as married women appear to be changing quite rapidly.

It is necessary to devise tests to distinguish between these various possible theories of the low pay of women, because they have quite different policy implications. Equal pay legislation can be expected to cause unemployment among women if productivity factors (e.g. education, market experience and motivation) do in fact largely account for women's unfavourable position. However, if employer monopsony power is important, such legislation can be shown simply to reduce monopsony profits and might even increase female employment opportunities. Again, if employer hiring standards are sub-optimal— due to male trade union power, or for 'informational' reasons—then fair employment legislation is appropriate. On the other hand, if hiring standards are optimal (cost minimising), then such legislation will raise costs. In sum, to the extent that productivity factors are important, the emphasis should not be placed upon fair employment legislation, but rather on measures to change women's motivations and educational position.

In the following section we consider the above implication of these theories and their shortcomings in more detail. In the third section we consider the tests which have been developed, and those which could be developed if data were more readily available. The fourth section presents some conclusions and recommendations.

THEORIES OF ECONOMIC DISCRIMINATION

PRE-ENTRY DISCRIMINATION

As noted earlier in Chapter 4 and elsewhere, prior to entering the labour market, women tend to invest in less training than men, and they can also be said to develop different tastes or motivations. Much research has been performed with respect to the former factor, but little with respect to the latter. How tastes are developed falls outside the realm of economics which traditionally takes tastes as 'given'. This should be an area for research by psychologists and sociologists, whose channels of communication with economists, unfortunately, are poor.[4] Yet the extent to which women wish to take on, say, light work and the extent to which they are constrained to do so ('the tyranny of the typewriter') is of basic importance. Further, apart from women entering the market with different tastes, there is also the question of whether these tastes are further shaped by market experience, i.e. the 'endogeneity' of tastes. Starting off 'badly' may shape tastes in an anti-work direction. Lack of sharp hypotheses in this field and consequent inadequate testing is an important shortcoming.

Turning to education, it is possible to be more concrete. In Britain women are considerably less well educated than men. Currently the proportion of men in the workforce with a degree is three times that of women, and there is similar relative under-representation of women in the workforce with 'A' levels. Reference can be made to Table 6.1 for the full picture. Given the high correlation of education with earnings, this can be shown to be an important factor in women's low average pay.

TABLE 6.1   Persons in the workforce by sex and highest qualification, GB 1972

	Male	%	Female
Degree or equivalent	5.5		2.0
Higher education but no degree	5.5		6.5
A level or equivalent	5.8		2.1
O level or equivalent	13.6		12.5
CSE/commercial qualification/ apprenticeship	10.7		9.5
No qualification	59.1		67.6

SOURCE
Office of Population Censuses and Surveys, *General Household Survey* (1975).

Different groups can have unequal levels of schooling for both supply and demand reasons. On the demand side, a group might face a lower return to *given* amounts of schooling and so decide to invest less. Among the reasons could be expectations of future discrimination once in the market and, for women, expectations of future family commitments. Thus we would expect the demand curve for education for women to be displaced to the left of that for men. This is shown in Fig. 6.1, where D_w and D_m represent women's and men's demand curves respectively. There is also the supply side—the terms on which funds for education are available. If these are the same for the two groups—represented, say, by the S_m curve—then in equilibrium the rate of return to education

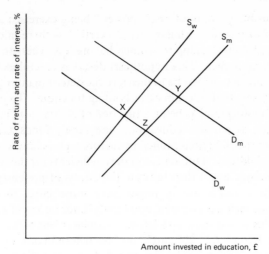

FIG. 6.1   Demand and supply schedules for education investments for males
and females

for women would be somewhat below that for men, as shown by the
equilibrium points Z and Y. Women would also invest less in education,
reflecting the lower productivity of education for them. If the supply
curve of funds for women were displaced to the left (say, to S_w), the
disparity in *amounts* of education would become more marked, but the
difference in equilibrium *rates of return* is less marked, as shown by
comparing equilibrium points X and Y. Thus, contrary to what is often
thought, a similar rate of return to education for men and women is
quite compatible with discrimination against women (leftward shifts of
the supply and demand curves). Indeed, a *higher* rate of return to
education for women than men would be more indicative of
discrimination—unless the implied higher cost of funds for women
could be rationalised in some other way.

In fact, one might expect the terms on which education funds are
available for women to be similar to those ruling for men. This is
because individual finance for education is largely a matter for
government in Britain, and government policy must to some degree be
responsive to the large numbers of female voters. The situation of
women here presents an interesting contrast with that of blacks in the
US, whose exclusion from political representation led to strong
discrimination in the provision of central government funds.[5] It is

hardly plausible to think of 'male power'[6] being exercised against the interests of women in a similar way. Nevertheless there might well be 'cultural traditions' leading to women having less access to education than comparable men. This hypothesis deserves careful examination. The procedure here would be to measure the determinants of schooling achieved by sex, that is, estimate 'schooling functions'. Thus we might think of schooling level as being a function of ability/taste/information factors (such as parents' education), and family funds available for education of the child (determined by factors such as family wealth and number of children).[7] Differences in the coefficients for the function for men and women could then indicate the effects of pre-entry discrimination. For example ability might have more effect in increasing education for men than women, and family funds be less of a constraint for men. This would show up a leftward displacement of the S curve for women in Figure 6.1. Research on the determinants of education achieved is, in Britain, under-developed. In view of the policy importance of education—because education and productivity are highly correlated—this is a gap which must be remedied.

A major difference between men and women, however, probably lies on the demand side. The research problem here is how to devise appropriate tests to show how much the lower productivity of women's education is due to (anticipated) market discrimination, and how much to the non-discriminatory factor of women's child rearing commitment. The only possible approach seems to be to assess the effect on female earnings of varying the level of family responsibility holding other things equal. American results[8] using this approach are considered below, and interestingly appear to bear out the hypothesis that education investments, and thus earnings, depend strongly for women on family commitments. To date there are no comparable British results due to lack of data on individual's work histories. Some appropriate data are collected in the course of the General Household Survey, but access to these has only slowly become available.[9] This is another important shortcoming.

FACTORS AFFECTING EMPLOYMENT GIVEN EDUCATION

Differences in the pattern of employment among groups are explained in part by differences in the amount of education, discussed above. Thus for a variety of reasons the better schooled are likely to be employed in the higher grade jobs. It might be because of the skills imparted by education, or because of its socialising effects (for example, in improving perseverance), or perhaps because some monopolistic employers can afford to indulge a 'taste' for educated employees. Whatever the reason however this positive correlation must exist if education is to pay its way as an investment and people are to continue to come forward to be trained. At the same time the pattern is clearly affected by other forces. These include power factors, as when unions enforce direct barriers to entering certain occupations, supply-side differences in motivation and/or job preferences, and informational factors or 'role stereotyping'.

On the question of direct barriers, craft unions and professional associations provide an institutional means for colluding against women and putting pressure on employers. Such organisations can be expected to have an economic motivation for discrimination against women, since restriction of entry can be expected to raise members' incomes in equilibrium. It can also be argued that once restriction of entry has begun there is an economic incentive for it to be continued. This is because new entrants will have 'paid' to enter (by waiting, or sitting extra examinations) in the expectation that the occupation's income flows, buttressed by restriction of entry, will continue. Lifting the restrictions will be akin to a capital loss for these persons.[10] There is unequivocal evidence of some craft associations barring entry to women, the best-known example being the printers.[11] Certainly the overall under-representation of women in skilled manual work and in the professions is marked. Current figures are given in Table 6.2, together with a comparison with 1961, which suggests the position is relatively stable.

However, the extent to which it is possible to attribute women's relatively unfavourable occupational composition to exclusion by craft and professional organisations is problematic. The main difficulty here, already referred to, is ascertaining what weight to put on differences in male and female employment preferences and ways of life. If preferences and consequently expectations of lifetime labour market experience differ then, it can be argued, so will the jobs for which women offer themselves. (On this point analysis of the determinants of occupational composition between colour groups is simpler: blacks cannot be said to have such a basic difference in tastes and social roles from whites, as women can from men.) This is because it is probable that periods of non-participation in the workforce cause skills to become 'rusty'.[12] It might be that the deterioration of earnings capability engendered by women's extended periods of non-participation is more marked for managerial and professional occupations than others. This

TABLE 6.2　Occupational distribution of employment by sex, GB 1961 and 1971

| | Numbers ('000), 1971 | | Measure[1] of Occupational representation, women | |
	Male	Female	1961	1971
Employers and managers	1936	419	.49	.48
Professional	790	85	.29	.26
Intermed. non-manual	875	985	1.66	1.44
Junior non-manual	1858	3397	1.81	1.75
Personal service	147	1125	2.69	2.40
Foremen and supervisors	549	51	.22	.23
Skilled manual	4601	533	.35	.28
Semi-skilled manual	1968	1109	1.07	.98
Unskilled manual	1071	698	.91	1.07
Agricultural workers	243	63	.38	.54
Armed forces	238	11	.11	.12
Own account	786	190	.70	.53

SOURCE
Department of Employment, *The Changing Structure of the Labour force* (1975).

NOTE
[1]. Calculated from $(L_{ij}/L_{ij}+L_{im})/(L_j/L)$ where L_{ij} (L_{im}) is the number of women (men) in the i th occupation, L_j is total number of women, and L is the size of the labour force. Thus the first entry in the 1971 column, 0.48, indicates that women in 1971 had a representation in the employer/manager category that was about half that 'expected' on the basis of their representation in the workforce as a whole.

could be because in these occupations knowledge must be continually up-dated, that is, continual post-schooling investments are required in addition to schooling. In some cases 'refresher courses' will be possible, but in others continuous on-the-job experience will be required. This would imply that a woman who expects to absent herself from the labour force for some time, and who wishes to minimise loss of capital, will opt against entering these occupations.

　　This human capital orientated reasoning leads to the expectation that women with anticipated breaks in labour force experience will be less well represented in, for example, professional and managerial jobs for reasons of income maximising choice. This is quite apart from possible discrimination in hiring or promotion practices. Another implication of this hypothesis is that the job opportunities of single women, while similar to those of men, will differ to some extent from those of married women, since the root of the supply-side difference is assumed to be the differential family care commitment of women (though this difference will tend to be lessened because single women anticipate marriage). There are also related demand side influences to be considered. Intermittent participation will count against women from the employer's point of view in jobs requiring much specific training. This could be a further factor accounting for women's low representation as managers, where much specific training is needed.[13] To test these hypotheses, data on work histories, cross-classified by marital status must be collected. Even at this stage, however, it can be said that the above reasoning is unlikely to explain the extremely low representation of women in the craft occupations.[14] There seems little reason to expect skills gained in an apprenticeship to depreciate particularly quickly as a result of non-participation. This serves to emphasise the part played by union barriers to entry.

A further aspect of the way market power can explain women's relatively unfavourable occupational composition is emphasised in monopsony theories. The basic point here is that wives' job choices will tend to be much more constrained than their husbands', so that wives will have less bargaining power in the labour market. This more limited job choice could arise from wives tending to search for jobs closer to home than do men, because of their child-care commitments. But it is also likely to arise even if no children are present, if the family's objective is to choose that pair of jobs in a single location which maximises joint family income. This is because the husband usually possesses the larger stock of human capital and can thus command the higher wage, so that the wife is likely to have to make a larger 'compromise' than the husband.[15] These forces can give rise not only to less favourable jobs, given productivity characteristics for married women, but also to lower pay, given the job. This latter possibility (covered in more detail below) is a result of the implied lower elasticity of wives' labour supply. Also conducive to this lower elasticity will be the lower degree of unionisation of women, which means they will be less subject to wage minima. This means that wives will be more subject to monopsony than husbands and, accordingly, are likely to receive lower wages in equilibrium.[16]

Monopsony considerations can be seen to provide a further reason for considering single women apart from married. Another empirical implication is that women should be at less of a disadvantage where a large number of employers are bunched together. In these circumstances the compromise required by married women will be lower, and the limited area of search engendered by family responsibilities of less consequence. It is, again, interesting to note that monopsony will not play much part in explaining black workers' labour market disadvantage. Some evidence that women's area of search is, in fact, markedly smaller than men's is presented in Table 6.3. The median distance between previous and current employer is almost twice as far in the case of males as females in Birmingham, though rather less in Glasgow.

TABLE 6.3 Distance of recruits' previous employer from case study plants, by sex 1966[a]

| | Birmingham | | Glasgow | |
	Male	Female	Male	Female
Under 2 miles	28.7%	55.1	39.0	47.0
2 to 4.9	47.8	32.1	33.1	31.8
5 to 19.9	17.2	10.6	20.7	17.8
20 and over	6.3	2.2	7.3	3.4
Median distance[b] miles	3.4	1.8	3.0	2.2

SOURCE
D. Mackay, *et. al.*, *Labour Markets Under Different Employment Conditions* (1971).
NOTES
[a] Figures relate to employees recruited over 1959–66 and still in employment in 1966.
[b] Medians estimated by linear interpolation.

However, what is required is comprehensive information on earnings (given sex and productivity characteristics), by size of conurbation and journey to work. Then it would be possible to develop pointers as to the importance of monopsony. Such data are not yet available,[17] marking a third shortcoming which should be remedied.

Imperfect information is likely to be another factor explaining the pattern of women's jobs. Informational theories of discrimination derive from the fact that employers have imperfect information about the productivity of individual workers. They will nevertheless have some idea, from past experience, of the probability distribution of productivity across individuals with given characteristics such as education, colour, sex and marital status. Employers must therefore act as statisticians and develop decision-rules—which might be called 'stereotypes'—in an attempt to predict applicants' performance on the basis of observable characteristics. Suppose the decision rule is unbiased, that is, *on average* individuals' actual productivity equals productivity (and wage) expected on the basis of the rule. Since the procedure is probabilistic, some individuals in fact will have higher or lower actual productivity than expected, and so can be said to be 'discriminated against' or 'preferred' in job assignment. This, however, is an inevitable consequence of imperfect information and will always be with us.[18]

Equally important is the possibility that the decision rule could be biased against one group or another. This is because the stereotypes developed by employers (and workers) need continual updating in the light of changes in the labour market. Since information about these changes is costly to obtain, the process of updating will rarely be complete. Consequently it would appear quite likely that the empirical rules developed will be outdated and that biased decisions (i.e. incorrect on average) will be made. The likelihood of this is clearly greater in periods of rapid change. Still, we would expect competitive pressures to cause employers to learn, for incorrect hiring decisions on average mean lower profits and thus the possibility of elimination by other firms. Also tight labour markets are likely to encourage learning via the induced experimentation and revision of stereotypes.

The empirical implication of the informational theory is that hiring and promotion policies might be sub-optimal over a much wider area than unionised and/or monopolistic firms. This is likely to be so particularly with respect to married women whose labour market participation has increased so dramatically over time. Married women formed only 15 per cent of the female labour force in 1931, but this had increased to 38 per cent in 1951, and 63 per cent in 1971,[19] and this must signify a large change in work expectations and commitment. Have the employers caught up? If they have, then enforcement of affirmative action programmes which over-ride employer hiring standards will simply raise costs. But if they have not, so that hiring standards are rather arbitrary, then the policy implication is that enforcing similar hiring standards for all the labour force groups will not much raise costs. It can safely be said, unfortunately, that tests for the optimality of employer hiring (and promotion) standards are under-developed.[20] Reder[21] pointed out long ago that hiring standards for the profit-maximising employer can be traded off against wage offers and the speed of filling a vacancy. Accordingly, standards will vary over the cycle (between regions), being higher in periods (areas) of high unemployment than low. This suggests one form of test. Again, human capital theory indicates that hiring requirements will be more stringent in circumstances where there is greater specificity of human capital. Factors which increase specificity such as the development of internal labour markets, or unionisation (which appears to reduce quits and thus increases the proportion of training investments which it is profitable for the employer to finance, i.e. increases specificity) should therefore be associated with more stringent screening. It has also been argued that small firms are more adroit in judging the quality of applicants[22]— indeed, this could be the reason why they appear to pay a lower wage, given quality. This suggests comparing small firms' hiring practices with larger firms. This should be done at the micro-level, by direct assessment of employer personnel policies,[23] though a large body of such studies would have to be made before generalisation were possible.

DIFFERENCES IN PAY GIVEN THE JOB

A major empirical question is the extent to which women's low average pay is a consequence of unequal pay, given the job, as opposed to their relatively unfavourable job distribution. The results of Chiplin and Sloane[24] (see below) indicate that the former is more important, i.e. women do receive less than men within 'occupations'. One major difficulty is assuming that the same job is in fact compared. It seems that women's low relative pay is more a consequence of their being employed in low paying firms than of receiving lower pay than men in the same job within a *given* firm. American evidence indicates that sex differentials, given the job *within* firms, are small.[25] Still, it should be pointed out that while we have American evidence on intra-firm sex differentials,[26] such studies have only just begun in Britain. This must therefore go on our list of shortcomings. From the analytical viewpoint, to the extent that women's unequal pay, given the job, is a matter of their high representation in low paying firms, pure wage discrimination is of secondary importance. Therefore we have to look for the reasons for women being employed in the low-paying firms, and this takes us back to the factors outlined earlier influencing employment patterns.

It has been held that factors such as entry barriers and informational imperfections which crowd women into a limited range of occupations will lower the relative wage of these occupations, thus changing the structure of wages. As seen earlier this is known as the 'crowding hypothesis'.[27] There seems in principle to be a simple way to test for such crowding effects on the wage structure. Holding productivity factors constant, we look to see whether the average wage is much lower in female-labour-intensive occupations than elsewhere. It must be emphasised, however, that it is essential to adjust as carefully as possible for productivity differences. It is by no means enough simply to demonstrate that average pay is relatively low in female-intensive industries or occupations. This could mean only that work in which women were concentrated was low-skill work. On the crowding argument, therefore, wage differences, given the job, occur as a result of women's unfavourable employment opportunities.

In a competitive labour market we would expect wage discrimination, in the sense of persistent differences in pay by sex for similar jobs within a firm to be limited not only because of legislation but because if women were really able to do the job more cheaply than men the profit maximising employer would employ women. There are, however, two ways in which an equilibrium wage differential might come about: women might be more likely to leave the employer than men, or they might be less elastic in supply to the firm (monopsony). Taking the case where the female separation rate is higher, for given marginal product this means that the equilibrium wage for women will have to be lower than for men so that the employer can earn a market rate of return on his training and hiring costs. A simple formula can be shown to be.[28]

$$W_m - W_f = \frac{C}{1+r}(S_f - S_m)$$

where: W is the wage rate
S is the separation rate
r is the discount rate,
C the hiring and training costs.

It can be seen that the wage differential varies directly with specific investment costs and with the difference in the probability of separation. Higher absenteeism among women can also be shown to increase the differential. We know that differences of the order of $15.00 to $25.00 per week have been observed in the US in 1971 for various clerical grades employing both men and women[29] (no comparable data yet exist for Britain). Assuming plausible values for C and r of $1000 and .06 respectively, and on the maximum assumption that the annual female (male) separation rate is 60 per cent (25 per cent) and that women work 95 per cent of the days worked by males we have an equilibrium differential of $8.00. Thus differences in male-female separation rates could conceivably explain a sizeable proportion of differences in pay, given the job. However, it is possible that the higher average separation rates evinced by women are mainly a consequence of their skill structure.[30] In this case, in fact, there might be very little difference between the sexes in their separation rates standardising for skill. A thorough study of male-female differences in separation rates has yet to be performed, though it is worth noting that the Department of Employment's Unit for Manpower Studies is currently investigating hiring costs.

The second possible factor causing wage discrimination is the differential experience of monopsony likely to be applicable, particularly to married women. If women are felt to be more inelastic in supply than men, then in order to stimulate a given increase in the supply of women a larger wage increase will have to be given to women than men. Thus the marginal cost curve of hiring women will be steeper than that for men, and this implies a lower wage for women. This fact has long been recognised.[31] It has the important policy implication that imposition of equal pay for equal work at the firm level need not necessarily reduce employment opportunities for women. We have already touched above on the type of tests needed to form a judgement as to the direction of impact of monopsony elements on women's pay.

EMPIRICAL ANALYSIS AND DATA SHORTCOMINGS

Many of the questions raised above could be much better approached by analysing a systematic body of data on earnings, cross-classified by sex and marital status, and the various characteristics such as education (and taste factors) known, or thought, to influence money earnings. Data with some of these advantages have existed in America for some time, and it is now 15 years since the first numerical estimates of the 'rate of return to education' were made.[32] This is basically because income and earnings questions are asked in the American population Censuses but, unfortunately for labour market research and policy, this is still not the case in Britain.[33] In an interesting recent study (of males only) Taubman has been able in fact to analyse earnings data cross-classified by over 30 relevant variables. These variables include measures of ability, family background including religion (thus Jewish respondents received over 30 per cent more than others, holding all other factors constant—is this the influence of upbringing or motivation?),[34] 'quality' of school attended, taste factors such as whether the respondent preferred salaried work, health, labour force experience, size of town and possession of business assets. This last is interesting because, since the dependent variable is labour earnings, possession of such assets *per se*, should not be associated with higher earnings. In fact it is, very significantly.[35] This might show nepotism in the labour market (the 'pull' of the rich). On the other hand it could be, as Marshall thought, a consequence of ability and possession of assets being correlated.[36]

Because such data have only recently begun to appear in the case of Britain, with the institution of the General Household Survey in the early 1970s, research here has lagged considerably. It was only in 1976 that an earnings function, for males only, was estimated for the British economy.[37] Economy-wide studies of the earnings relationship for women in Britain based on individual data,[38] on industry data,[39] and on personnel records of individual firms,[40] still remain limited. This would appear to be a considerable shortcoming and efforts should be directed toward improving British data in this respect, and to making them more widely available. For example, in America data tapes have long been commercially available but it is only recently that a similar service with respect to General Household Survey data has been initiated.

THE HOUSEHOLD DIVISION OF LABOUR AS A FACTOR IN THE LOW PAY OF WOMEN

As we have seen, there is the expectation that craft and professional associations will impose direct barriers to the entry of women, as indeed for other minorities. However, outside the areas where barriers to entry are plain, a major difficulty in comparing the male pattern of employment with the female is to ascertain what weight to put on differences in male and female employment preferences and ways of life. A way of gauging the overall impact of entry barriers in women's pay is to find out how closely human capital variables 'explain' pay. If the fit is good (compared say to a comparable male earnings function) the scope for market discrimination is reduced, through differences in coefficients would also be indicative of discrimination. Care must be taken, however, in controlling for married women's periods of labour market absence—full data on working histories are required. We can also test to see if women in 'women's jobs' are less well paid *ceteris paribus*, so examining the 'crowding' hypothesis. As for the tastes factor, a crude way of allowing for possible taste differences is to separate out married women. We would expect married women to have very different jobs from men, though single women should be more similar.

This latter expectation is quite dramatically borne out when we compare male to female pay ratios among marital status groups.

Adjusting for differences in age, education and hours worked, the expected ratio for single persons is nearly the same as the actual. For married persons, however, there is still a large 'unexplained' difference after adjustment. This is shown in Table 6.4. The unexplained difference cannot simply reflect discrimination against women, for there appears to be little discrimination against single women. This shows the real difficulty of disentangling discrimination against women from their very different role in society. However, this method can hardly be said to be a sharp test of the market effect of taste differences, and clearly more work on tastes is required.

TABLE 6.4 Median income ratios, by sex and marital status, United States 1959

	Single, never married	Married, spouse present
Actual	.98	.33
Adjusted using:		
female earnings function	.91	.51
male earnings function	.96	.50

SOURCE
Gwartney, J., and Stroup, A., 'Measurement of Employment Discrimination According to Sex', *Southern Economic Journal* (1973) p. 578.

As for the 'fit' of earnings functions for women, one of the advances in analysing women's earnings has been the development of the 'segmented' earnings function. This is a function which permits adjustment for the fact that some women spend a considerable part of their potential working life outside the labour force. During such time they invest less in market skills, perhaps not even enough to offset the 'depreciation' of their human capital. For example, a US study[41] of a national sample of women aged 30 to 44, taken in 1967, showed white married women with children to have spent 6.4 years in the labour force since school and 10.4 years out of it, compared to 14.5 and 1.5 years respectively for never-married women. The figures for black married women were 9.1 years in and 10.3 years out of the labour force, and for single women, 13.4 and 4.7 years respectively. Consequently instead of assuming a monotonic decline in post-school investments, Mincer proposes a segmented post-school investment function. Let us assume there are three segments: the first ending with the birth of the first child, the second comprising a broad non-participation interval in which children are reared, and the third defining the period of re-entry to continuous work. There is likely to be little training undertaken during the first segment, and even disinvestment (depreciation being greater than investment) in the second. There will be a certain amount of new investment, for example, refresher courses, within the third segment. Some results of the 'segmentation' approach are given in Table 6.5

The equations reveal that for white married women the coefficient on current job tenure is higher than in other segments and the home time

TABLE 6.5 Regression of log female earnings on schooling, segmented work experience and other variables, USA 1967

Variable	White Married with children (a)	White Never married (a)	White Never married (b)	Black Married with children (a)	Black Never married (a)
Constant	0.09	0.55	1.48	−0.02	−0.48
Schooling	0.064[a]	0.077[a]	0.054[a]	0.095[a]	0.110[a]
Work before first child	0.008[a]			0.005	
Work after first child	0.001			0.001	
Current job tenure	0.012[a]	0.009		0.006	0.001
Total years worked		0.026	0.036[a]		0.004
Square of total years worked		−0.0007	−0.0005[a]		−0.0003
Home time after first child	−0.012[a]			−0.006	
Other home time	−0.003			−0.005	
Total home time		−0.009			−0.02
In hours per week on current job	−0.11[a]	−0.43[a]		−0.30[a]	−0.13
In hours per year on current job	0.03	0.21	0.666[a]	0.08[a]	0.03
R^2	0.28[b]	0.41[b]	0.67[b]	0.39[b]	0.46[b]

SOURCES
(a) Mincer and Polachek (*op. cit.*)—for hourly earnings.
(b) Polachek, S., 'Potential Biases in Measuring Male/Female Discrimination', *Journal of Human Resources* (1975) 10, p. 215—for annual earnings.
NOTES
[a] Indicates $|t| \geqslant 2$
[b] Indicates inclusion of other variables in the regression (for example, illness, years resident in state, etc.)

coefficient is actually negative. This appears to bear out the hypothesis that investment and earnings depend strongly, for women, on family commitments. Investment in the current job, since it takes place for most women when children have grown up, is higher than in the early jobs when there is presumably anticipation of dropping out of the labour force. The negative coefficient on home time indicates a net depreciation of earning power of about 1.2 per cent per annum. However, it is interesting to note that the home time coefficient for never-married women is not significantly negative. This could perhaps be explained by their periods of non-participation being search-oriented. For black women the experience coefficients are smaller and there is less variation between segments (though it is in the same direction as for whites). The greater family responsibilities of black than white women might be part of the explanation for their investing less on the job. But that there are other factors, such as discrimination, at work however is shown by black *single* women also having lower experience coefficients than white.

The equations also indicate that for women as for men the human capital framework is quite successful in explaining the distribution of annual earnings, as column 3 indicates. In fact, the coefficient of determination (0.67) compares favourably with coefficients for male earnings functions. In male earnings functions using schooling, labour force experience and weeks worked per year as independent variables to explain log annual earnings, the multiple correlation coefficient has turned out to be 0.525 in the case of America, and 0.665 in the case of England and Wales.[42] Thus the productivity component underlying single women's earnings appears no less systematic than in the case of males, which is not consistent with the hypothesis of much market discrimination against this group of women at least. Moreover, as would be expected given optimising behaviour, the rate of return to education appears slightly higher for blacks than whites. In accordance with the analysis of Figure 6.1 above, we could interpret this as indicating a higher marginal cost of funds for the former.

DUALISM AND CROWDING

As seen in Chapter 4 sometimes an effort is made to test for the effect of direct barriers to given groups entering the better jobs, that is, 'primary' labour market jobs, not by comparing earnings functions for the groups as above. Rather, individuals are separated into groups according to whether their job is felt to be 'primary' or 'secondary', and then separate earnings functions are run for these two groups. The test here seems to have the rationale that productivity factors such as education might have lower coefficients in the secondary labour market regression, indicating that individual differences in productivity in this sector do not matter. This has the implication that emphasis on improving individuals' human capital is misplaced.[43] This procedure, however, is not appropriate. This is because considering high skill and low skill groups separately means that the effect of increasing education on earnings in increasing the chance of moving from a low to a high skill group is missed. This imparts a downward bias to the correlation between education and earnings.

As for the effect of 'crowding' on earnings, the test here is to see if occupations in which women are over-represented have lower average earnings than other occupations, standardising for productivity differences between individuals. Jusenius has recently performed such an exercise using American data on female earnings, controlling for education, vocational training, tenure, and labour force experience. The experiment is marred by separating individuals into 'low skill', 'medium skill' and 'high skill' groups. However, it does appear that women working in female-intensive occupations (defined as those occupations with more than 43 per cent employees female) have lower earnings than other women. For example, from these results it seems that a woman in a typically female occupation such as chambermaid earns nearly 20 per cent less than a woman in a typically male occupation such as janitor. This appears to support the crowding hypothesis. The difference is insignificant among the 'high skill' category, however. This could mean that the crude standardising factors included in the regressions are appropriate for high skill jobs, but not for low skill jobs, in which case this estimate of the crowding effect would be biased upwards.

SCHOOLING FUNCTIONS

The level of education achieved is an important determinant of earnings, as we have seen. Therefore it is necessary to inquire into the determinants of levels of education. In the past what British work there has been has concentrated on males, and been focused on the contribution of family background factors to level of schooling. In the inter-war period males with fathers in white collar jobs had a markedly greater chance of completing secondary education,[44] though the difference appears since to have narrowed, presumably because schooling is now paid for out of taxes, with no attendance fees (however, the foregone earnings costs of attending further schooling, and university, remain). Some idea of the current position may be gained from Table 6.6. Family background still influences schooling completed, but this is clearly impressionistic. What is needed here is systematic analysis using modern statistical techniques, so that we can meaningfully compare male and female access to education.

TABLE 6.6   Male and female students by occupation of father, GB 1972

| | Occupation of father | | |
	Non-manual	Manual and personal service	Total
Percentage of fathers in sample	39.2	60.8	100
Percentage of students over 15 years in:			
Secondary school	53.4	46.6	100
University/college	57.7	42.3	100

SOURCE
Office of Population Censuses and Surveys, *General Household Survey* (1973).

In America there has been some very interesting research into schooling functions. Using an economic model, we would expect the level of schooling completed to be a function of returns achievable from education both in the market and at home (consumption benefits of education) and costs. Here is not the place to develop a full model. It is simpler to comment on the results obtained already. Such results are presented in Table 6.7, though unfortunately only one study is available which contrasts men with women. All the regressions indicate parents' education to be a significant determinant of schooling. This could be because parents' education is an indicator of the market benefits the student expects from education, as would be the case if better-off parents could exert 'pull' for their children in the market. In fact this is probably not the case: family background factors do not seem very important for individuals' earnings *once* human capital has been gained.[45] It seems more to be the case that parents' education (particularly mothers') increases the ability to learn (that is, IQ), and possibly also increases the taste for education. It is also likely that parents' education is related to family financial support and hence enters on the costs side. Parsons shows for his sample, for example, that individuals are much less likely to take part-time jobs while at school (an indicator of support) if the father is well educated *ceteris paribus*.

TABLE 6.7 Determinants of Schooling Level, Dependent variable years of schooling completed, US 1940 and 1966

	Const.	Father's education	Mother's education	Father's occupational status	Family income	No. of sibs.	I.Q.	Birth order (1 = 1st born, 0 otherwise)	R^2
US males 1966	8.43	.187 (7.55)	.153 (5.46)	.005 (1.78)	insig.	−.212 (7.83)	—	—	.27 (.40)
California males 1940	10.38	.122 (3.22)	.131 (3.18)	—	−.782 (.58)	−.123 (2.09)	.023 (2.29)	insig.	.080
Females	9.31	.085 (2.73)	.163 (4.67)	—	1.52 (1.30)	−.136 (2.42)	.011 (1.28)	.349 (1.97)	.166

SOURCES
Leibowitz, A., 'Home investments in children', *Journal of Political Economy* (1974) p. S122; Parsons, D., 'Intergenerational wealth transfers and the educational decisions of male youth', *Quarterly Journal of Economics* (1975) p. 608.

NOTES
|t| statistics in parenthesis.

Finally, all the regressions show a negative sign on the size of family variable. This could indicate that students from large families can less afford to continue long at school/university than those from small, and/or that children from large families receive less mother's attention than those from small.

There are some interesting differences between the male and female functions. It should be emphasised, however, that not only is the sample American, it is also unrepresentative, coming from the top 1 per cent of the Californian IQ distribution. These regressions are therefore simply brought forward to give some idea of the potential of the approach, not as the last word. It seems that the cost constraints are more important and ability a less important factor in determining schooling for women than men. On the costs side it can be seen that size of family has more impact for women; so does birth order—and family income has a large, though poorly determined, coefficient. On the benefits side, it can be seen that the coefficient for IQ is large and significant for men but insignificant for women. There is the suggestion, therefore, that differences in education level for men are mainly a consequence of shifts in the demand curve (due to differences in ability, see fig. 6.1) around a common supply curve, while for women it is shifts in the supply curve, given demand, which are prominent. However, this is a subject which needs to be examined in the British context.

MONOPSONY

Women, as we have seen, are more likely to be subject to monopsony than are men. Since monopsony is likely to apply more to married than single women, it provides an additional reason to expect different rates of pay for these groups. Unfortunately there is little direct evidence on the monopsony question. Nursing, within the US, appears to conform to the monopsony model due to the tendency toward concentration of nursing employment among a few hospitals in a given area.[46] But this is hardly comprehensive evidence of monopsony influence. A British study of male and female pay among industries finds that the pay of both males and females is higher in conurbations, *ceteris paribus* but male pay increases slightly more.[47] We would expect male pay to increase less, however, (if it varies at all) as size of town increases, because males have more mobility. This is, in fact, the finding in a nationwide study of librarians in Britain[48] and also in a recent American paper,[49] so the matter is still open. In the American study, holding region, education and labour force experience constant, women in towns of less than 250 thousand population earned 35 per cent less than those in towns of over 750 thousand. The comparable figure for males was 20 per cent. In a British study, this time of earnings in the teaching profession, it was found that most of the differential in pay between single men and women could be explained on the basis of measured differences in education and experience. No such satisfactory explanation existed in the case of married women. This latter result was interpreted in terms of 'the lower supply price' of married female teachers due either to their lower ambition or their lower geographic mobility.[50]

An attractive possibility would be to estimate women's and men's elasticity of supply to firms and relate this to earnings differences given skill. This would enable direct testing of the monopsony hypothesis. An attempt has been made to do this by estimating sex differences in elasticity of labour supply to the market in given metropolitan areas and relating this to wage differentials by metropolitan area.[51] Unfortunately this approach founders because there is no reason to expect the elasticity of labour supply to the metropolitan area and to the firm to be related. For example, males might be quite inelastic in supply to the market, but elastic in supply to the firm because of, say, union-determined minimum wages. Hopefully further tests of this important hypothesis will be forthcoming. ·

HIRING STANDARDS AND IMPERFECT INFORMATION

If the employer can be shown to labour under large information imperfections, this will lower the 'price' (in terms of lost output and higher costs) of enforcing similar hiring standards for different labour force groups. It is, however, very difficult to judge hiring standards because, as we have pointed out, they will vary according to the state of the labour market,[52] and factors relating to skill specificity such as unionisation and firm size. The US Department of Labour has prepared lists of 'General Education Development' and 'Specific Vocational Preparation' required for 4000 different jobs. However, these 'requirements' can hardly be used to judge employers' standards, because of their wide margin of error.[53] In another Department of Labour sponsored study, hiring standards between firms in different areas were compared and much made of the variability in standards between regions.[54] However, only if excess demand for labour were held constant would such a study prove informative.

Research into hiring standards does not to date appear to have had a firm enough theoretical base. Economists have tended to ignore this area because of a belief in the perfect competition paradigm—an employer whose hiring decisions are consistently inappropriate will be forced out of business. But this ignores the fact that adaptation to change takes time. There would seem to be good reasons to expect particular disequilibria in the market as far as married women are concerned. There is also the fact that monopolistic firms do not, by definition, suffer so immediately if their hiring rules are biased. This suggests two possible correlates of inappropriate hiring decisions, but they have not yet been tested.

CONCLUSIONS

In considering problems for theory and data collection in the field of women's low pay, special attention has been drawn to the following areas: the development of tastes, the role of women's family responsibilities, differential access to schooling between the sexes, 'crowding' and imperfect information. Male-female differences in separation rates have also been touched upon. Let us summarise first the main theoretical shortcomings, then consider what might be done as far as collection of data is concerned.

THEORETICAL SHORTCOMINGS

The main theoretical shortcomings uncovered in the paper can be said to relate to the areas of tastes formation, monopsony, and hiring standards. Economics traditionally takes tastes as 'given' yet tastes might well be endogenous, that is, formed by labour-market experience. This would seem a fruitful field for future cooperation between economists and psychologists/sociologists. One major benefit of such work would hopefully be the development of ways of measuring motivation, a characteristic relevant to productivity about which we can only speculate at the moment.

In the area of monopsony, the theory is under-developed inasmuch as clear empirical implications have not yet been derived. To some extent testing of the impact of monopsony is hampered by lack of data (see below). But it is also likely that the importance of the problem is only now beginning to be recognised, so that existing data have not been used as fruitfully as they might.

Finally there are the problems associated with testing for the optimality or otherwise of employer hiring 'requirements'. Since this has been an area left very much to the personnel specialist, economic considerations have tended to be ignored. Thus too much emphasis has tended to be placed on the technical specification of a 'job' and too little on the fact that employers can substitute more or less qualified people in a given job according to how wage rates for skill vary, and according to the urgency of filling the job. In devising tests for employer hiring standards consideration must therefore be given to such factors as the level of excess labour demand in the market and the degree of competition in the market.

DATA PROBLEMS

Lack of data appears, however, as a more significant constraint on explaining the low pay of women. Lack of data means that 'schooling functions', that is, the systematic comparison of male and female access to education, have not yet been estimated for Britain. Just as serious, measurement of 'earnings functions', the relation of earnings to characteristics thought to influence productivity (such as education) has lagged far behind America.[55] It is only recently that attempts have been made to measure such an earnings function for men and women in Britain.

Apart from the above major gaps, lack of national data on earnings by size of town and journey to work have meant that the impact of monopsony cannot be adequately judged. Further, the presence or otherwise of unionisation is highly relevant in the context of monopsony. Unfortunately no union membership question is asked in the General Household Survey. There is also lack of information as far as measuring male/female differences in pay, given the job, is concerned. For this it is important to be able to gauge the sex differential in pay, given the job, *within* and among firms. As far as inter-firm comparison is concerned it would be useful to obtain data on employment by sex by size of establishment. At the present, Census of Production employment data do not distinguish sex. It would also be interesting to be able to compare male/female differences in turnover and absenteeism more fully than is possible with existing published data.

Much of the above information is, or could be, relatively easily collected. As far as the material that is currently being collected is concerned, the General Household Survey represents a major source for further work. This survey has only been carried out since 1971, and there is scope for further analyses by researchers To obtain access it used to be necessary to have a research programme which was sponsored by a government department. Fortunately some of these data are now commercially available in the form of a computer tape, though there is a long (five year) time lag between data collection and availability.

Going on to the question of material that could be collected, the major difficulty for research is the lack of an income question in the decennial Census. It would be enormously helpful if such a question could be asked—as it is in many other countries. Income tax data, another comprehensive source, are not very useful for the purposes considered in this paper because they are not cross-classified by the respondent's characteristics. Finally, evidence from intra-establishment studies[56] of male and female earnings suggests that marital status can be as important as sex in explaining earnings differences. At the present time no published earnings data are available classified by marital status and consideration should be given to including a question on marital status in the New Earnings Survey.

NOTES

1. See Cain (1976) p. 1236.
2. Though anticipated market discrimination will also deter individuals' investment in education.
3. Becker (1971).
4. Thus Becker has said: 'Economists generally take tastes as "given" and work out the consequences of changes in prices, incomes and other variables under the assumption that tastes do not change. When pressed either they engage in *ad hoc* theorising or they explicitly delegate the discussion of tastes to the sociologist, psychologist or anthropologist. Unfortunately these disciplines have not developed much in the way of systematic usable knowledge about tastes' (Becker [1975], p. 817). However, psychologists are researching in this direction. See, for example, M. Tuck (1976). We are greateful to Mary Farmer for bringing this reference to our attention.
5. See Myrdal (1962) p. 1271 and Owen (1972) p. 30.
6. See Madden, J., 'Discrimination—a Manifestation of Male Market Power?' in Lloyd (1975) p. 159.
7. See Liebowitz, A., (1974) p. 5112ff.
8. Mincer and Polachek (1974).
9. See Office of Population Censuses and Surveys (1978).
10. For a fuller analysis, with particular reference to the British medical profession, see Siebert (1977). It should be emphasised that the above relates to craft, not industrial unions. Industrial unions rely on extensive organisation and the strike threat, rather than restriction of entry.

11. McCarthy, *The Closed Shop in Britain* (Oxford: Blackwell, 1964) p. 39.
12. Polachek (1975).
13. Mancke (1971) p. 320.
14. Thus, only 8 per cent of girls aged 15 to 17 entered apprenticeship in Great Britain in 1972. The comparable figure for boys was 39 per cent. Moreover, the vast majority of girl apprentices were in hairdressing—see Department of Employment, *Women and Work—A Review* (1975) p. 5.
15. See Frank (1976) p. 3.
16. See Reagan (1975) and Gordon and Morton (1974).
17. Work on monopsony in the case of librarians is in progress, however: see Siebert and Young (1978).
18. Aigner and Cain (1977) p. 178.
19. Department of Employment (1975) Table 1.
20. See Chapter 4.
21. Reder (1955).
22. Stigler, G. J., 'Information in the Labour Market', *Journal of Political Economy* (1962) p. 102.
23. See Sloane and Siebert (1977) part III.
24. Chiplin and Sloane (1976(a)) p. 78.
25. See Buckley (1975) Table 1 and Chapter 5.
26. For references see Jusenius (1977) p. 107.
27. Note that no evidence was found for this in Chapter 2 using a simple test.
28. Goldfarb and Hosek (1978) p. 99.
29. Buckley (op. cit.).
30. In 1976, according to the New Earnings Survey, 11.5 per cent (14.7) of manual men (women) were estimated to have been with their employer less than a year. For non-manual workers the corresponding figures were 9.3 per cent (16.2). As for loss of pay due to absence, 11.8 per cent (17.3) of manual men (women) lost pay in 1973, the corresponding figure for non-manuals being 3.2 per cent (5.1 per cent).
31. Sargent Florence (1930).
32. Becker (1962) pp. 13–21.
33. However, a voluntary survey on income has been performed as a follow-up to the 1971 Census. See OPCS (1978).
34. Taubman (1975) pp. 39ff.
35. Ibid., Chapter 10.
36. Marshall, Principles of Economics, p. 312, cited in Becker (op. cit.) p. 85.
37. Psacharopoulos and Layard (forthcoming).
38. See Greenhalgh, C., 'Is Marriage an Equal Opportunity', Centre for Labour Economics, *London School of Economics Discussion Paper*, no. 14, 1977 and Layard, R., Piachaud, D. and Stewart, M., *The Causes of Poverty*, A Background Paper for Report no. 6, Royal Commission on the Distribution of Income and Wealth, HMSO (1978).
39. Nickell (1974), Chiplin and Sloane (1976(b)).
40. Chiplin and Sloane, 'Personal Characteristics and Sex Differentials in Professional Employment', *Economic Journal* (December 1976); Sloane and Siebert (op. cit.).
41. Mincer and Polachek (op. cit.) p. 578.
42. Mincer (1974) Table 1, Psacharopoulos and Layard (op. cit.) Table 2.

43. For example see Jusenius (op. cit.).
44. See Floud in Glass (1954) p. 120–1.
45. Some support for this contention is to be found in the high R^2 shown in earnings functions. If nepotism were widespread, then some individuals with low human capital would earn more than others with high and R^2 would be low. Liebowitz also finds that the addition of family background variables does not much increase explained earnings variance for her sample of white males (op. cit., p. S127). Comparable British results would be interesting.
46. Hurd (1973) p. 237.
47. Nickell (op. cit.) Table 1.
48. See Siebert and Young (op. cit.).
49. Frank (op. cit.) Table 1.
50. Turnbull (1974) p. 255.
51. Cardwell and Rosenweig (1975).
52. Gaston (1972) p. 273.
53. One such attempt is contained in Berg (1970) p. 46.
54. US Department of Labor (1970).
55. The absence of education data in the New Earnings Survey is an important ommission.
56. See Chapter 4.

REFERENCES

Aigner, D., and Cain, G., 'Statistical theories of discrimination in labour markets', *Industrial and Labor Relations Review* (1977).
Becker, G., 'Investment in human capital—a theoretical analysis', *Journal of Political Economy* (1962).
—— *Human Capital* (Chicago: University of Chicago Press, 1964 [2nd ed., 1971]).
—— 'Altruism, egoism and genetic fitness: economics and sociobiology', *Journal of Economic Literature* (1975).
Berg, I., *Education and Jobs: The Great Training Robbery* (1970).
Buckley, T., 'Equal pay: progress and problems (America)', *International Journal of Social Economics* (1975).
Cain, G. C., 'The challenge of segmented labor market theories to orthodox theory: a survey', *Journal of Economic Literature* (1976).
Cardwell, L. and Rosenweig, M., 'Monopolistic discrimination and sex differences in wages', *Yale University Economic Growth Centre, Discussion Paper no. 222* (1975).
Chiplin, B. and Sloane, P., 'Male-female earnings differences: a further analysis', *British Journal of Industrial Relations* (1976(a)).
—— 'Sex differences and the inter-industry wage structure for manual workers in UK manufacturing', *Paisley College Working Paper no. 22* (1976(b)).
Department of Employment, *The Changing Structure of the Labour Force* (London: HMSO, 1975).
——, *Women and Work—A Review* (London: HMSO, 1975).

Frank, R. H., 'Sources of male-female wage differentials—the theory and estimation of differential over-qualification', *Cornell University Discussion Paper no. 133* (1976).

Gaston, R., 'Labour market conditions and employer hiring standards', *Industrial Relations* (1972).

Glass, D., *Social Mobility in Britain* (London: Routledge and Kegan Paul, 1954).

Goldfarb and Hosek, 'Explaining male female wage differentials for the "same" job', *Journal of Human Resources* (1976).

Gordon, M. and Morton, T., 'A low mobility model of wage discrimination with special reference to sex differentials', *Journal of Economic Theory* (1974).

Hurd, R., 'Equilibrium vacancies in a market dominated by non-profit firms: the "shortage" of nurses', *Review of Economics and Statistics* (1973).

Jusenius, C., 'The influence of work experience, skill requirement, and occupational segregation on women's earnings', *Journal of Economics and Business* (1977).

Leibowitz, A., 'Home investments in children', *Journal of Political Economy* (1974).

Lloyd, C. B., *Sex Discrimination and the Division of Labor* (New York and London: Columbia University Press, 1975).

Mancke, R., 'Lower pay for women: a case of economic discrimination?' *Industrial Relations* (1971).

Mincer, J., *Schooling, Experience and Earnings* (New York: NBER, 1974).

Mincer, J. and Polachek, S., 'Family investments in human capital: earnings of women', *Journal of Political Economy* (1974).

Myrdal, G., *The American Dilemma*, 2nd ed. (New York: Harper and Row 1962).

Nickell, S., 'An analysis of the industrial wage structure for both men and women', *mimeo.*, London School of Economics (1974).

Office of Population Censuses and Surveys, *Bulletin no. 8* (1978).

—— *Population Trends* (Summer 1978).

Owen, J. D., 'The distribution of educational resources in large American cities', *Journal of Human Resources* (1972).

Parsons, D., 'Intergenerational wealth transfers and the educational decision of male youth', *Quarterly Journal of Economics* (1975).

Polachek, S., 'Potential biases in measuring male-female discrimination', *Journal of Human Resources* (1975).

Psacharopoulos, G. and Layard, P. R., 'Human capital and earnings: British evidence and a critique', *Review of Economic Studies* (forthcoming).

Reagan, B. R., 'Two supply curves for economists?', *American Economic Review* (1975).

Reder, M., 'The theory of occupational wage differentials', *American Economic Review* (1955).

Sargent Florence, P., 'A statistical contribution to the theory of women's wages', *Economic Journal* (1930).

Siebert, W. S., 'Occupational licensing: the Merrison Report on the regulation of the medical profession', *British Journal of Industrial Relations* (1977).

Siebert, W. S. and Young A., 'Sex differentials and professional earnings', *Paisley College Working Paper*, no. 28 (1978).

Sloane, P. and Siebert, W., 'Hiring standards and the employment of women', *mimeo.*, prepared for Manpower Services Commission, Paisley College (1977).

Taubman, P., *Sources of Inequality in Earnings* (Amsterdam and New York: North Holland and American Review, 1975).

Tuck, A., *How Do We Choose?* (London: Methuen, 1976).

Turnbull, R. and Williams, G., 'Sex differentials in teachers' pay', *Journal of the Royal Statistical Society*, Series A (1974).

US Department of Labor, 'Hiring standards and job performance', *Manpower Research Monograph*, no. 18 (1970).

Index

absenteeism, 10, 178, 235
Addison, J. T., 36
affirmative action, 119, 124, 152; programmes, 233
Agarwal, N. and Jain, H. C., 172, 178
age, 6–7, 86–7, 136, 147, 168, 190; analysis by, 28; common starting, 10; earnings profiles, 94–106, 136, 142, 149; experience, 192–4; profiles, 26–34
Aigner, D. and Cain, E. G., 249
Alexander, A. J., 129, 144
Andresani, P. J., 139, 151
apprenticeship, 195, 249
Ashenfelter, O., 107–10, 120, 124, 125
Atkinson, A. B., 105, 159

Bain, G. S., 110
baking, 145
barriers to entry, 237
Barron, R. D., 16, 34; and Norris, 150, 161
Becker, G., 11, 108–9, 124, 127–8, 142, 161, 224, 248–9
behaviour; reward, contingencies, 142; self confirming, 148
Berg, I., 250
Bergmann, Barbara R., 53, 142
Bergquist, V. A., 221
bipolarity, 161
Birnbaum, 148–9; see also Edwards et al.
birth order, 244
Blau and Justenius, 158, 162; see also Edwards et al.
Blaug, M., 135, 146, 159
Blaxall, M. and Reagan, B., 158
Blinder, A., 194, 196–7
Bosanquet, N., 144; and Doeringer, 149

bricks, pottery, glass, 71
Buckley, T., 249
bureaucratic control, 130

Cain, G. G., 160, 248; see also Aigner, D.
Cairnes, 140
California, 244
Canada, 3–4, 108, 165–222; Census, 168, 172, 182–3, 186–8, 191, 196; Department of Labour, 176, 190; Labour, 192; Statistics, 167, 169, 172, 186–7, 203, 205
capital; intensity, 129; investment, 24; substitution, 118
capitalistic development, 137
Cardwell, L. and Rosenzweig, 250
career hierarchy, 16, 130
Cassell, F. H. et al., 147–8
catering, 16
Census; Canada, 168, 172, 182–3, 186–8,191, 196; of Population, 3, 17, 22–3, 109–10, 223, 248; of Population, U.S., 236; of Production, 22, 247
Central Arbitration Committee, 107
channels of recruitment, 133
chemicals, 145
Chicago labour market, 147
child; care, 119, 178, 194, 228, 238–9; rearing, 136, 192
children, 97
Chiplin, B. and Sloane, P. J., 47, 53–4, 125, 140, 143, 146–7, 155, 158, 234, 249
cleaning, 16; contract, 17; dry, 17
clerical activities, 16
cluster analysis, 150
coefficient of Skewness, 102, 104; Gini, 105

coefficient of Variation, 102, 104–5, 185
collective; agreement, 7, 37; bargaining, 17, 37, 43, 52, 145
Communications Administration, 71
community colleges, 195
comparative advantage, 184
competition, 247; perfect, 246
Conservative policy, 115
construction, 71
Consumer Finances, Survey of, 173
contract; cleaning, 17; compliance programme, 17
conurbations, 47, 54
Co-operative societies, retail, 36
cost; of education, 148; of funds, marginal, 240; of information, 129; non-wage, 140; training, 161; transactions, 130
craft unions, 248
credentialism, 132, 159
Crowding Hypothesis, 7, 11–12, 128, 142, 196, 234, 237
customer discrimination, 127

data; income tax, 248; problems, 247–8; shortcomings; 236–46
Dean, A. J. H., 125
Demand and Supply Schedules for education, 226–7
Department of Employment, 53, 115, 249; Gazette, 58–9, 121–2; Unit of Manpower Studies, 236
Department of Labour, 120
Department of Manpower and Immigration, 186, 187
dexterity, manual, 16
differential; extent of, 57, 62; pay, evidence of, 172, 180
discontinuous labour force experience, 30, 94, 97, 119, 152
discrimination, 134, 224, 238; coefficient, 108–10; employment, 223; indirect, 132; non-labour market, 179; pre-entry, 225–8; reverse, 132; statistical, 132, 134, 139; Theory of Economic, 225–36; wage, 224, 235
distribution, 12; industrial, 7, 15, 24,

30, 47, 171; occupational, 31–3; retail, 16
Doeringer, P. B. and Piore, M. J., 129, 137–41, 144, 152; see also Bosanquet
Doughty, 8
dry cleaning, 17
Dual Labour Market, 2–3, 5–7, 127–8, 138, 149–52, 160, 162
Dualism and Crowding, 240–1

earnings, 10, 122–3; change in relative, 63–70; dispersion, 101; distribution, 10, 22; female, 47, 57; full-time, 23; function, 247; hourly, 10, 57; lifetime, 135, 141, 173; male, 33, 57; mean, 27; median, 44, 47, 52, 58; of labourers, 116; of male and female, distribution, 101–6; of skilled workers, 116; overall, distribution, 11–15; percentage of, 17, 21; profiles, 94–106, 136, 142, 149; ratio, 58–68, 172, 180–99; regional, 47; segmented, 238; unadjusted and adjusted, ratio, 172–3
Earnings Survey, Distribution of, 21
East and West Midlands, 47
East Anglia, 45
Economic Discrimination, Theory of, 225–36
education, 3–4, 36, 47–52; 136, 146–7, 158, 160, 168, 194–7, 201, 220, 223–4; attainment, 195; cost of, 148; Demand and Supply schedules for, 226–7; educators, 226; given, factors affecting employment, 228; investment in, 152; rate of return to, 236
Edwards, R. C. *et al.*, 130, 137, 140, 148–9, 152, 161
efficiency, 130
elasticity of labour supply, 128, 236, 245
empirical analysis, 236–46
employee(s); adult, 10; clerical, 148; discrimination, 127; manual, 10–11, 60; referral, 145; white-collar, 147

employer; discrimination, 127; personnel policies, 234

employment, 15; Appeal Tribunal, 107; by occupation, 24–5; Department of, 53, 115, 249; discrimination, 223; factors affecting, given education, 228–234; female, 170–2; Gazette, Department of, 58–9, 121–4, 159; level of, 8; part-time, 189, 220; Protection Act, 107; tests, 6, 133

employment distribution, 12, 15; female, 12–13, 14, 15, 24

engineering, 17, 20, 144–5; civil, 141; industry, 116

enterprise, size of, 144

entry; barriers to, 237; into the ILM, 131–4; ports of, 144; restrictions on, 229; tests, 145

equal; Employment Opportunity Commission, 120, 124, 180, 225; opportunity, 52; opportunity laws, 184, 200; pay, 52, 55, 124, 180, 225; Pay Act, 36, 53, 106–7, 112–14, 116, 118, 121

equity theory, 158

establishment, 22, 177; employment in, 22; profitability, 177; size, 22–3, 54, 177; small, 40, 53–4; studies, 219

executive orders, 119

experience, 136, 146–8, 159, 223, 230; age, 193–4; intermittant work, 240; work, segmented, 239

exploitation, 40

extent of Differential, 57–62; male and female earnings, 57–62

factor(s); affecting change in relative earnings, 63–70; analysis, 149; associated with low earnings of women, 180–99; sociological, 138, 141

Factory Acts, 34

family; background, 241, 242, 250; income, 169, 195, 244; size of, 244

Family Expenditure Survey,

Farmer, H., 248

feedback, positive, 142

female; employment, 170, 172; and poverty, 166, 172; headed families, 166, 219; intensive industry, 235

Ferber, M. A. and Lowry, H. M., 136, 147, 160

firm; size of, 130, 151, 245; small, 22, 131, 141, 144, 151, 198, 234

Flanagan, R., 120, 159, 160

Floud, 250

Frank, R. H., 249, 250

full-time, 24; employee, 24, 52; females, 24

Gaston, R., 250

General Household Survey, 9, 47, 146, 223, 226, 228, 237, 241, 247

Gini coefficient, 105

Glass, D., 250

Glucklick, P. *et al.*, 55

G.N.P., growth of, 124

Goldfarb and Hosek, 249

Goldstein, M., 125

Gordon, D. M. and Morton, J. E., 136, 141, 147, 149, 160–1, 249

government; policy, 148; policy, the effect of, 106–21; sector, 227

Greenhalgh, C., 249

Gunderson, M., 124, 170, 172–3, 177–8, 180, 184, 191, 193, 196–7

Gwartney, J. and Stroup, A., 136, 238

Hall, C. R. J., 55

Hamermesh, D., 54

Hamilton, G. S. and Roessner, J. D., 159

Harris, A., 150

Heckman, J., 125

hiring; costs, 236; standards, 225, 233, 245–6

Holmes, R., 173, 195

Horowitz, Anne R., 124

Hosek, see Goldfarb

hours, 25, 37, 54, 57, 63–8, 71, 86–7, 109, 112–3, 141, 149, 180; and weeks worked, 189–92

household, Division, 237–40; duties, 7; versus Wage Discrimination, 178–9

Human Capital, 7, 36, 52, 97, 127–8, 142, 146, 148, 152, 159, 230, 233, 240; investment, 134–7, 151; models, 6; Theory, 26, 43

imperfect information, 3, 232, 245–6
incentive pay system, 177–8
income(s), average, 58; distribution, 58; family, 169, 195; policy, 7, 109, 114, 116; tax data, 248
indices, 132
indirect discrimination, 132
industrial, analysis, 12, 14, 16–17, 23, 26; Data, 71–87; distribution, 86–7, 171; pattern, 184–8; Relations Act, 107; Training Act, 107; unions, 248
industry, female intensive, 235
inflation, 8
information, 179, 224, 229, 233; imperfections, 245; marginal cost of, 240
intensity, capital, 129
interviews, personnel, 133
intra-firm sex differentials, 234
investment, capital, 24; in education and training, 152
Inter Industry Study, 47
I.Q., 242, 244

Jain, H. C., 159, and Pettman, 130, 220; and Sloane, P. J., 219 see also Agarwal
job(s), evaluation, 107; given, Differences in Pay, 234–6; grade, 148; low pay, 170–2; search, 6, 47, 133, 232; segregation, 110, 177
Jones, N., 53
journey to work, 47, 232
Justinius, C., 241, 249, 250, see also Blau

Kahne, H., 219
Kerr, C., 129
Klitgaard, R. A., 142
KOS occupational classification, 15
Kumar, P., see Wood, W. D.

labour; allocation of, 134; as factor in low pay of women, 237–40; Canada, 192, 193, 199; Department of, 120; mobility, 144, 150; supply, elasticity of, 236
labour force; intermittant experience of, 178, 192, 198, 201–2, 230; participation, 169, 170, 219; Survey, 185, 188
labour market; casual, 139; Chicago, 147; competitive, 129; dual, 2, 3, 5, 6, 7, 17, 127, 128, 138, 149, 150, 151, 152, 160, 162; empirical evidence on structured, 143–151; external, 129, 130–1; imperfections, 129, 137; internal, 5, 7, 128, 129–37, 144, 146, 150, 159, 234; local, 145; primary, 138, 139; secondary, 138, 139; segmentation, 128, 137–43, 148, 198
laundry, 17
Laws, 158
Layard, R. *et al.*, 125; see also Psacharopoulos
learning-by-doing, 159
legislation; equal pay, 225; government, 57; impact of, 57; protective, 134; social, 152
Leibowitz, A., 243, 248, 250
Leigh, D. R., 162
Lerner, S. W. *et al.*, 145
librarians, 244
Lloyd, C., 248
location, 6, 177
locational factors, 43–7
Lorenz Curve, 105
low pay, 9, 11, 17, 52; and make up of pay, 35; and size of establishment, 23; by occupational group, 18–19; by type of collective agreement, 38–40; concentration of, 20–1; definition of, 1, 3, 10, 27, 106; jobs, and female employment, 170–2; ranked by industry, 20–1; regression results, 41; threshold, 10; weekly, 22
Lowry, H. M., see Ferber, M. A.

McCall, J. J., 124
McCarthy, W. E. J., 49

McEaddy, see Waldman
Mackay, D. I. *et al.*, 144–5, 150, 232
Madden, J., 248
Make-up of Pay, 34–7
male/female; changes in earnings, 179–80; earnings ratio, 58–63; evidence of pay differentials, 172–80; hours ratio, 63
Malkiel, B. G. and J. A., 136, 147
management organisation, 17
Mancke, R., 249
manpower; Economics, Office of, 9, 125; policy, 152; Studies, Department of Employment's, 236
manual, 10–11; dexterity, 16; empolyee(s), 10–11, 60; ratio, 62; women, 45
manufacturing, 59; ratio, 60–2
marginal; cost of funds, 240; productivity, 19, 127
marital status, 6, 27, 136–7, 141, 146–7, 159, 161, 170, 190, 230–1, 233, 237–9, 245, 248
market; environment, 17; guild, 129, 144; imperfections, 139; open, 129; primary, 140, 142–3, 149–51, 240–1; secondary, 140–3, 149–51, 240–1
Marquand, J., 21, 53
Marshall, A., 237, 249
Masters, S. H., 124
mean, 57, 101
median, 33, 57
medical profession, 248
Meltz, N., 185, 187
merit, 36
Mincer, J., 135, 146, 159, 238–9, 249; and Polachek, 248–9
Ministry of Labour, 21
minority group, size of, 109
miscellaneous services, 71
misconception(s), 132–3, 143
mobility, 7, 151; barriers to, 138–9, 152; claims, 140–1; geographical, 245; labour, 144, 150; potential, 128; upward, 162
monetary and fiscal policy, 106
monopoly, 229

monopsony, 2–3, 6–7, 128, 179, 224–5, 232, 235–6, 244–7, 249
moonlighting, 141
Morton, T. E., see Gordon, D. M.
motivation, 142, 229, 246; to work, 128
multicollinearity, 112
multiple regression, 53
Myrdal, J., 248

national; agreements, 37; Board for Prices and Incomes (N.B.P.I.), 11, 17, 52–4, 106; Health Service, 17; Longitudinal Survey, 146, 151; minimum wage, 8
neoclassical theory, 137
nepotism, 108, 237, 250
net; advantages, 129; investment, 118
New Earnings Survey (N.E.S.), 2–3, 6–11, 22–3, 36–7, 47, 52, 58, 115, 121–2, 124, 161, 223, 248–50
Nickell, S. J., 33, 42, 47, 53–4, 249–50
non-competing groups, 140
non-labour market; discrimination, 179; institutions, 179
non-manual, 10–11; employees, 10–11, 14, 27–8; employment, 27; occupations, 16, 151; ratio, 61; women, 45
non-manufacturing; manual workers, 59; ratio, 60, 62; sector, 62
non-parametric test, 15
non-wage cost, 140
Norris, C. M., 16, 54, see also Barron, R. D.
nursery provisions, 4
nursing, 16, 181, 195, 244

Oaxaca, R., 194, 196–8
occupational; analysis, 12, 16–17, 25; classification (K.O.S.), 15; data, 87–94; distribution, 31–3; group, low pay by, 9, 11, 17, 52; pattern, 181–4; segregation, 181–4; structure, 96
Office; of Manpower Economics, 9, 125; of Population Censuses and Surveys, 248

opportunity, equal, 52
Osterman, P., 140, 150, 160, 162
Ostry, S., 172–3, 191
Owen, J. D., 248
overtime, 6, 10, 34, 36, 52, 54–5, 63, 66–9, 71, 87, 108, 111–3, 122, 124

Parrish, J. B., 220
Parsons, D., 242–3
part-time; employment, 22, 189, 220; female employment, 27; women, 22–6; work, 5, 54, 159, 191, 201; workers, 100–1
pay, 9; basic, 36; Board, 115; differences in, given the job, 234–6; differentials, evidence of, 172–80; equal, 52, 55, 124, 180, 225; longer period of, 9; low hourly, 45, 53; low weekly, 45, 63; make-up of, 34–7; scheme, 23; single period, 9; system, incentive, 177–8
Payment, method of, 148
Payment-by-Results, 6, 34, 36, 68–71, 87, 122–3, 148
perfect competition, 246
personnel interviews, 133
Pettman, B. O., see Jain, H. C.
Piachaud, D. and Stewart, M., 249
Piore, M. J., 142, 150, 160, see also Doeringer
placement activities, 152
Polachek, S., 146, 239, 249, see also Mincer, J.
policy; Conservative, 115; employer personnel, 234; government, 227; manpower, 152; monetary and fiscal, 106
Population, Census of, 3, 17, 23, 109–10, 223, 248–9
positive feedback, 142
Povall, M., 55
poverty, 1, 3, 8, 165, 200; and female employment, 116–72
pre-entry discrimination, 225–8
Price, R., 110
private and public sector, 20, 37
probability of separation, 235
productivity, 7, 143, 147, 172–3, 177–9, 225; marginal, 19, 127

profession, medical, 248
Professional and Scientific Industries, 71
profits, 142
promotion, 134, 138, 148
Psacharopoulos, G. and Layard, R., 146, 249
psychologists, 225, 246
Public Administration, 71

quit rates, 143, 150
quota, 134

race, 110, 112, 120, 149, 152, 227, 232, 239
radical economists, 138
Raphael, 221
Rasmussen, D., 108
ratio; female/male earnings, 58–63; female/male hours, 63; manual hours, 63; manufacturing, 60–1; non-manual hours, 61–3; unadjusted and adjusted earnings, 172–3
Reagan, B., 249, see also Blaxall, M.
recruitment, channels of, 133
Reder, M., 233, 249
redundancy procedures, 150
Rees, A. and Schultz, 145–7
Region, 71; South East, 71; Yorkshire and Humberside, 71
Regional; distribution, 47; earnings differences, 47
Regional Analysis, 43–7
regression, multiple, 53
restriction, 152; on entry, 229
restrictive practices, 110
retail; co-operative societies, 36; distribution, 16; trades, 188
reverse discrimination, 132
Robb, A. and Spencer, B., 195–7
Robinson, O., 16, 36
Roessner, J. D., see Hamilton, G. S.
Rosen, S., 135, 137
Rosenweig, see Cardwell
Royal Commission, 3–4, 7, 53, 249
Routh, G. G. C., 53

Salop, J. and Salop, S., 132, 158
Sargent, Florence P., 249

Sawhill, I. W., 219
schooling functions, 228, 241–4, 247
Schultz, G. P., see Rees, A.
screening; devices, 131, 152; hypothesis, 135, 159; processes, 110
secondary workers, 162
secretarial activities, 16
segregation, 7, 17, 27; by firm, 149; industrial, 5; intra-occupational, 149; job, 110, 177; occupational, 18, 184
self-confirming behaviour, 148
self-selection, 132, 143, 152, 229
selling, 33
seniority, 130, 140–1, 145–7, 152
separation; probability of, 235; rates, 236
service(s), 20; increments, 36; industries, 23; length of, 7, 42–5, 54; miscellaneous, 71; sector, 220; trades, 188
sewing machining, 174
sex; differentials, intra-firm, 234; Discrimination Act, 1, 55, 106, 118, 121, 132; stereotyping, 233
shift; pay, 34, 36, 87; work, 6, 34, 36, 52, 68–71, 122
shortcomings, theoretical, 246–7
side factors; demand, 34; supply, 34
Siebert, W. S., 147, 248; and Young, A., 249–50; see also Sloane, P. J.
signalling, 119, 132
single parent women, 1
skill(s), 151; adaptive, 143; differentials, 114, 116–7; functional, 143; general, 136; hierarchy, 131; mix, 34; specific, 131–2, 136, 143
Sloane, P. J., 47, 53–4, 125; and Siebert, W. S., 146, 249; see also Chiplin, B.; see also Jain, H. C.
Smith, S. P., 125, 147–8, 160
Snell, M. N., 55
Soap, 145
Social; Contract, 115; Security, work history file, 144; welfare, functions, 105–6
social legislation, 152; work, 16

socialisation, 138
sociological factors, 138, 141
sociologists, 225–46
Sommers, D., 220
South East, 44–5, 47, 71
Spence, M., 119, 132–3, 158
Spencer, B. G., 170; see also Robb, A.
spillover effect, 40, 198
standards, hiring, 3, 225, 233
Standing, G., 159
Statistics Canada, 167, 169, 172, 182–3, 186–7, 203–5, 212–7
statistical discrimination, 132, 134, 139
status, 36
Steinberg, F., 159
stereotyping, sex, 233
Stewart, M., see Piachaud, D.
Stigler, G. J., 249
Stiglitz, J., 132
Stroup, R., see Gwartney, J.
substitution, capital, 118
Survey of Consumer Finances, 173

Taira, K., 130–1
tastes, 246, 248
Taubman, P., 236, 249
teaching, 181, 245; primary, 16
technology, 141
test, non-parametric, 15
textiles, 182
Theory of Economic Discrimination, 225–36
theoretical shortcomings, 246–7
Thomson, A. J. W., *et al.*, 37, 40, 42
threshold payments, 115
'tipping' phenomenon, 133
town, size of, 244, 247
trades, service and retail, 188
tradition, 183
training, 52, 140, 180, 195; costs, 161; general, 130, 159; investment in, 152; opportunities, 34; specific, 5, 129, 130, 159
transactions cost, 130
Transport Administration, 71
Tuck, M., 248
Turnbull, R., 250
turnover cost, 142, 149

unemployment, 24, 110, 112–4, 118, 123, 180; males, 149
union, 130, 224; craft and industrial, 248; management of, 199; membership, 42, 144; organisation, 17, 54; trade, 42; white-collar, 42
unionisation, 6–7, 25, 42, 130, 134, 139, 152, 158, 188, 197–9, 201–2, 220–1, 229, 234, 245, 247
U.S. (United States), 119; Census of Population, 236; Department of Commerce, 206–9; Department of Labour, 219, 245, 250; Survey of Economic Opportunity,
U.S.A., 3, 108, 112, 120, 145–6, 151, 165, 194, 222, 234, 238, 244

Vroman, W., 124

Wachter, M., 134, 138, 142, 148, 158, 160–1
wage; Board, 37; council(s), 1, 37; determination, 141; differentials, 142, 173–8; discrimination, 173, 177, 178–9, 224, 235; dispersion,

131; drift, 36; rates and earnings relationship, 36
Waldman and McEaddy, 220
Wallace, J., 16, 36
Wedderburn, 8
Week(s) worked, 189–92
white-collar; employees, 147; union, 42
Whybrew, E., 54
Williamson, *et al.*,159
Wolpin, K. I., 125
Wood, W. C. D. and Kumar, P., 221
work; aspiration of women, 128; experience, 6, 193–4; experience, intermittant, 240; experience, segmented, 238; journey to, 47, 232, 247; motivation to, 128; part-time, 159, 191, 201; same or broadly similar, 107
worker, secondary, 162
workforce, 42

Yorkshire and Humberside, 44–5, 71
Young, A., see Siebert, W. S.